Our Haunted Kingdom

Andrew Green founded the Ealing Psychical Research Society and co-founded both the Lewisham Psychical Research Society and the National Federation of Psychical Research Societies. He is also a member of the Society for Psychical Research, and of the Paraphysical Society of Downton, Wiltshire.

Well known as a lecturer on psychic phenomena, he lives in an eighteenth century cottage in Robertsbridge, Sussex, which – naturally – is reputed to be haunted.

Pass me on when you've finished reading me

Healthy Planet

www.healthyplanet.org

Our Haunted Kingdom

Andrew Green

FONTANA/COLLINS

First published by Wolfe Publishing Ltd, 1973
First issued in Fontana 1974
Copyright © Andrew Green 1973

Made and Printed in Great Britain by
William Collins Sons & Co Ltd Glasgow

Contents

Introduction   17

Bedfordshire   19
Chicksands Priory, Clophill   19
Great Park, Ampthill   21
Luton Museum, Luton   22
Markyate   22
Union Street, Bedford   23
Woburn Abbey, Woburn   24

Berkshire   26
Church of All Saints, Faringdon   26
Littlecote House, Nr. Hungerford   27
Shoppenhangers Manor Restaurant, Maidenhead   28

Buckinghamshire   29
Aston Sandford Church, Nr. Haddenham   29
Bucks Standard, Newport Pagnell   30
Castle House, Buckingham   30
Chequers Inn, Amersham   32
Ellesborough Parish Church, Ellesborough   32
George & Dragon, West Wycombe   33
Lane End   34
Little Abbey Hotel, Gt. Missenden   34
Loakes Road, High Wycombe   36
Missenden Abbey, Gt. Missenden   36
St. Mary's Abbey, Medmenham   37
Stony Green, Nr. Prestwood   38
Vatche's Farm, Aston Clinton   38

Cambridgeshire   39
Cambridge   39
Old Cottage, Little Abington   41
Sawston Hall, Nr. Cambridge   42

Cheshire   43
Boys Club, Hyde   43
Capesthorne, Macclesfield   4

Gawsworth Hall, Macclesfield   45
House of Bewlay, Chester   46
Poulton Road, Birkenhead   47

Cornwall   48
Manor House, Newquay   48
Manor House Inn, Rilla Mill   49
Roche Chapel, Nr. St. Austell   50
Smugglers Cottage Guest House, Portreath   50

Cumberland   52
Citadel Restaurant, Carlisle   52
Lorton Hall, Cockermouth   53

Derbyshire   56
Haunted Mansion, Belper   56

Devonshire   58
Berry Pomeroy Castle, Berry Pomeroy   58
Cheriton Cross   59
Cowick Barton Inn, Exeter   60
Exeter University, Exeter   60
Haldon House Guest House, Dunchideock   61
Kilworthy House School, Tavistock   62
Modbury   62
Moretonhampstead   63
Old Smugglers Inn, Nr. Teignmouth   64
Parish Church, Weare Giffard   65
Royal Castle Hotel, Dartmouth   65
St. Johns Church, Torquay   66
Spanish Barn, Torquay   67
Topsham Churchyard, Topsham   68

Dorset   69
Athelhampton   69
Corfe Castle   71
Crown Hotel, Poole   72
Godlingston Manor, Nr. Herston   72
Manor House, Sandford Orcas   74
Monmouth Ash Tree, Horton/Woodlands   74
Rectory, Pimperne   75

Durham   76
Darlington & Simpson Rolling Mills, Durham   76
East House Farm, Washington   77
W H Smith, Gateshead   78
Social Club, Greatham   78
Spring Lane, Consett   79
Vestry, Sunderland   80
Washington Old Hall, Washington   81

Essex   82
Ambassador Bowling Club, Basildon   83
Beeleigh Abbey, Maldon   83
Bell Hotel, Thorpe-le-Soken   84
Borley, Nr. Long Melford   86
Church of the Holy Cross, Basildon   88
Cold Norton, Nr. Maldon   88
Fountains Head, Brentwood   89
Golden Fleece, Brentwood   90
High Street, Brentwood   91
Larkhill Road, Canewdon   92
Marchings, Chigwell   92
Moat House Motel, Brentwood   93
New World Inn, Great Warley   93
Oil Refinery, Coryton   94
Prittlewell Priory, Nr. Southend   95
St. Osyth's Priory, Coggeshall   97
Swann, Brentwood   97
Upminster Gold Club, Upminster   98
Warley Lea Farm, Nr. Brentwood   99
White Hart, Brentwood   99

Gloucestershire   101
Berkeley Arms, Tewkesbury   101
Blackfriars Priory, Gloucester   102
Gloucester Jail, Gloucester   102
Prestbury   103
St. Mary's Vicarage, Kempsford   104
Shaw Green Lane, Prestbury   105
Swan Pool, Redbrook   106
Tudor House Hotel, Tewkesbury   107
Vicarage, Arlingham   107

Hampshire 108
Bagwell Lane, Fleet 108
Beaulieu Abbey, Beaulieu 109
Church of All Saints, Crondall 110
Ebenezer Lane, Ringwood 110
Fort Wallington, Fareham 111
Marriage Guidance Council, Southsea 112
Moyles Court, Nr. Ringwood 112
Poplar Farm Inn, Nr. Andover 113
Royal Oak, Havant 114
Rumasa, Totton 115
Selborne, Nr. Petersfield 115
Tudor Rose Inn, Nr. Fordingbridge 116
Wherwell Priory, Nr. Andover 117
White Hart Hotel, Andover 117

Herefordshire 118
Goodrich Castle 118

Hertfordshire 120
Bramfield Road, Datchworth 120
Brocket Arms, Ayot St. Lawrence 121
Hawkins Hall Lane, Datchworth 122
Mardleybury Manor, Nr. Welwyn Garden City 122
Old Pest House, Near Knebworth 123
Palace Theatre, Watford 124
Rectory Lane, Datchworth 125
Watford Rail Tunnel 125
Mathews, St. Albans 126
Westminster Bank, Stevenage 126
White Hart, Hemel Hempstead 127
Whitehorse Lane, Datchworth 128
Wicked Lady, St. Albans 129

Huntingdonshire 130
Golden Lion Hotel, St. Ives 130

Ireland 132
Castlegarde, Co. Limerick 132
Kilkea Castle Hotel, Co. Kildare 133
Killakee Art Centre, Co. Dublin 134

Isle of Man   *136*
Castle Rushen, Castletown   *136*
Falcon Cliff Hotel, Douglas   *138*
Hill Fort, Nr. Castletown   *138*
Tantaloo, Ramsey   *139*

Kent   *141*
Boys Hall, Willesborough   *141*
Bridge Place Country Club, Bridge   *144*
Court Mount Hotel, Birchington   *145*
Downe Court Manor, Bromley   *145*
Kings Head, Staplehurst   *146*
Lympne Castle, Nr. Hythe   *147*
Pennis Lane, Fawkham Green   *148*
Dering Woods, Pluckley   *149*
Elvey Farm, Pluckley   *149*
St. Nicholas Church, Pluckley   *151*
High Street, Pluckley   *151*
Smarden Road, Pluckley   *151*
Crossroad, Pluckley   *152*
Dicky Buss's Lane, Pluckley   *152*
Rooks Cottage, Westerham   *152*
Shorne Lodge, Nr. Gravesend   *153*
Snob Boutique, Chatham   *154*
Thanet House, Broadstairs   *156*
Theatre Royal, Margate   *156*
Timerden Bottom, Nr. Shoreham   *157*

Lancashire   *159*
Chingle Hall, Nr. Preston   *159*
C Claridge, Manchester   *161*
Dean Road, Bolton   *162*
Hall-i'-th'-Wood, Bolton   *162*
Lawrence Gardens, Liverpool   *163*
Peel Hall Farm, Astley Green   *164*
Penny Lane, Liverpool   *165*
Railway Inn, Waterfoot   *165*
Samlesbury Hall, Nr. Preston   *166*
Smithills Hall, Nr. Bolton   *167*
Speke Hall, Speke   *168*
Stork Hotel, Billinge   *169*

Leicestershire 170
Belper Arms, Newton Burgoland 170

Lincolnshire 171
Ye Old White Swanne, Louth 171

London 172
Aldgate Station 172
Baker Street 173
Bank of England 173
Barnes Common 174
Berkeley Square 174
Blackheath 175
Boston Manor House 175
Bruce Castle Museum 176
Chingford Mount Cemetery 177
Chiswick House 177
Covent Garden Station 178
Dental Surgery, Regents Park 179
Doughty Street 180
First Floor Flat, Admiralty 180
Fisheries Inn, Harefield 181
Hall Place, Bexley 181
Hampton Court Palace 182
Highgate Cemetery 183
Ickenham Station 184
Montpelier Road, Ealing 184
Nag's Head, Hackney 187
Old Palace, Croydon 187
Plough Inn, Clapham 188
Ratcliff Wharf, Stepney 189
Roundshaw Estate, Croydon 190
St. Giles Church, Camberwell 191
St. Mary's Church, Neasden 192
Second-hand City, Kensington 192
Sheppey's Restaurant, Mayfair 193
Temple, Fleet Street 194
Thamesmead, Woolwich 195
Theatre Royal, Drury Lane 196
Tower of London 197
Volunteer, Baker Street 199

Westminster Abbey   199
Wig and Pen Club, Strand   200
Wycliffe Road, Battersea   201

Norfolk   203
Aylmerton, Sheringham   203
Bircham Newton Aerodrome   204
Caravan, Great Yarmouth   205
Castle Rising Castle, Castle Rising   206
Happisburgh   207
Mission Hall Cottage, Briningham   207

Northamptonshire   209
Castle Street, Wellingborough   209
Great Oxendon   210
Nene Cottage, Oundle   210
Old House, Higham Ferrers   211
Pig Lane, Northampton   211
St. John the Baptist, Boughton   212

Northern Ireland   213
Antrim Castle, Co. Antrim   213
Ballgally Castle Hotel, Co. Antrim   214
Crom Castle, Co. Fermanagh   215
Drumbeg, Co. Down   216
Ecclesville, Co. Tyrone   216
Lambeg, Co. Antrim   217
Springhill, Co. Londonderry   217

Northumberland   219
Alwinton   219
Buckton   220
Craster Tower, Alnwick   221
Holy Island   222
Lord Crewe Arms, Blanchland   223

Nottinghamshire   225
A A Headquarters, Nottingham   225
Denewood Crescent, Nottingham   226
Hippo Restaurant, Nottingham   227
Newstead Abbey, Linby   228

Oxfordshire   229
Blandy House, Henley-on-Thames   229
Church of St. Michael, Rycote   230
Minster Lovell Hall, Minster Lovell   230
White Hart, Minster Lovell   231

Rutland   232
Bluebell Inn, Belmesthorpe   232

Scotland   233
Alison Hutchison & Partners, Midlothian   233
Bedlay Castle, Lanarkshire   234
Benalder Cottage, Inverness   235
Cape Wrath, Sutherland   236
Careston Castle, Angus   237
Crathes Castle, Kincardineshire   238
Duntrune Castle, Argyll   238
Former Youth Hostel, Perthshire   240
Glamis Castle, Angus   241
Hermitage Castle, Roxburghshire   242
Inverawe House, Argyll   243
Moncreiffe Arms Hotel, Perthshire   244
Muchalls Castle, Kincardineshire   245
St. Andrews Cathedral, Fifeshire   246
Sandwood Bay, Sutherlandshire   247

Shropshire   248
Lilleshall Abbey, Nr. Newport   248
Swan Hotel, Dawley   249

Somerset   250
Cashman's Store, Keynsham   250
Cedar Avenue, Butleigh Wootton   251
Court Hotel, Chilcompton   252
Forde Abbey, Nr. Chard   252
Grey House, Nr. Bath   253
New Road, Taunton   254
Rumbling Tum Restaurant, Chilton Polden   254
Youth Club, Shepton Mallet   255

Staffordshire   256
Hills House Farm, Bloxwich   256
Tudor Bingo Hall, Longton   257
White Hart Inn, Walsall   257

Suffolk   259
Abbeygate Street, Bury St. Edmunds   259
Birds Eye Foods, Lowestoft   260
Worlingham, Nr. Beccles   260

Surrey   262
Angel Hotel, Guildford   263
Antique Shop, Bramley   263
Boughton Hall, Send   264
Brooklands, Weybridge   264
Car Park, Guildford   265
Castle Restaurant, Sunbury-on-Thames   265
Cedars Museum, Chertsey   266
Chertsey Offset Printers, Chertsey   267
Chinthurst Woods, Bramley   268
George, Chertsey   269
Godstone Road, Caterham   270
Golden Grove, Chertsey   270
Hayes Lane, Kenley   271
Heathside Road, Woking   272
High Street, Woking   272
S C Johnson, Nr. Camberley   273
Lion & Lamb Café, Farnham   273
Loseley House, Nr. Guildford   274
Maldwyns Antiques, Ewell   274
Nonsuch Park, Ewell   276
Old Vicarage, Kingswood   276
Old Woking Road, Woking   277
Parish Church, Woking   278
Puttenden Manor, Nr. Lingfield   278
Riddlesdown, Kenley   279
Roebuck, Richmond   280
Slines Oak Road, Warlingham   281
Top Rank Bingo Hall, Nr. Morden   281

Vicarage, Kingswood   282
William IV, Ewell   283
Wonersh, Nr. Guildford   284

Sussex   285
Battle Abbey, Battle   285
Beggars Bush, Nr. Wadhurst   286
Blackboys Inn, Blackboys   287
Busheygate, Robertsbridge   287
Classic Cinema, East Grinstead   288
Eridge Green   289
Farm Cottages, Staplecross   289
Fletchers House, Rye   290
George Inn, Robertsbridge   291
Lion Hotel, Nr. Bognor   291
Michelham Priory, Nr. Hailsham   292
Nan Tucks Lane, Buxted   294
St. Michaels School, East Grinstead   295
Seven Stars Inn, Robertsbridge   295
Turkey Cock Lane, Rye   296
Winchelsea   297
Wyke Gardens, Worthing   298

Wales   300
Beach House Club, Glamorgan   300
Blue Lion Inn, Flintshire   301
Cegin-y-Mynach, Denbighshire   302
Clwch Dernog, Carmarthenshire   302
Farm, Monmouthshire   303
Glynne Arms, Flintshire   303
Penalt, Monmouthshire   304
Rockfield, Monmouthshire   304
Watery Lane, Monmouthshire   305
White Hill, Monmouthshire   305

Warwickshire   307
Ettington Park Hotel, Stratford-upon-Avon   307
Harrow Hill, Longcompton   308
Jack & Jill Inn, Lillington   309
Warley Abbey Grounds, Nr. Birmingham   309

Westmorland   *311*
Levens Hall, Nr. Kendal   *311*

Wiltshire   *313*
King & Queen Inn, Highworth   *313*
Maddington, Shrewton   *314*
St. Michael's Church, Swindon   *315*
Savernake Forest   *316*
Tudor Tea Rooms, Mere   *317*

Worcestershire   *318*
Dudley Castle, Dudley   *318*
Mount Pleasant Hotel, Gt. Malvern   *320*
Old Court House, Shelsley Walsh   *320*
Walcott Lane, Drakes Broughton   *321*

Yorkshire   *322*
Air Heating Ltd, Nr. Leeds   *322*
Bailey Club, Barnsley   *323*
Bramham   *324*
Brompton Road, Sheffield   *325*
Fountains Abbey, Nr. Studley Park   *325*
Glebe Cottage, Nr. Leeds   *326*
Golden Lion, Leeds   *326*
Haworth Parsonage, Haworth   *327*
Howley Hall Golf Club, Nr. Batley   *327*
Long Marston, Marston Moor   *328*
Spofforth Castle, Nr. Harrogate   *329*
Synagogue, Leeds   *330*
White Rose Salon, Hull   *331*

More Books   *332*

Acknowledgements   *334*

Introduction

In 1961 it was stated that there were 10,000 haunted sites in the British Isles but on examination the majority of these cases would, perhaps regrettably, prove to be no longer active. The aim of this collection is to provide a major selection of genuine hauntings experienced in the last 25 years.

As with any catalogue of this nature a few private houses have had to be included and I can only hope that their privacy will be respected.

The cases marked with an asterisk* have been personally investigated by the author or the witnesses involved have been interviewed, but because poltergeist activity is usually associated with individuals and not property only a couple of 'sample' cases of this type of phenomenon have been included.

There are many fascinating books providing information on old ghostly tales and legends, from the famous Cock Lane Ghost of London to the numerous stories of sprites and hobgoblins of the West Country and the islands. This work offers a wide selection of phantoms from the horror of Happisburgh in Norfolk to the ghostly trousers of Somerset, but all seen and experienced by sensible well-balanced people who are alive today, and many of the entries deal with previously unpublished cases.

Sites include open fields, country lanes, cinemas, warehouses, offices, power-houses and of course numerous castles and ruins, in other words wherever people work, live or play.

From my investigations it seems that Pluckley in Kent retains the title of the most haunted village in Britain but one aspect that also results from this survey is that there appears, thankfully, to be a far greater acceptance of the authenticity and existence of ghosts. No doubt due to this there is a surprising increase in the number of hauntings that are reported annually.

For the statistician it is interesting to see from the number of cases published in this book that London retains the title of the most haunted county in the country and the most haunted capital city in the world, with 33 current ghosts. Surrey may appear to be the second most affected county with 30 cases, but this could be due to more time having been spent here. Essex with 22 was expected, but it was disappointing to find that Leicestershire failed to provide more than one haunting in time for inclusion in this catalogue, for even the smallest county of Rutland has at least one genuine phantom.

For those wishing to read more about ghosts a selected list of some publications is given at the end of this collection.

Occasionally when lecturing on psychic experiences I am asked whether I really believe in ghosts. I hope this book will provide a conclusive answer.

Naturally I would welcome any genuine and reliable reports concerning haunted sites, but to those who still scoff at ghosties, do please remember that you may be one yourself some day.

Andrew M Green, Robertsbridge, Sussex

Bedfordshire

Home of the famous Woburn Abbey

Open to the public during normal hours or by appointment	5
Private houses	1
Historic buildings, museums, ruins	3
Open spaces, roads	3
Phenomena	
Noises	1
Moving objects	1
Apparitions	
Females	1
Monks	1
Males	4
Horses	1

Chicksands Priory*

Clophill, Bedfordshire
Private property, please respect

Part of an RAF/USAAF base which is owned by the Air Ministry, Chicksands Priory was founded by the Countess Rohese in 1150 but now acts as the Officers' Mess for the USAAF personnel on the site.

The Countess's first husband was Geoffrey de Mandeville, first Earl of Essex and founder of Walden Abbey, but on his death in 1144 she turned her attentions to Cudessand, the original name for the area in the 11th century.

The priory was well endowed, being the third largest religious house of the Gilbertine Order in the country, and was one of the two cloistered establishments which accommodated both canons and nuns. At one time it may well have housed over a hundred people.

In March 1536 the suppression of small monasteries commenced and in October 1538 John Orrey, prior of Chicksands' six canons and 17 nuns, and Margaret Burton, the prioress, surrendered the building and were 'pensioned off'. New owners followed in rapid succession, Richard Snowe in 1540, Sir Peter Osborn in 1587 and many others until Sir Algernon Osborn, who died in 1948, sold the estate to the Government in 1936.

Three years later the Air Ministry gave the use of Chicksands to the Royal Navy and after a lapse of only nine months the RAF took it over. In November 1950 they were joined by United States Air Force personnel.

There are numerous legends about the priory, the most popular being that of 'the fallen Nun'. The usual romance is supposed to have occurred between one of the nuns and a canon and on the resultant pregnancy both parties were put to death. The man was beheaded, the execution being watched by his lover who was enclosed in a wall up to her neck and then completely sealed up to die. The story claims that on the 17th of each month the ghost of the nun walks the priory area searching for the boy friend.

Set over one of the windows in the eastern wall of the remaining cloister one can see a plaque to the nun, Berta Rosata, 'By virtues guarded and by manners graced, Here alas is fair Rosata placed'. An oddity of the building is that there are more windows appearing on the outside than can be seen from within, due no doubt to the rebuilding that took place in the 18th and 19th centuries.

Of the authenticity of the plaque one expert claims 'it appears to be an obvious invention of the late 18th century. I can find no mediaeval use of the Christian name "Rosata". It may well have been an 18th century invention for what they believed a name of the period should have been.' Even the wording of the inscription is hardly suitable for a disgraced nun.

True Dr Richard Layton wrote to Cromwell in 1534 saying that on visiting the Priory he discovered 'two of the said nunnes not baron', one of them having been impregnated by a serving man, the other by a superior.

Of the ghost one learns of a local story that a man was scared to death after seeing the apparition, but official records disprove this. Some facts of the haunting, however, are that in the 1960's a figure of a woman dressed in black was seen disappearing through a wall in the picture gallery adjoining the King James's Room. The apparition had long hair covering most of its features—hardly that of the normal appearance of a nun.

One of the female staff, however, saw a 'fascinating woman dressed in white glide past me. I heard the rustle of her dress and saw the long white train as she moved past. It was about ten o'clock in the evening, some time in January.'

In August 1954 a Flight Lieutenant on coming off duty at ten went to his room to read but fell asleep. He awoke at 3.45am and decided to read again and switched on a light. 'There at the side of my bed a woman with a ruddy face and untidy hair, wearing a dark dress with a white lace collar. She appeared to be holding a note pad. She moved to the foot of my bed and vanished.'

Three years later in March 1957 another officer saw a 'motionless head and shoulders of a middle-aged woman dressed in what we associate as a nun's head-dress. She was looking past me with an expression of serious thought'.

Both these experiences, like the others, were witnessed in the picture gallery.

What is puzzling is that out of the numerous statements by witnesses, in one of which an American officer felt a pair of hands around his ankles, only two seem to match the description of a nun and the experiences involved vary considerably.

Great Park

Ampthill, Bedfordshire
Open to the public during normal hours
on A5120
1¾ miles from Flitwick station

What must be a unique and one of the most romantic looking ghosts in the country is that which haunts this 300 acre park. Charles II presented the huge plot to the Ashburnham family and Lord Ashburnham built the house there in 1694, mainly to replace the ancient castle which had become too ruinous.

Sir John Cornwall had built the fortress for his wife, and Catherine of Aragon was sent there pending Henry's divorce arrangements. It seems a pity that all that is left of what must have been a magnificent building is an 18th century cross which marks its site.

Most, if not all, of the material went to construct the new home for the Ashburnhams which, incidentally, is not open to the public.

The apparition starts his tour within feet of the castle's site and rides down towards a small brook where it vanishes. Described by some as 'a knight in full armour with a plumed helmet and on a magnificent white steed', he is seen by more mature witnesses as a 'white shape of a man riding a horse'. The latter description was that given by an ex-policeman who was on holiday in the area in September 1965.

Whatever the phantom looks like, he remains unidentified.

Luton Museum and Art Gallery*

Wardown Park, Luton, Bedfordshire
Open to the public during normal hours
Junction of A6/A505
Nearest station—Luton

The Luton museum building was originally a Victorian home, but was taken over by the Corporation in 1904 and opened as the town's art gallery and museum in 1929. It contains many fine collections including those of musical instruments, archaeological exhibits and local witchcraft finds.

For some years the building has been haunted by phantom footsteps heard both early in the morning and in the evening. Several of the staff and a few visitors have heard the sounds of an unseen person walking gently up the back staircase and the curator, Mr P Smith, admitted that he too thought he heard the noise.

'But,' he hastened to add, 'I don't really believe it was any sort of psychic phenomena. I just don't believe in ghosts.' He has been the administrator of the museum for seven years and had often heard reports by witnesses and feels that his own repeated experience was caused by auto-suggestion'.

'The romantic story associated with the footsteps is unfortunately untrue,' he pointed out. 'The tale is that the ghost is of a Victorian housemaid who, after an unsuccessful romance, drowned herself in a lake in the grounds. In fact, the lake was not constructed until after the Council had taken over the building.'

Nevertheless auto-suggestion cannot account for all the reports received, surely?

Markyate

Bedfordshire
Open to the public
On A5
5 miles from Luton station

It is not unusual to see a ghost in quiet country lanes, but to encounter an apparition on a busy trunk road is slightly out of the ordinary.

The site of a shattering experience in 1970 was on the A5, close to the Pack Horse Inn, between Dunstable and Markyate. It was early one Sunday morning when a taxi driver on his way to collect a fare had the fright of seeing a figure 'about six feet tall, dressed in white' suddenly stepping out in front of his vehicle. 'I braked,' he told a local news reporter, but I was going too fast and went straight through him.' The driver was so confident he had hit the ghostly pedestrian that he parked his car and went back to search the area.

But 'there wasn't a sign of anyone and the car was unmarked'. The figure's clothes were those of a cricketer and it was established that in 1958 the cricket team of Kenwood Manufacturing Co Ltd were returning to Surrey after a match at Milton Bryan by way of the A5.

Exactly on the spot where 'the man in white' had been seen the group swerved to overtake a car and were involved in a severe crash, killing two of the team, Sidney Moulder and Jerry Rycham of Woking, and injuring three others.

What is perhaps remarkable about this case is that several reports have been made by motorists passing the site stating that they had noticed a cricketer on the side of the road whom they presumed was a hitch-hiker having just left the local pub.

Union Street

Bedford, Bedfordshire
Open to the public
On A428/A6
Nearest station—Bedford

Joining Tavistock Street with Dame Alice Street, about 100 yards from the prison, Union Street is now popular with motorists for it offers parking space for busy shoppers. In earlier years, however, the road, then much wider, was the site of the public gallows and it was here that 'Black Tom', a disreputable highwayman, was hanged for his crimes in 1607.

Occasionally workers who have been working overtime when going to collect their cars have seen the figure of 'Black Tom' near one corner of the parking area, 'wavering about as if drunk with his head lolling on one side like a loose puppet' was what one witness described it as in 1963. But as soon as anyone curious enough moves towards the figure it 'just disappears'.

Woburn Abbey*

Woburn, Bedfordshire
Open to the public during normal hours
On A50
6 miles from Leighton Buzzard station

Thanks to the publicity minded Duke of Bedford, this historical house must be one of Britain's best known mansions. Now with a large collection of wild animals which compete with Longleat's game reserve, practically every interest is catered for.

A famous collection of art treasures from renowned oil paintings to furniture and silver, 14 state apartments and a 3,000 acre park vie with each other to attract the thousands of tourists who visit this splendid and picturesque property each year.

When the thirteenth Duke found himself owner of Woburn Abbey in 1953 he found some hefty problems—death duties of 4½ million pounds, a house that costs £150,000 a year to maintain and some ghosts. Despite the huge difficulties he chose to remain and promote the Abbey as 'the stately centre of the world'.

But it is only occasionally that one hears about the spectres which inhabit the 18th century building. Even in his own autobiography, *A Silver Plated Spoon*, the Duke made no mention of the haunting atmosphere which pervades certain areas.

Although no actual apparition has been seen by the Duke he has often been aware of a presence in certain rooms. The main problem, however, has been the persistence of the door opening phantom.

So frequent was it (doors of a television room were constantly opened and seconds later a facing door at the other end of the room was affected) that the wing of the building was reconstructed turning it into bedrooms with a passage where the doors used to be.

In an attempt to stop the activities the doors were constantly being locked and finally new locks were fitted, but to no avail.

Unfortunately the door opening sessions have now moved and communicating doors of the Green and Roses bedrooms are now affected. Her Grace, the Duchess of Bedford, told me that 'guests who do not know about the presence of the ghost in the rooms came to me quite perturbed the following morning as they have had to get up several times in the night to close the doors—there are three doors to the rooms to open'. As to the identity of the unseen inhabitant 'it is supposed to be a young man who was strangled, but not killed, and kept in what was called the masquerade cupboard, then thrown unconscious from the window, dragged through the park and finally drowned in one of the lakes'.

Why the poor lad should have a mania for doors though is not known.

An apparition that haunts 'mostly the north wing and corridors' and has had the great pleasure of 'meeting' Her Grace the Duchess unfortunately 'frightens the dogs out of their wits'.

The Abbey was built in 1744 on the site of a Cistercian house which like so many others, was seized under the Dissolution. The Abbot had spoken out against the King's marriage to Anne Boleyn and was hung for his indiscretion from one of the oak trees still to be seen in the south front.

This may well be the cause of the apparition often seen in the crypt by the Duchess, visitors and, more especially, workmen and cleaning staff who have described the figure as 'wearing a brown habit'. An identical ghost was witnessed in the magnificent Sculpture Gallery during a special Club dinner in March 1971. He was seen 'standing between the entrance pillars with his back to the room. Then he just glided through the door'. The Duchess said that 'our Irish chef who lives over the room has also seen the Sculpture Gallery ghost and two ladies who went through the wrong door found him peering at them'. She adds further details of the phantom's clothing for he 'wears a long brown cloak and an enormous hat'.

According to the 'Bedfordshire and Buckinghamshire Observer' other guests reported 'an icy blast' at the time when the ghostly monk made his appearance.

One explanation offered for the 'new' ghost is that considerable repair work has been carried out recently and 'possibly this has disturbed the conditions'.

Another recent haunting is that in the Antique Centre. 'A tall man in "antique clothes" with a top hat' has been witnessed by a painter who had no prior knowledge of the ghost, several visitors and a female member of the staff.

Berkshire

Where the phantom of Littlecote House haunts

Open to the public during normal hours or by appointment	3
Historic buildings	1
Churches	1
Shops	1
Apparitions	
Female	1
Male	2
Others	1

Church of All Saints

Faringdon, Berkshire
Open to the public during normal hours
Junction of A420/417
11 miles from Swindon station

This unusual building, a cruciform church with a central tower that lost its spire, dates from the 12th/13th centuries. Inside visitors can see on the south door ancient ironwork with dragon motifs to the Unton and Pye families.

In the graveyard, nearest the adjoining Faringdon House, the ghost of a headless man has been seen at dusk walking slowly along the north wall of the church. Some locals believe he is one of the 15th century Unton family who was beheaded during the Civil War.

Littlecote House*

Near Hungerford, Berkshire
Open to the public during normal hours
Off A4
3 miles from Hungerford station

During my few years in The Life Guards one of my squadron leaders, Major John Wills, a member of the tobacco family, told me of the ghost of this historic building which has been owned by the family for some fifty years.

It is a Tudor mansion of the 1490-1520 period housing many beautiful items of furniture and tapestries and, with its six acres of grounds which contain a Tudor Mount and a trout stream, is situated in the open unspoiled countryside of the attractive Kennet Valley. One of the attractions to visitors is the magnificent Great Hall in which is displayed a fabulous collection of unique Cromwellian armoury.

The oft told legend of the ghosts is that concerning the Darrell family who used to own the house in Elizabethan times. 'Will' Darrell, the black sheep of the family, was charged with the murder of a new born baby, having told the midwife within minutes of the birth to throw the child on the fire. Despite protests the baby was grabbed from her arms, tossed into the fireplace and held down by Darrell's well polished boot until the flames had consumed it. Somehow Darrell was acquitted though the local belief was that the child was his, born to one of his several mistresses, possibly even his own sister.

John told me that occasionally bloodstains were supposed to have appeared on the floor of the haunted bedroom, and the ghost of the tragic unidentified fair-haired mother carrying a torch used to be seen in the Long Gallery. The apparition of Mrs Barnes of Great Shefford, the midwife, carrying the babe in her arms was seen in the bedroom.

It was the ghost of the child that caused the death of 'Wild Will', for it is supposed to have appeared suddenly in front of him when riding in the park startling his horse to such an extent he was thrown from the saddle and broke his neck. 'Darrell's Stile' is a spot which still frightens horses.

Sir Edward Wills, elder brother of the present owner, definitely saw the apparition of the mother in 1927, but more recently other spectres have been witnessed. A female figure walked along a narrow passage, through a doorway on the north side and out into the garden in 1968, and in 1969 footsteps were heard by guides in the Long Gallery when all visitors had left.

A year later Joe Milburn, a National Trust lecturer, took two photographs of the four-poster bed in the haunted 'murder room'. When the film was developed an unusual semi-transparent shape could be seen leaning through the curtains surrounding the bed. Kodak assured Joe that there was nothing wrong with the film, their technicians had checked it and found it perfect.

One of the most recent incidents was in September 1970 when a journalist saw the apparition of the midwife and child in the bedroom.

Shoppenhangers Manor Restaurant

Maidenhead, Berkshire
Open to the public during normal hours
Exit from 9A on the M4. Just past the Esso Motel
Nearest station—Maidenhead

Though the restaurant of this highly attractive building is new, the ancient manor house linked to it dates back to the 13th century. It was originally the home of the de Shoppenhangere family, but has been completely rebuilt twice since its construction though the huge barns in the courtyard, built mainly from ships' timbers, are the originals.

Surrounded by a typical old English garden the manor offers a really baronial atmosphere and food.

Late in 1971 one of the waiters, during the preparation of an evening meal, was disturbed at seeing the ghostly figure of a tall man 'in grey clothes' silently glide across a landing on the first floor. Upon reporting the matter he learnt that several of the staff had seen the apparition at 2am and believed it to be that of an old servant of the Tudor lord who died after falling down a stairway.

Buckinghamshire

With two haunted abbeys and a training school

Open to the public during normal hours or by appointment	11
Private houses	2

Historic buildings	1
Churches	2
Inns, hotels	3
Private houses, offices, factories	3
Open spaces, roads	3
Schools, universities, colleges	1

Phenomena	
Noises	3
Moving objects	1

Apparitions	
Females	6
Monks	1
Males	4
Horses	2
Others	1

Aston Sandford Church

Near Haddenham, Buckinghamshire
Open to the public during normal hours
Off A4129
3 miles from Monks Risborough station

Here in this 13th century church the ghost of a former 19th century vicar and diarist, the Rev Thomas Scott, has been seen shortly before evensong. He appears standing beside the pulpit and remains, according to one recent witness, 'for some minutes' before 'gently fading away'.

He is known to have spent many years of his life in the village and took a considerable interest in the church and the welfare of the local residents.

He visits the parish less frequently now and has only been seen about a dozen times in the last 25 years.

Bucks Standard

10 St John Street, Newport Pagnall, Buckinghamshire
Private property, please respect

Newspapermen and journalists are renowned for their scepticism of ghosts and most of them are prone to dismissing tales of the paranormal as imagination. Occasionally however, as in the case of the haunting of Worley Lea Farm in Essex, the reporters are forced by their own experience to admit to the phenomena.

In this instance, in Buckinghamshire, the ghost is so infrequently experienced as practically to be ignored by the staff of the weekly newspaper. But nevertheless some employees working late in the folding department have heard 'definite footsteps and a scratching' coming from an empty storeroom on the top floor.

If this had been the only experience it would have been dismissed, but a few years earlier, a young printing apprentice hurrying into the building one evening enquired about the 'figure in white looking through the window upstairs'. The room in question was at the time empty and had been locked for some months.

Confirming the haunting by an unknown spectre was the report by the previous tenant of the 120 year old building of hearing footsteps, 'rather like those of a woman', issuing from the top floor.

Castle House

West Street, Buckingham, Buckinghamshire
Open to the public by appointment only
Junction A413/A422
12 miles from Bletchley station

In 1965 Buckingham Town Council moved into this ancient house, unaware that the property had been haunted for many years by the ghost of a priestly confessor to Catherine of Aragon. It was here that Catherine gave birth to a son, who died within hours, and waited patiently for her divorce from Henry VIII.

The 12th century Castle House was built with stones from an ancient castle destroyed by the Danes and was originally the seat of John Barton, one of the county's Knights. In 1431 he left the house to his brother, but shortly afterwards it was taken over by the Fowler family and it was Edward Fowler who entertained Henry's first wife.

By 1592 Theophilus Adams had claimed the estate because it had been used for 'superstitious purposes', John Barton having let it to a priest who was later to celebrate mass in the local church. It is probably this gentleman who has been seen in one of the upper corridors.

Considerable alterations were carried out in 1619 by the new owners William and Mary Lambard, but when William died his widow married Sir Edward Richardson and counted among her guests King Charles I. On one visit here he held a council of war on the premises with Prince Rupert and the Prince of Wales before going to Oxford and defeat.

Further alterations were made in the 1700's, all the front rooms of the building being re-designed, but some years later about 1830 the north wing was so dilapidated it was pulled down. In 1881 further improvements were made and when electricity was incorporated into the amenities (in 1908) a priests' hole over the entrance to what was 'The Great Parlour', was discovered containing a male skeleton. This was at the time believed to be the remains of the priest who had been locked up in the hiding place while attempting to escape.

The house by the 1960's was owned by John Bristow Bull, a descendent of the Prince of Wales, whose father had been instrumental in the discovery of the ancient hiding place. Because the racing track at Silverstone is only a few miles away several of the famous drivers, including Stirling Moss and John Surtees, used the house as temporary accommodation and it was during this period that the ghost was seen again gliding along the corridor leading to his eventual grave.

Council employees have seen nothing unusual, but reports are that the ghost only appears after normal working hours.

Chequers Inn*

London Road, Burry End, Amersham, Buckinghamshire
Open to the public during normal hours
Off A413
Nearest station—Amersham

Is it coincidence or is it due to the ghost that landlords of this charming old pub stay only a few years? The previous guv'nor, a former private detective, left after numerous nights of being interrupted by the sounds of moaning. His daughter was scared on one occasion by a 'white hooded' figure floating silently into her bedroom.

The inn was built in the 15th century and has undergone little alteration since, though gas fires now occupy spaces that were originally open ingle-nooks. It was one day in 1971 that a Scots barman described to the current licensee, Mrs Vera Hill, the figure of a man wearing a long dark cloak that he could see 'trying to get up the chimney'.

'I could see nothing myself,' she told me, 'but I am convinced the place has a ghost. We discussed the description of the apparition with some locals immediately afterwards and they assured us that it was that of Mr Osman who had been seen numerous times over the last few years.'

Shortly after the hostelry was initially opened, a group of religious martyrs, six men and a woman, spent the night there under the guard of Osman, a warder. The following morning the seven were burned at the stake about a mile away in Rectory Woods.

Ellesborough Parish Church

Ellesborough, Buckinghamshire
Open to the public during normal hours
Off 4010
3 miles from Wendover station

Overlooked by Beacon Hill at Great Kimble is the small but ancient parish church of Ellesborough and here, shortly after the war, the church organist witnessed a seldom seen phantom of a 'tallish man dressed in mediaeval garb'.

Whilst practising at the instrument, he heard the front door of the church open and turned round to see the ghost 'just glide in and move over to one of the memorial tablets where he vanished'.

A few years later, a lady arranging some flowers at the altar had the chequer experience, and early in 1970 a visitor to the church reported a similar incident. He was interested enough to walk over to where the apparition had disappeared and found that the only object of interest there was the Hawtrey Memorial plaque.

George and Dragon Hotel*

High Street, West Wycombe, Buckinghamshire
Open to the public during normal hours
Junction A40/A4010
2 miles from High Wycombe station

Not very far from the notorious Hell Fire Caves, the site of Sir Francis Dashwood's diabolical orgies in the 18th century, lies this attractive hotel the proprietor of which, Mr James, is a puzzled man. So many people have seen the ghost of Susie (or Sukie) in recent years that he is at a loss to understand why he has not witnessed her activities or even heard the ghostly footsteps treading the main stairway.

One of the most recent reports of the haunting was in January 1972 he told me when one of his guests saw the apparition of the young woman in a 'glorious white dress' gliding along an upstairs passage. Also, at certain times of the year, dogs refuse to enter the bedroom from which the ghost emerges, usually between two and three o'clock in the morning.

The ghost is strongly believed to be that of a young and attractive serving wench who was accidentally killed in the caves by three jealous admirers some 200 years ago. Her attentions were directed towards one of the more generous and prosperous clients and no doubt she had been lured to the assignation in the belief she was meeting her lover. One can imagine the horror with which she viewed a trio of half drunk sneering locals and must have fought fiercely before tripping and striking her head on the cave wall.

Her body was brought back to the bedroom, still in a dress which resembled a wedding gown, where it was found the next morning.

Mr James also reminded me of a report, published in *Readers Digest* in 1966, made by an American guest who slept in the affected room before being awoken by a 'column of light hovering near the doorway. The light ballooned forward and seemed to reach towards me'. He had already got out of bed armed with a heavy book, but when the swishing opaqueness moved towards him he jumped back and switched on the electric light.

The footsteps are those of a traveller who, it is claimed was robbed, murdered and locked up in another room in the latter half of the 18th century.

The proprietor has also heard it said that a tunnel exists joining the hotel to the Hell Fire Caves which would suggest that at least part of the building is very much older than the extensive re-building work that took place in 1720.

Lane end

Buckinghamshire
Open to the public
On B482
5 miles from High Wycombe station

During the latter half of the 19th century a young village girl whose favourite colour was deep red and was always seen wearing dresses of that colour had announced her forthcoming marriage to another resident of the village. He was one of the workers on Muswell Farm near Hanover Hill, about a mile south of the village.

Anna, the bride to be, often worked in a pub at Wheelerend Common, north of Lane End. Tragedy struck the couple, however, for only ten days before the ceremony Anna fell ill and died from an unknown illness.

Only a few years later her ghost was reported having been seen on country paths in the locality of Park Lane leading from the pub at Wheelerend Common. It was in this area that the couple used to meet during their courting days.

Eventually stories of her wanderings died out until the 1940's when Anna's phantom became extremely active and was seen by some of the villagers no less than 30 times in one year.

Now it seems that she has changed her haunting locality, for in December 1961 a girl in a 'red wine coloured dress' was seen drifting across a field travelling towards Hanover Hill. Her appearance was also recorded in December the following year and on both occasions she appeared early in the afternoon 'about half past three'.

Little Abbey Hotel*

Great Missenden, Buckinghamshire
Open to the public during normal hours
On A4128
1 mile from Great Missenden station

What could be better than having a haunted hotel within yards of a haunted Abbey? This country house hotel, believed to be at one time part of Missenden Abbey and therefore dating back to the 12th century, has been regularly visited by a phantom monk since the turn of the century.

In 1955 the owner wrote that 'some 50 years ago servants could not be persuaded to enter what is now the lounge', but when I spoke to the assistant manager here in September 1972 she told me that 'only last week there was an unusual incident'.

Early one morning during the week of the 18th September Mr Allison, the hotel handyman, was 'fixing a window' on a half landing when he saw the figure of 'a gentleman in a brown hooded cloak coming up the stairs. He had his hands together as if in prayer and as he passed me I wished him a 'good morning' and turned back to my work'.

A few minutes went by and no-one came up or down the stairs. Mr Allison was puzzled as to where 'the guest' was going to for, other than a toilet, the rooms on the top floor are those of the staff and are all locked. The handyman checked the doors and the toilet and reported that he had been unable to find the gentleman or explain his disappearance.

Mrs Potten, the assistant manageress, was quite convinced that the figure was that of the monk who, years earlier, kept the staff away from the lounge.

An unknown monk of the Augustinian Abbey is believed to have committed suicide in 1297 for fear of the disciplinary action that would be taken against him for some misdemeanour, but it may well have been Roger Palmer. This incumbent was, according to one work, seen leaving a married woman's house early one morning clad only in 'hose and a doublet and a sword'.

The appalling scandal which resulted from this incident is understood to have been the cause of closing the Abbey.

The water supply to the hotel once came from a well inside the building, but this eventually dried up when the river Misbourne shifted its course after a flood.

Little Abbey Hotel was once used as a preparatory school and it was during this period that a secret passage was discovered leading to the Great Abbey. The entrance to it, a trapdoor in the ballroom bar, was blocked and cemented over.

Although there is no mention of 'Little Abbey' in official documents, local belief is that it was built for nuns of the same Augustian order and this tunnel was used by the monks to gain entry into the building to provide the Sacrament to the women without breaking numerous vows.

Loakes Road

High Wycombe, Buckinghamshire
Open to the public
Off A40
Nearest station—High Wycombe

In the 17th century one of the manors of High Wycombe, Loakes House, was known as the home of a keen horse rider. She was killed in the lane leading to the property when her mount threw her during an early morning canter, and occasionally early riders have seen the ghost of a woman riding furiously down Loakes Road disappearing at a spot near the football ground.

The house, built by the Marquess of Lansbury, is now Wycombe Abbey School for Girls and the road in which it stands leads to Wycombe Hospital, a useful facility should any witness suffer from shock at the sight of an apparition vanishing into thin air.

Missenden Abbey*

Great Missenden, Buckinghamshire
Open to the public by appointment only
On A4128
Nearest station—Great Missenden

Does a ghost need educating one wonders, for Missenden Abbey is owned by the Buckinghamshire Education Committee and run as an Adult Education College offering weekend courses on folklore, ballet and dressmaking as well as evening meetings for the general public and courses for teachers.

The Abbey was founded in 1133 by Augustinian monks from Northern France. Henry III stayed here several times offering as payment for the hospitality timber for the rebuilding of the Abbey Church. Princess Elizabeth inherited the property from her father Henry VIII, after the dissolution, but soon after her coronation the new queen gave the Abbey and its lands to her favourite the Earl of Leicester known, as all television watchers will know, as 'Robin'.

The Earl obviously decided to make some profit on the gift and sold it in 1574 to the Recorder of London, Sir William Fleetwood, whose family lived in it until the 18th century and had altered it to become more of a manor house than a religious establishment.

On the death of the last Fleetwood, James Oldham Oldham purchased the property and demolished much of the original

Abbey, but in 1806 the new owner carried out considerable renovation and it is the result of his work that is seen today.

In 1946 the descendants of the Carringtons, who had bought the Abbey from John Ayton, sold it to the County Council for use as a college.

The Warden of the Abbey, Mr M Lloyd, tells me that one wing of the house still retains mediaeval timbers in its roof and a late mediaeval chimney, but that's about all that is left of the original building.

There have been numerous stories of apparitions having been witnessed in the building but, as Mr Lloyd points out, 'the only one that appears to have survived relates to the figure of a woman' who has at various times been seen on the main staircase. She is usually seen wearing a black crinoline, though some witnesses describe the apparition as in 'grey Victorian dress'.

In July 1972 one of the students reported that during a course she had taken the previous year a female figure in 'light grey' was seen near the ladies' cloakroom in a different part of the house. A similar incident had been reported about 10 years earlier.

Sometime in 1958 one of the teachers stated that a vase had been thrown down the stairway by unseen hands and in July 1971 a heavy glass ashtray was found split in two, lying on the carpeted floor of one of the bedrooms, by one of the students. Perhaps the 'lady in grey' is trying to persuade people not to smoke or the authorities to organise a flower arranging course?

St Mary's Abbey

Medmenham, Buckinghamshire
Open to the public by appointment only
Off A4155
2 miles from Marlow station

Another of the sites associated with the notorious Hell Fire Club are these ruins of a 12th century Cistercian Abbey which Sir Francis Dashwood ironically used as one of his meeting places. It was here that he, with his young cronies, practised their motto of 'Do what you will'.

What is believed to be a large number of brutal and sadistic murders were carried out in the locality and it is rather puzzling that the area is not teeming with ghosts, phantoms and wraiths of the hapless victims.

There is one, though, and that is thought to be unconnected with the Club. It is of a young woman in a 'light blue gown' seen on the river bank within yards of the ruins. She appears to be bending down searching for something and has been witnessed more often at dusk during the summer months.

The last recorded incident was in June 1968.

Stony Green

Bryant's Bottom, Near Prestwood, Buckinghamshire
Open to the public
Off A4128
2 miles from Great Missenden station

Two miles north of High Wycombe, just after Hughenden, the A4128 turns sharp right at Bottom's Farm, but the ghost hunting driver should carry straight on. Two miles north the traveller will find himself at Stony Green and on his left a hill, Denner Hill. The other side of this is Bryant's Bottom.

As one can imagine, roads in this area are little used and therefore the haunting of Stony Green is hardly known. But in 1961 a farm worker driving his tractor through this bit of the Chilterns slowed at seeing the apparition of a woman in grey riding on the southern hillside.

Her head was bowed and held with one hand whilst her other hand concentrated on controlling her speeding horse galloping to the hillcrest and over the top, presumably down to the Bottom.

The local legend is that the rider is of a 'Lady of the manor' who was killed when her horse threw her, and the cause of her apparent misery was an argument with her husband who had accused her of being unfaithful. She has seldom been seen since the mid 19th century, when the incident was supposed to have occurred, and the 1961 witness is believed to be the most recent.

Vatche's Farm

Aston Clinton, Buckinghamshire
Private property, please respect

Within a few yards of an ancient moat and situated on the Roman road known as Akeman Street, is this old farmhouse. In the courtyard here an apparition in an 'old fashioned dark brown coat' is sometimes seen during Autumn evenings gliding from the gateway to behind one of the outbuildings.

On one occasion three people all saw the figure. The area has a long history but there appears to be no record of any incident which could account for the haunting.

Cambridgeshire

The seat of learning and nine ghosts

Open to the public during normal hours or by appointment	4
Private houses	4

Historic buildings, museums, ruins	1
Inns, hotels	1
Private houses, offices, factories	1
Open spaces, roads	1
School, universities, colleges	4

Phenomena	
Noises	1

Apparitions	
Females	3
Males	4
Others	1

Cambridge

Cambridgeshire
On A10
Nearest station—Cambridge

Practically in the centre of the university complex is Christ's College and here, late in the Easter term each year, a few under-graduates are disturbed at seeing the wraith of a former Don gliding down a narrow lane leading from Parker Street into St Andrew's Street. He has also been seen in Jesus Lane, the area surrounding Sidney Sussex College, off Sidney Street and more often in the Second Court of the College.

There is some evidence for the belief that the apparition, 'a tall young man in grey clothing', is that of a don who was drowned earlier this century in a bathing pool by a jealous and disappointed rival lover of a local girl. Because the murder appeared to be accidental the culprit was never brought to trial, but his conscience overpowered him and he left the town shortly afterwards.

Among the attractions of Trumpington Street, the main road through the town from Royston, is Peterhouse College, the Fitzwilliam Museum and the popular buttery.

The area between Peterhouse and the museum and strongly associated with the nearby inn is haunted by the ghost of a former master's wife who, although not seen for some years, was witnessed in the early 1960's. There are numerous stories as to the reason for her gliding round that particular locality, the most likely one being that one of the students had gained her affections and used to meet her at the pub.

Not far away lies Barnwell Abbey House which was built in 1678, part timber and part brick. It was here that what must be the greatest variety of ghosts ever existed. Unfortunately for the ghost hunter, however, they were all exorcised earlier this century so no longer can visitors expect to experience a poltergeist, clanking chains, a solitary head, a phantom squirrel, a ghostly hare or the apparitions of the white lady or Squire Butler who died here in 1765.

In 1968, however, the ghost of a lady in 'a grey cloak' and believed to be one of the nuns of St Radegunds, was reported to have been witnessed and two further reports in the following year suggests that either a new haunting has started or that she was not previously noticed.

The house in Abbey Road was built on the site of an Augustinian Priory and local belief is that an underground passage exists leading to Jesus College, originally St Radegunds Nunnery. Some evidence for this tradition is that there is a bricked up archway in the basement which could possibly conceal an entrance to the tunnel.

A 'closed haunt' is that of a 'presence' felt in a hostel in St Peter's Terrace. Because of the frightening atmosphere which pervaded the accommodation, the affected room was permanently closed in 1960.

The phantom figure of an undergraduate 'in 18th century clothes' is seen on a staircase in the second court of St John's College. Tradition has it that the ghost is of Dr James Wood who eventually became master of the College. It seems that when a student he was so short of 'the ready' that he had to sit on the stairs wrapped in straw to keep warm and used the staircase light, a candle, to study by.

Yet another haunted area in this seat of learning are the upper rooms of a portion at the Old Court at Corpus Christi. The most interesting explanation for the figure seen somewhat infrequently is that it is of a 17th century student who fell in love with a master's daughter. Surprised during a rendezvous with his lover, the lad hid in a kitchen cupboard immediately below the 'haunted quarters', was trapped and unable to get out. His starved, suffocated body was discovered several weeks later.

The Old Cottage

Little Abington, Cambridgeshire
Private property, please respect

In the small village of Little Abington two buildings are historically linked with the ghost of 'a highwayman' who never was. Jeremiah Lagden, born in 1740, was the son of the owner of the now demolished White Hart Inn at Bourn Bridge. After spending 40 years in the hotel he moved with his mother, brother, sister-in-law and their family to The Old Cottage. His mother, an attractive woman, died in 1785 and was buried in a vault in the garden. The law at that time is supposed to have decreed that people buried in churchyards had to be clothed in wool and those in other material should be entombed elsewhere. Mrs Lagden was able to enjoy her craving for fine silks to the last, having been enshrouded in them before being lowered into her grave.

But the source of the silks aroused curiosity for a number of rolls of the fine cloth were found hidden in the White Hart and were believed to be a smugglers' cache. Suspicion must have fallen on Jeremiah but he died with the rest of the family in 1804, probably from an infectious disease. They were all buried in 'Jeremiah's grave' in the family tomb in the garden. When alterations were carried out in the Old Cottage over a hundred years later, some 18th century perfume bottles were found in a secret cupboard which seemed to confirm the smuggling activities of 'young Lagden'.

Several local residents have seen the ghost of 'a highwayman at dusk' in the garden of the cottage which adds to the earlier, but incorrect, belief that Jeremiah lived by his wits as a 'Gentleman of the road'. There is no evidence of this.

The other building associated with the former post boy of the local hotel is 'Jeremiah's Cottage', but the only real relationship is the name for he was not in any way connected with the property.

Sawston Hall

Near Cambridge, Cambridgeshire
Open to the public by appointment only
On A130
Nearest station—Cambridge

Like Borley Rectory, so much has been written about the haunting here that it has become 'one of the classics' for any catalogue of ghosts.

Sawston Hall itself is of the Tudor period though remains of earlier occupation of the site include Neolithic, Roman and Saxon. It has been the home of the Huddleston family for nearly 450 years and the ghosts include Queen Mary who slept there one night: her bed is one of the highlights of the many exhibits displayed there. Because the Duke of Northumberland's men were unable to capture the Queen they set light to the hall in 1553, but Mary Tudor kept her promise to rebuild it and in 1584 the restored mansion was complete.

One of the witnesses of the phantom queen saw the 'figure in grey' both in the grounds and, as many people have done, in the Tapestry Room where the Queen slept.

Tom Corbet, the renowned clairvoyant, in common with at least two other visitors had heard someone at the door when he stayed there a few years ago and believes that another of the spectres that inhabits the Hall is that of a watchman named either Cutlass, or more likely Cutriss. There is a family named Cutriss in the village.

Mrs Huddleston, the owner's wife, used to hear the sounds of a spinet being played, but that was before the war and the 'tinkling notes' have not been heard since.

Cheshire

With two haunted manors and a tobacconist's shop

Open to the public during normal hours or by appointment	5
Private houses	–
Clubs, cinemas	1
Historic buildings, museums, ruins	2
Shops, stores	1
Open spaces, roads	1
Phenomena	
Smells	1
Noises	2
Apparitions	
Females	2
Males	1

Boys Club

Hyde, Cheshire
Open to the public by appointment only
On A560
Nearest station—Hyde

As with a lot of youth clubs, accommodation is provided for the club leader, in this case in 1968 Mr Andre Davis and his wife. 'Fairly frequently' they have heard the sound of billiard balls clicking in the room below. 'This goes on for, it seems, some minutes, then we hear a loud crash, then silence'.

Mr Davis has given up investigating for on the occasions he has been downstairs nothing unusual is to be seen, though his dog refuses to enter the billiard room.

When they first arrived at the Club, Andre went into the room and saw an old man playing at the table. He looked towards the club leader, but continued with his solitary game. Assuming it was a friend or relative of one of the lads Mr Davis ignored him, but later when he went to lock up there was no sign of the old gentleman and the table was boarded over.

Perhaps confirming the belief that the phantom is that of a previous club leader who dropped dead whilst playing billiards, is that in the morning after the sounds have been heard the wall clock, given in his memory, is found to be going backwards.

Capesthorne

Macclesfield, Cheshire
Open to the public during normal hours
On A34
Nearest station—Macclesfield

Believed to have been built by the renowned John Wood of Bath in 1722, this huge mansion lies close to the modern example of the space age, the radio telescope of Jodrell Bank. The chapel of the estate is understood to be the earliest surviving work of John Wood, though the house itself was later altered by Blore and Salvin.

In 1861 a disastrous fire destroyed much of the centre section of the vast establishment, but it was successfully rebuilt with hardly a trace of the damage that was caused.

It is not surprising that of the people who have experienced unusual phenomena here, several of them are parliamentary representatives for the owner of Capesthorne, Lt Colonel Sir Walter Bromley-Davenport, was an MP himself for many years. Sir Charles Taylor, member for Eastbourne, when staying with Sir Walter, saw the figure of 'a lady in grey' float past when he was about to walk up a stairway in the west wing, but this incident seems unconnected with the other apparitions seen by the owner.

'A number of spectre-like figures' was how he described the wraiths he saw gliding down the stairway into the vault of the chapel, but he also witnessed another ghost in one of the many corridors.

It was his son who suffered a harrowing experience in 1958. He was awoken by the sound of his bedroom window rattling. Turning to see the cause of the noise, he saw what appeared to be a man's arm reaching towards the frame. He jumped out of his bed, strode to the window and, as he reached the glass, the arm vanished. The window was still shut and all that he could see on looking out was a moonlit courtyard empty and still, thirty feet below him.

In March 1967 the butler, Mr Elio Cenzaleghe, told the *Manchester Evening News* that the 'family ghost', 'she is a lady in a greyish dress', has been seen so many times that there can be no doubt as to her authenticity.

Gawsworth Hall*

Macclesfield, Cheshire
Open to the public during normal hours
On A536
4 miles from Macclesfield station

Only a few miles from another haunted manor, that of Capesthorne Hall, is this beautiful half-timbered house of the ancient Manor of Gawsworth held by only five families since the Normans.

In September 1972 I asked the current owner, Mr Raymond Richards, his views concerning the numerous tales of ghosts in the building. He replied that the Hall, the Church and the Rectory 'all 15th century buildings, have been associated with manifestations at one time or another'.

In accepting the phenomena known to occur he said, 'perhaps because we know so much of the occupants of this house living here down the centuries, we have come to attach no importance to happenings which occur from time to time.

At all events they are all part of the household and Gawsworth has a rich heritage of history. We would not have it otherwise.'

One of the most recent manifestations was when Monica Richards reported in February 1971 the smell of incense occasionally creeping into her bedroom which is situated immediately below a priests' hole. It was some 50 years ago that a skeleton was found behind a cupboard near an oratory which leads from the hiding place and an escape hatch to the cellars.

Truly the house has seen many stirring events since the de Orreby family first took up residence in their 'new home in 1130'. This historic manor was the subject of England's famous duel in 1712 between Lord Mohun and the Duke of Hamilton when both contestants were killed. The fighting Fittons lived here from 1316 to 1662 and it is believed that it is from that period that the recently seen ghost 'of a lady in ancient costume' derives.

In 1579 Sir Edward Fitton inherited Gawsworth from his father. He married Alice, daughter of Sir John Holcroft, and many of the letters written to their daughters Anne and Mary survive to this day.

Anne married Sir John Newdigate of Arbury, but it was Mary who was to gain notoriety. In 1596 she was appointed Maid of

Honour to Queen Elizabeth as a result of her father's influence at
the Royal Court, but her career was not to be a long one. She was
believed already to have been termed as 'The dark Lady' by
Shakespeare in his sonnets and in 1602 Sir Robert Cecil reported
to the Queen that her Maid of Honour was pregnant.

The Queen, outraged at 'the efffrontery', sent Mary and the
Earl of Pembroke to the Tower where they 'would both dwell
awhile'. There knowledge of the 'famed beauty' seems to fade,
but it is certainly possible Shakespeare, or was it Bacon, came to
Gawsworth when journeying to Rufford.

Even if one were to ignore the fairly frequent hauntings, Gawsworth itself is a magnificent building rich in exposed timbers of
mediaeval times.

It has been said 'to see Cheshire, you must see Gawsworth'.
I agree.

House of Bewlay (shop)*

Eastgate Street, Chester, Cheshire
Open to the public during normal hours
On A5115
Nearest station—Chester

Many branches of the tobacconists known as the House of Bewlay,
owned in fact by Finlays, are situated in attractive old buildings.
This one in Chester is no exception, but its proximity to recently
excavated ruins of an old religious building or a 100 year old
suicide may be the reason for it being haunted by an unseen
phantom.

On several occasions in the last few years staff have heard someone come into the shop though no-one is to be seen, even when an
assistant is behind the counter.

What has proved a little disturbing to customers and staff alike
is, however, the unusual 'wailing' that has been heard in the centre
of the shop. 'It sounds like a woman moaning', said one customer.

Heavy 'stamping and thumping' has also been heard on occasions
coming from an empty room over the sales area and members of the
staff have often heard someone walking behind them when going
into the storeroom.

According to Mrs L Jones, the manageress, the pitiful cries
heard now, only very infrequently since an exorcism, are believed
to be that of a young woman who hanged herself many years ago
after her husband deserted her. 'It used to be a glass shop,' she
told me, 'but before then was an old burial ground. Doors still
open by themselves and lights come on and off, but we have got

quite used to it now. We accept her as a member of the staff and call her Sarah'.

Mr Wakefield, sales director of Finlay, said that the premises are part of a modernised block of shops which are about 30 to 40 years old. 'I understand that the phenomenon is much quieter these days. But I must admit it's a bit unusual to have a member of the staff both unpaid and unseen.'

Mrs Jones feels that 'there is a queer feeling of friendliness' towards the ghost and no-one is worried any more. 'In fact, there is an atmosphere of confidence' that Sarah will eventually leave, but in the meantime causes no serious problems.

Poulton Road

Bebington, Birkenhead, Cheshire
Open to the public
Off A41
Nearest station—Bebington

One evening in August 1970 a motorist driving along Poulton Road from Higher Bebington had just left the area illuminated by the street lights when he saw a figure of a girl 'with long hair and a long dark coat' standing on the verge.

The driver stopped to offer her a lift, but as he opened the passenger door 'the girl slowly vanished into thin air'.

This was not an isolated incident for only three weeks earlier another motorist had had a similar experience, and earlier in the year a woman walking home from Clatterbridge Hospital had seen the same lonely figure standing at the roadside.

Some many years ago a novice on her way to a nunnery from Poulton Hall is known to have died in the locality and the belief is that the apparition now being seen is of this youngster. She was a local girl and believed to have suffered from a broken romance.

Cornwall

An ancient county in the West

Open to the public during normal hours or by appointment	4
Private houses	–
Historic buildings, museums, ruins	3
Inns, hotels	1
Phenomena	
Noises	2
Moving objects	1
Apparitions	
Males	2
Others	1

―――――――――――――――

The Manor House*

West Pentire, Newquay, Cornwall
Open to the public during normal hours
On A3059
Nearest station—Newquay

This attractive 15th century guest house is known to be haunted by the ghost of Dr John Pussey, former vicar of Crantock. The house was originally owned by the Duke of Falmouth, but it was in the mid 1800's that the reverend gentleman lived and died there.

Among the many reports of the vicar's activities was in September 1970 when a couple saw the figure standing in the lounge looking out of one of the windows across the front lawns.

It was only a few weeks earlier that another pair of guests had seen him for the first time when they were walking to the front door. So convinced were they that it was 'a local priest looking at them' they waved in friendly greeting, but were a little puzzled to learn later that they were the only people in the house.

Mr and Mrs Nash had been staying there for a few days holiday, but on the night before their departure their bedroom became so cold that they slept in their car. They had during their stay noticed doors opened by unseen hands, lights switched on and off and the oven in the kitchen switched off—sometimes at the most inconvenient times!

One of the highlights of their holiday was when Mr Nash had, by mistake, left his 'day' shirt in the bathroom before 'changing and going down for dinner'. It was necessary for Mrs Nash to visit their bedroom after the meal where she was surprised to find her husband's shirt 'neatly folded on the back of a chair'. They questioned the staff and the owners and even other guests as to who had returned the shirt. The only explanation was that the vicar, a very tidy and methodical man, had carried out the service.

When watching television in the lounge the sound of cases being moved was heard in the empty bedroom by several guests. On another occasion Mrs Nash's sister saw a table lamp move just before switching it on to illuminate her sewing.

A honeymoon couple were embarrassed by finding a fire extinguisher outside their bedroom door late one morning. After much questioning it was found that it had been moved from its original site on the ground floor.

The vicar has even been heard to reply to a question put by a guest to her son. She called out to the youngster in number 4 bedroom, 'are you coming down to dinner?' and received the answer, 'yes' from behind the door.

She went immediately to the dining room only to find her son waiting for her. Together they returned to his room but it was locked and empty.

The owners of the guest house are not in any way disturbed by 'their ghost' for it is 'quite friendly and has never scared anyone'.

Manor House Inn

Rilla Mill, Cornwall
Open to the public during normal hours
Off B3257
17 miles from Plymouth station

Well off the beaten track on a small road leading to the mysterious yet romantic Bodmin Moor is the small hamlet of Rilla Mill.

Here in 1965 the licensee of the local pub, Mrs McCloy, reported that phantom footsteps have been heard for several years in an up-stairs room which is always empty at the time of the phenomenon. Many of her regulars who have heard the noises accept them as part of the interest of the old inn, but are not always happy at the very obvious drop in temperature that occurs. 'It gets really icy cold', Mrs McCloy said.

This atmospheric phenomenon may well be caused by the closeness of the river Linner, but however near the river flows it cannot account for heavy footsteps walking on the floorboards of an empty room.

Roche Chapel

Near St Austell, Cornwall
Open to the public
Near junction of B3274 and A30
6 miles from St Austell station

In this ruined 15th century chapel, set high on a pinnacle among the rocks, locals have on occasions heard the sounds of something unseen moving around and infrequently glanced at a 'fleeting shadow' in its precincts.

According to legend it is supposed to be the ghost of a miner who fled for sanctuary to the building after being attacked by demons. It is more likely he was suffering from an overdose of cider, but, whatever the cause, the ghost continues to seek peace in the solitude of this ancient ruin.

Smugglers Cottage Guest House*

West Beach, Portreath, Cornwall
Open to the public during normal hours
On B3300
4 miles from Redruth station

Situated within a few feet of the beach of this north Cornish village this small haunted hotel has a long and interesting history. It was built as a fisherman's cottage in the 16th century and for many years was a private residence. It gained publicity in the 1940/50's as the location for the film *Rake's Progress* starring Rex Harrison and Lili Palmer.

Soon afterwards, during alterations, a minute secret room was discovered between the floors adjoining the central staircase. In it was found a small table seated at which was a skeleton of a man, still wearing remnants of a black cloak, and an old 'sea-chest'. Beside the bones was an old rusty sword and this, with the table, were presented to Exeter Museum.

Contents of the chest were unexciting consisting only of a few coins of the 1700's and some cloth, probably silk. It was assumed that the man had been one of the many smugglers who used to inhabit the area, but how and why he was trapped in the room will never be known.

The house had been haunted for many years before this discovery, however, and continues to be so. The ghost is of a small young man, presumably a smuggler, dressed in 'Jacobean style' clothes who appears from the wall panelling in a first floor corridor and walks furtively towards the staircase where he vanishes. The spot from where he originates is in fact the original entrance to a tunnel leading down to the beach. This had to be sealed by the hotel owners to prevent unexpected and unrecorded late night visitors from entering the building from the seashore.

His appearance was last witnessed by two nurses and a dog staying at the hotel in the 1960's, but some ten years earlier, together with a teacher, a sales executive, a probationary officer and a great dane, I stayed on the affected landing from 10.30pm to 2.30 in the morning in the hope of gaining some psychic experience. At 1.30 we all felt a sudden drop in temperature and watched as the huge dog suddenly bristled, snarled and growled at the wall panelling covering the tunnel entrance.

Though we observed nothing unusual the dog was obviously scared at what he could see. He got up from the floor and, still with his hackles raised and teeth bared, backed against the stairway turning his head slowly as the unseen presence passed within feet of us.

For a few seconds he stood growling savagely at a spot on the floor next to the staircase and then, as if a curtain had been lowered, regained his normal composure and lay down on the boards again between our feet.

Nothing further happened, so after an hour we all went to bed. Wiser? I don't really know.

Cumberland

Has an atomic power station, a miniature railway and three ghosts

Open to the public during normal hours or by appointment	2
Historic buildings, museums, ruins	1
Shops, stores	1
Apparitions	
Females	2
Males	1

Citadel Restaurant*

77 English Street, Carlisle, Cumberland
Open to the public during normal hours
On A6
Nearest station—Carlisle (Citadel)

If the original builders of this establishment knew its use today they would probably turn in their graves for it was designed about 100 years ago as a Temperance Hall, with all the puritanical associations of the Victorian era.

Now it is a large, lively and fully licensed restaurant run by Mr and Mrs Tiidus who have no qualms about housing a couple of ghosts.

In 1966 the *Carlisle Journal* reported that a Mr Don Reid was sitting by the fireside waiting for a friend in the Arcade Bar at about 5.45pm. He saw 'someone' enter the doorway and, assuming it was his colleague, went to order some beer but stopped before reaching the bar for he realized that he was wrong. The figure 'was a grey-black shape about 5ft 7in tall and it came straight through the wall, across the room and seemed to disappear, just as if it had been poured into the ground, about seven feet from me.

It had no recognisable facial features, but was plain enough at the time.'

The barmaid, Mrs Thomlinson of Charles Street, also saw the phantom 'out of the corner of my eye' but it was so real to her that she went into the 'little dispense bar and looked there for what I thought was a customer. But there was nobody'.

On chatting to Mrs Tiidus about the report six years later, she confirmed the details of the incident for she had witnessed not the phantom but the actions of her customer, Mr Reid, and the barmaid.

'The restaurant was altered a year later,' she told me 'and nothing happened until about 18 months ago when my six-year old daughter asked me about the old woman in grey. Was she my baby sitter, she wanted to know. Obviously I have made no mention of ghosts to her but it certainly sounds as if we now have another one.'

Mrs Tiidus also informed me that several cellars and tunnels below the old hall were 'closed up some time ago. Some of them led across the road, others in the direction of the old Abbey'. Upon enquiring as to what building had existed opposite, she replied 'Oh, it was the old town gaol'.

She believes that the old woman seen by her daughter was associated with the prison, but the 'figure of a man could be that of a monk, perhaps?' But English Street is only a few yards from the castle built by William Rufus in the 12th century, so there might be a connection there also.

Lorton Hall*

Lorton, Cockermouth, Cumberland
Open to the public during normal hours
On B5289
14 miles from Workington station

I think here that I can do no better than quote direct from the Rev J A Woodhead-Keith-Dixon's detailed and informative letter to me in September 1972. This followed a report that since his occupation of the Hall in 1961 he and several others have seen the ghost and heard the rustling of phantom skirts in this 17th century manor house.

'The Grey Lady of Lorton Hall would appear to be a member of the family living here in the latter years of the 18th century. This family (which eventually died out in 1851 but was descended as I am from the family of Winder, the original owners of the estate), produced a generation of mongoloid children.

'Two of the boys had keepers and died fairly young. One girl, Elizabeth, was a half mongoloid child but as she grew older became gradually more and more insane. She lived, we think, into her early sixties but, as there is no record of her burial in the churchyard, her age is open to question. We have a grave in the garden at the Hall—always supposed to be that of the Grey Lady. I have a plan eventually to exhume this and take any remains to the churchyard. The reason given for her being buried in the garden is that the then Vicar refused to allow a lunatic to be buried in consecrated ground.

'The appearances are always connected with the full moon—opening and closing of doors between 5 and 7.30 in the morning. Only once, however, have I actually *seen* the apparition during one of these periods. This was at the unexpected time of 9.20am. I thought it was my wife coming down the stairs, as these were distinct feminine footsteps, and I went towards the library door to speak to her. All I saw was a grey gauzy figure carrying a lighted candle—completely ignoring me and going on down the corridor. I recovered quickly enough to get down the corridor in time to see the figure pass through the dining room window (where the front door used to be in the days when she lived in the house). I never really believed the stories until then, but I am now quite convinced of the truth of the stories. The tenant of the home farm, who was a very down-to-earth old Cumbrian and not given to romancing in any way, said he had seen the ghost on several occasions and simply accepted her as a fact. At the end of the war a company of Girl Guides was allowed to camp in the grounds. They were packing up in the early hours of the morning when one of the Guides saw the ghost coming out of the front door and walking in the garden.

'Only one attempt has been made to exorcise the ghost—in 1923—but on the morning this was to be done the priest who was to officiate dropped dead. This was taken to be an indication that nothing should be done so nothing further has taken place since that time.

'The earliest owners of this estate that we can trace were a Norse family called Huthwaite ("the hall in the clearing") who had a dwelling here as far back as the 800's. In 850 AD the monks carrying the coffin of St Cuthbert from Lindisfarne on their fantastic journey fleeing from the Danish invasion rested here—and in their record described the place as "next to" the little tower of Lortona. This must have been a simple "motte and bailey" construction but by 1089 had grown to twin towers. In the autumn of that year King Malcolm III of Scotland and his Queen, Saint Margaret, made a pilgrimage to the holy places in the south of their kingdom of Strathclyde and stayed in the tower of the Hall. They attended Mass in the chapel built on the site of the resting place of St Cuthbert's coffin, celebrated by the chaplain to my ancestor's family. The family living there then was called Swinburn—having married the heiress of the Huthwaites. In or around 1127 the Swinburn heiress married Peter Winder and at the same time this area of Strathclyde was ceded to Stephen of England by David I of Scotland. Coming under the Norman system Peter Winder had the manors of Lorton, Whinfell and Brigham conferred upon him in return for knight's service and allegiance to William de Meschines, Lord of the Honour of Cochermouth. We still hold these three manors within the Honour of Cochermouth, the present Lord Paramount being Lord Egremont.'

The Winder family remained here till 1722, then came the Braggs the last of whom, Elizabeth, died without issue and the estates went to the next in line, the Dixon family, who can trace their descent back to 1541.

Derbyshire

A busy industrial county famous for china

Private houses

Phenomena
Noises

A Haunted Mansion

Belper, Derbyshire
Private property, please respect

Immediately to the north of the industrial town of Derby one
finds Belper and it was in a large house here that some 175 years
ago a murder was committed by a 'large man with a beard'. Below
the building a tunnel leading to a weir is believed to have been the
path through which the victim's body was dragged, finally to be
thrown into the swirling waters of the Derwent.

During the war a Mrs Danbury, who had been evacuated to the
area, found herself, her daughter and another married couple
staying in the property. It had been requisitioned by the Council
to house 'refugee' families from the south.

Her bedroom was at the end of a corridor adjoining a narrow
staircase leading to the communal wash-houses. The next room
was occupied by her 14 year old daughter.

One September night she awoke suddenly at 11.30pm 'fighting
for breath. I felt I was being strangled or suffocated. Whilst still
struggling to regain my senses I felt coarse hair brushing against
my face and neck, and heard the sounds of a man panting. There
was nothing to see even though the moon was bright. This
frightened me even more, of course'.

Gradually she recovered and was able to call out to her companions who were both asleep. The husband, Bill, on visiting the room a few minutes later, calmed her and explained that there was nothing in the room.

Two days later a neighbour suggested that schoolboys had been telling her about the history of the property. Mrs Danbury assured her that she had no knowledge of the place and was then told that she was sleeping in the room 'in which a man had smothered his wife many years ago'.

She remained for another three months, but 'always with the light on and there was no re-occurrence. But another friend who stayed there years afterwards told me they too had the same experience'.

So frequent were the reports of similar incidents that the room was 'never rented to local people'.

Devonshire

For cream teas and thatched cottages

Open to the public during normal hours or by appointment	14
Historic buildings, museums, ruins	2
Inns, hotels	4
Churches, abbeys, rectories	3
Open spaces, roads	3
Schools, universities, colleges	2
Phenomena	
Noises	3
Apparitions	
Females	3
Monks	1
Males	3
Dogs	1
Cars	1
Others	4

Berry Pomeroy Castle*

Berry Pomeroy, Devonshire
Open to the Public during normal hours
On A381
2 miles from Totnes station

The tiny village was named after a Norman family who were responsible for the building of the attractive castle on the peak of a wood-covered cliff. Between 1506 and 1552 the Duke of Somerset, brother of Jane Seymour, constructed a large mansion within the castle walls whilst acting as Regent for Edward VI.

The Seymours remained there until late in the 1600's when it was evacuated due to damage caused during the Civil War. However, His Grace the Duke, the second senior duke in the country, preceded only by the Duke of Norfolk, still owns the castle which suffered further damage from a disastrous fire in 1708.

Reports of apparitions having been seen here extend back for about 50 years, but the most persistent experience is that of a baby's cries.

Occasionally the cause of the pitiful sounds is seen for the babe, an illegitimate child, was murdered shortly after birth by the mother who is believed to be one of the Pomeroy daughters. And it is the woman, dressed in a long blue cape with a hood, that has been witnessed several times close to some arches near the gatehouse.

As well as the phantom and the cries, an appalling sense of loneliness and dread, 'even of stark evil', is often felt by visitors to this particular spot.

Edward Pratt, an engineer friend of mine, was one who suffered from this in 1965 and although he saw nothing he told me that 'the feeling of absolute desolation in those arches is overpowering'. When he visited the castle he had no knowledge of the haunting and was surprised to learn of the infanticide that had occurred several hundred years ago.

Three years later the curator here was given photographs by two separate groups of visitors which show in one print the ghost-like figure of a man in a tricorn hat, and the other the profile of a young woman. Both photographs were taken near the entrance to St Margaret's Tower.

One is to presume that the latter is of the murderess, but that of the man is a mystery which is likely to remain so for some time.

Cheriton Cross

Devonshire
Open to the public during normal hours
On A30
9 miles from Exeter station

Dartmoor is a desolate, rugged and mysterious spot at any time yet with a peculiar romantic aura which in yester-year caused tales of hobgoblins, sprites and, for Sherlock Holmes, the *Hound of the Baskervilles*.

In his *Ghost Hunter's Game Book* (Muller 1958), James Wentworth Day, a renowned writer on fascinating topics, devotes a complete chapter to 'The Black Hound of Mid-Devon' and details much of the research into this phenomenon carried out by Mrs Barbara Carbonnell.

He also publishes the report of Mrs Drummond of Budleigh Salterton who experienced a 'totally new animal ghost, the White Dog of Dartmoor', that she witnessed in the 1930's.

Whether this has any connection with an incident in 1969 is a matter of conjecture.

Ivor Potter was driving back to London along the A30 at 7.30 one evening in October, when he suddenly spotted a light coloured great dane in his headlights standing in the road in his path. He braked hard but was too late to miss the dog, or at least so it seemed. When he went to find the animal, to confirm that he had not imagined it had vanished as he crashed into it, nothing was to be found. 'It really did disappear into thin air'.

Cowick Barton Inn

Cowick Lane, Exeter, Devonshire
Open to the public during normal hours
On A30
Nearest station—Exeter

Some 500 years ago the monastery of St Thomas was sited in this area and when in the 19th century the 'railway came' the name was perpetuated by St Thomas Station. Close to the monastery and possibly part of the estate was Cowick Barton Farm which was mentioned in the Domesday Book.

Eventually the farm fell into decay and in 1963 the ruins were renovated and transformed into this pub. Despite the intensive amount of work involved, however, the apparition of a phantom monk continues to be seen occasionally in the precincts of the modernised construction.

In 1965 Mrs Hayman of 89 and Mrs Jenkins of 95 Wellington Road, which practically adjoins the pub, reported to the *Exeter Express* that they had seen the monk in their bedrooms—most unorthodox. The apparition has been witnessed in 'broad daylight' walking across nearby fields on the river bank by numerous residents and visitors to this ancient old town.

Exeter University

Prince of Wales Road, Exeter, Devonshire
Open to the public during normal hours
Off A377
Nearest station—Exeter

Adding a new interest to the chief city of the south-west, the still expanding Exeter University is a collection of very modern buildings situated in some 300 acres of magnificent grounds offering a choice to the visitor of an arboretum or the new Northcott Theatre opened in 1967.

In the same year several students at the University reported seeing an apparition of a 'tall man in a long white coat' in one of the corridors. Although his identity remains a mystery, he was seen again in 1969 and 1970 and could possibly be one of the decorators who helped complete the building a few years earlier.

It is known that one of the team of workers was a man devoted to his craft and had often expressed his great enthusiasm for the work involved.

Haldon House Guest House*

Haldon Drive, Dunchideock, Near Exeter, Devonshire
Open to the public during normal hours
Off A38
4 miles from Exeter station

The village of Dunchideock, sounding more Scottish than Devonian is described by the AA as 'a handful of cottages near a church, standing alone in a field. A few minutes walk away is Haldon House, built in 1900'. This, unfortunately, is where the confusion starts for Sir Robert Palk, at one time Governor of Madras, is known to have purchased Haldon House and what was then the village of Tor Key for £12,000 from the Earl of Donegal about 1770.

Jim McDougall, writing a feature article in the local paper, *Herald Express*, of 28th April 1972, says that an estimated £120,000 was spent by Sir Robert on Haldon to create a small replica of Buckingham Palace. It was this part that was demolished when the Palks were suffering from financial troubles in 1923. Although on the face of it little should have remained, according to the new owners, however, who moved in during Christmas 1971, the house which was originally the 'servants' quarters' has 22 bedrooms and is now a flourishing guest house.

Efforts have been made by Mrs Parmenter and her family to establish the identity of the numerous ghosts that have been reported there. She told me that one tale was that Sir Robert, later to become Lord Haldon, fathered two sons who were continually fighting until one of them 'disappeared', but despite searches in local records mention of only one son can be found.

Former owners, Mr and Mrs Martin, reported in November

61

1970 that their '300-year-old house' was haunted by the 'head and shoulders of a faceless figure which has been seen gliding past a ground floor glass panel'. This may be connected with the story of a monk 'who was buried alive at Haldon' but where, when and why is not known.

The Martins also told of guests who were woken at 3am by taps on their bedroom doors and, incredibly, a voice calling their first names.

Mrs Parmenter, one of the directors of J H Stone Ltd, the new company formed to administer the small hotel, admitted that some guests had mentioned hearing the sound of horses hooves in the early hours and that the 'apparition had been seen in the bar', but emphasised she had witnessed nothing.

'But with six adults, four boys, three girls and five dogs permanently living here, it's silence that would be unusual'.

Kilworthy House School*

Tavistock, Devonshire
Open to the public by appointment
On A384
15 miles from Plymouth station

Converted from an Elizabethan manor in about 1830 and changed into a school by the Rev John Lyon in 1963, this building will now be seeing even further changes for the new American headmaster, Stephen Cawdray, has great plans to enlarge on the progressive co-education he introduced in September 1972. Mike Reece, the house-master, told me that they cater for about a couple of dozen youngsters between 12 and 17 years of age and two of them have already reported seeing the same ghostly figure that the Rev Lyon reported a year earlier.

The headmaster had seen a 'slim shape dressed in a long grey cloak with a sort of head-dress and from the shape it was obviously a young woman'. Some months earlier a former matron also saw the spectre and a pupil had witnessed the impression of an unseen figure sitting in a chair.

Modbury

Devonshire
Open to the public
On B3207
12 miles from Plymouth station

Built on a steep hill, Modbury is a charming and picturesque market town with several Georgian houses and the attractive half-timbered Exeter Inn which has been a popular meeting place since the days of Good Queen Bess.

In the early days of motoring, Devon was a favourite county only for the wealthy tourist who could occasionally be seen being driven through the country lanes by a liveried chauffeur in the latest Rolls or Daimler. Often picnic baskets would be stored in weird contraptions attached to the boot of the magnificent vehicles or on the roof in personally designed racks.

The gentry of the county travelling to the nearest town would no doubt use less elaborate storage equipment—perhaps just wire netting.

In 1967, whilst driving from Modbury to Gara Bridge over the River Avon at 7.30 one clear evening, a driver from Chudleigh was surprised to see a black 1920 Daimler Laudaulette approaching him. Coming to a bend in the road he looked for the old vehicle, but there was no sign of it. Puzzled by the disappearance of the old model he drove on.

A week later when approaching the same spot, he again saw the Daimler and was able to see that it was fitted with a 'wire netting roof rack' before he reached the turning. On reaching the bend, the man was even more puzzled for again the vehicle had vanished.

This incident was repeated on three occasions during the year and the witness found that two other locals had seen the car. They had, however, noted that the driver was wearing a dark jacket and the peaked cap of the chauffeur, but his features appeared 'misty'.

There is no turning off the road and no lay-bys where the 'phantom' car could have been taken.

Moretonhampstead*

Devonshire
Open to the public
On B3212
13 miles from Exeter station

On April 4th 1969 Mr and Mrs Hunter of Richmond were driving along the winding road from Exeter making their way to relatives at Yelverton. It was 4am in the morning for Mr Hunter prefers driving at night and was keen on seeing the sun rise over the Dartmoor peaks.

'It was fairly misty though', he told me, 'and of course we had our headlights on. We were about half a mile from Moretonhamp-stead coming down a twisting road when Gemma, my wife, pointed out that a car was coming up the hill towards us. We saw the headlights approaching a couple of hundred yards away.

'They were sweeping up round the bend at such a speed that I thought the car would hit us, so swung the wheel over and we landed up in the ditch.'

What puzzled the couple was that no car passed them and when Mr Hunter tried to re-start their own vehicle he found the battery was flat, yet they had travelled over 50 miles without a stop. Eventually they were able to get a tow into Moretonhampstead. 'It took just about 15 minutes', and on reaching the garage the mechanic was as puzzled as the Hunters.

'I can't understand it,' he said, 'every bit of energy has been drained out'. He also told them that no car, as far as he knew, had travelled that particular road in the 'last two hours' since he had been on duty.

Days later the Hunters learnt that 'there have been quite a few drivers who have experienced the same sort of mysterious incident at the spot—but it only happens when there is a mist and early in the morning'.

One of the local AA patrolmen recalled an accident on the bend 'about five years ago. The driver of the vehicle was killed'.

Mr Hunter is a librarian at a university and his wife is a publicity executive.

Old Smugglers Inn*

Coombe Cellars, Near Teignmouth, Devonshire
Open to the public during normal hours
On A379
Nearest station—Teignmouth

In its early days this old pub was known as the Ferry Boat Inn and was much frequented by the lightermen taking loads of Dartmoor stone to London for 'the new bridge' which now resides in America.

Before then it was a rendezvous point for Lord Nelson who is known to have met his lover, Lady Hamilton, here whilst his boat rode at anchor in the nearby harbour. Letters on view in Torquay museum prove this.

Another reason for its local fame is that in the 18th century a woman resident was murdered in a bedroom and the occasion was perpetuated in a drawing made shortly afterwards. This picture was purchased by the landlord a few years ago following complaints by a resident barmaid that she was terrified by an unseen presence in her bedroom.

The licensee at the time did not realise that the bedroom concerned was the 'murder room'. Now it is let out as normal accommodation to tourists and holidaymakers, none of whom have made any comment about 'an atmosphere'.

But in 1970 two television aerial erectors went into the attic to fix a new aerial. One returned to the landing to act as 'adviser' to his colleague, shouting instructions as to the best direction in which to turn the pole. After some minutes the mechanic in the loft hurried down the step-ladder 'white as a sheet and obviously terrified. He flatly refused to go up again without someone with him, but', the landlord told me, 'he also refused point blank to tell me what had caused his trouble. I gather it was something he had seen'.

The site of his work is directly over the bed in the 'haunted' room below.

Parish Church

Weare Giffard, Devonshire
Open to the public during normal hours
Off A386
10 miles from Barnstaple station

Many years ago the nearby Weare Giffard Hall, now a hotel, was haunted by the ghost of a crusader and 'an objectionable woman' who used to bid visitors 'get you gone'. The proprietress of the hotel stated in 1967 that very occasionally reports were received by her guests that they had seen one or the other of the phantoms which, at that time, still lingered in the modernised premises.

A few yards away however, a tall figure of a man has been seen more recently gliding from the gatehouse of the old hall to the parish church. 'He appears to be looking for something', one witness said.

Local belief is that it is the ghost of Sir Walter Giffard who continues to look for his wife who vanished in Edwardian times.

Royal Castle Hotel

The Quay, Dartmouth, Devonshire
Open to the public during normal hours
On A379
Nearest station—Dartmouth

The 1584 Galleon Bar of this old coaching inn was built, it is said, from ships' timbers salvaged from the wrecked Armada fleet and contains a famous Lidstone iron cooking range, locally made 300 years ago. The Bar was formerly two kitchens.

Re-creating a feeling of genuine antiquity is the Adam dining room with an unusual staircase and a magnificent view of the river.

Among many famous guests who have stayed here were Sir Francis Drake, Edward VII, Charles II and Queen Victoria, but the phantom noises of horses' hooves and the crunching of a coach wheels are believed to be associated with William and Mary.

Princess Mary had travelled to Britain to await her husband's arrival, but details of his changed plans (he had landed at Torbay) were brought by a courier at two in the morning. At that time access was through a pair of doors into the courtyard which was closed many years ago and has now become part of the hallway. It is here that the noises are heard by guests and the staff, usually in October.

St John's Church

Torquay, Devonshire
Open to the public during normal hours
On B3199
Nearest station—Torquay

It cannot often be the case when a church organist threatens to go on strike because of a ghost, yet this is what happened here in 1956.

Rehearsals of a choral society also had to be abandoned because of the sudden appearance of an apparition who for weeks had been playing the organ in the empty building. Among the locals who had heard the sounds were the vicar who, like several members of the choir, witnessed the shadowy figure of a man in the vicinity of the instrument.

First reports of the phantom however were made shortly after the death of the former organist, Henry Ditton-Newman. He had died from pleurisy on November 19th 1883 in Babbacombe Road and was buried in the Torquay cemetery. Henry, a dedicated organist, was a former pupil of Dr Samuel Wesley and had improved the standard of the services in the church with several innovations he introduced. He also organised numerous concerts and was an accomplished composer. One of his collections, 'Hymn-Tunes and other Music', was published after his death.

The Rev Hitchcock had admitted to seeing the ghost of Henry several times standing near the organ. Numerous visitors had also mentioned the appearance of the organist, but for a period the reports ceased. It was only in 1956 that the phantom resumed his haunting. One temporary organist complained about the figure who joined him when playing, and refused to return to the church.

The reason for Henry's return is believed to be that he was in the middle of writing some more music when he died. The current vicar, the Rev Rouse, found it necessary to remove the old organ 'because it was worn out' in October 1956. Since then poor Henry has only occasionally been seen.

Montpelier House, the former choir school adjoining the church and a place much used by Mr Ditton-Newman, was also haunted for a period. Footsteps were heard and on one occasion the vicar thought there was a burglar in the house. He chased the footsteps down the stairs into the dining-room where he realised they were made by 'one of the unseen'. A 'locum' vicar often saw Henry in the building until an exorcising service was given on the top floor of the house 'where the atmosphere was strongest'.

Spanish Barn

Torre Abbey, Torbay Road, Torquay, Devonshire
Open to the public during normal hours
On A379
Nearest station—Torquay

Within only a few yards of the railway station in this very popular south coast resort one can visit the ruins of the 14th century Abbey and the Spanish Barn in the grounds of the Abbey park.

The old tithe barn, used at one time to store the produce of the Home Farm for use later by the monks, was also a temporary prison in 1588 for the crew of the *Nuestra Senor del Rosario*. This vessel, one of the ships in the Great Spanish Armada like so many of its companions, was disabled in the Channel, captured and towed to the nearest port—in this case, Torquay.

The entire crew of 397 were quickly taken ashore and held captive in the barn, but only for a few weeks. In the severely cramped and unhealthy atmosphere among the rotting straw inhabited by hundreds of rats, sickness and disease took their rapid toll and few Spaniards survived.

One of the victims was not in fact a member of the crew but a woman disguised as a page to a nobleman acting as Captain of the vessel. The reason for her presence there was that her lover Don Pedro de Valdez, a typical Spanish romantic, was unable to part from her and had smuggled her aboard with the hope of handing her over to some Catholic friends, possibly the Careys, following the conquest of England.

However, she was not discovered until nearing death when a Catholic priest in the Abbey was requested to perform the last rites. Even though nearly 400 years have passed she has often been seen drifting wearily, slowly and with downcast face through the Park to the entrance of the Barn.

Several witnesses whilst in the King's Drive, which adjoins the grounds have seen the apparition—usually about midnight.

Incidentally, Sir George Carey had found it necessary to post a strong guard round the barn to prevent the local residents murdering the crew, for Devon folk had no love for the Spaniards. Some of the survivors of the internment were ransomed and returned to Spain, others sent back to their ship which was taken under escort to Dartmouth and where they were put to work on Sir John Gilbert's estate, and the remainder were despatched in small groups to other parts of the country. Many land-owners benefitted from this free prisoner-of-war labour, but comment is occasionally made of the swarthy Spanish appearance of some Devonians—perhaps not all the prisoners were unloved.

Topsham Churchyard

Topsham, Devonshire
Open to the public
On A377
Nearest station—Topsham

Topsham village stands on a promontory at the mouth of the River Clyst about two miles south of Exeter and for many years has been haunted.

In the road near the Parish church an apparition of 'a grey figure' has been seen usually about 11.30 at night. It moves slowly down the street until reaching the graveyard where it vanishes.

The latest recorded witnessing of this phantom was in June 1968 when a bold resident 'tried to grab it', but it just slipped through his fingers and 'drifted onwards' until reaching the church.

One wonders if there was a fatal accident nearby for this witness stated 'it seemed to rise up from the road surface'. Or is it just steam from a drain?

Dorset

Home of the headless phantom of the Duke of Monmouth

Open to the public during normal hours or by appointment	6
Private houses	2

Historic buildings, museums, ruins	3
Inns, hotels	1
Private houses, offices, factories	2
Open spaces, roads	2

Phenomena	
Noises	3
Moving objects	1

Apparitions	
Females	4
Males	2
Others	1

Athelhampton*

Dorset
Open to the public during normal hours
5 miles from Dorchester station

In August 1972 Robert Cooke, MP for Bristol West and owner of this Manor told me that some three years previously he had woken in the early hours to see the door of his bedroom, 'the grey room', open and close and a very strong glaring light in the room. He believed the incident was connected with the ghost of 'the grey lady' who inhabits the house. 'My wife told me it was due to the cheese that I had eaten the night before, but I can assure you it was not imagination or a tummy upset. My wife was asleep at the time anyway'

Another unusual incident that he personally experienced was in 1957 when he was working in the study. He heard sounds of his cat padding down the stairway and wondering where it was planning to go, went to have a look for the animal. After searching for about half an hour he gave up and returned to his work. The following morning he told the gardener about the incident, for the cat had been ill and he was pleased to realise it had recovered. The gardener's reply, however, was that the cat had died the previous week and was buried in the garden.

The rattling doors which used to disturb the occupants have now been stopped, 'ever since I fitted draught excluders to them', Mr Cooke said. 'But both my housekeeper, Mrs Chinchen, and myself have heard the hammering of the cooper in the wine cellar adjoining the Great Hall. Mrs Chinchen has also seen the grey lady in our bedroom. The room was originally grey, became green, was painted blue and is now yellow.'

The phantom of the 'Black Monk' was dismissed by Mr Cooke. 'I think that turned out to be a priest who was acting as a guide for a party of visitors. He was certainly seen outside the bathroom, but I don't think it was any ghost, just a gentleman wanting to "wash his hands".' There is no historical reason for such an apparition anyway, 'though as far as I am concerned the house which has been inhabited for some 500 years must have some reminders of the past—some of the previous occupants must have left their mark upon it'.

One of the finest mediaeval houses in England with ten acres of landscape gardens, Athelhampton has a unique timbered roof, heraldic glass and a magnificent Tudor Great Chamber. In the grounds the River Piddle wends its rippling way to the coast and nearly encircles the building.

The Manor also has several secret staircases and priests' holes made by Owen, the renowned priest hole maker. One of these, behind some wall panelling, was bricked up many years ago and in the course of the work a pet monkey was accidentally walled up alive in the aperture. 'The animal's scratchings are still heard, despite quarterly payments to Rentokil. It can't be rats.'

'Phantom duellists were seen in the Great Chamber, or Great Hall, before the first world war and there are other stories of headless men at the dinner table', Mr Cooke continued, but exactly who the characters are is difficult to establish.

'The Great Hall itself is one of the finest examples of 15th century domestic architecture in the Kingdom.'

In its early days the de Loundres family occupied the manor and in the reign of Richard II the de Pydeles had taken over. One can assume that the name of the river Piddle is derived from them. Sir Richard Martyn married a de Pydele in the 1350's and the

70

Martyns remained Lords of the Manor for the following 250 years.

The present owner received Athelhampton from his father, Robert Cooke, Sheriff of the City and County of Bristol 1971-72 'on the occasion of his marriage in July 1966 to Jenifer Evelyn King, daughter of Evelyn Mansfield King, MP for South Dorset'.

One of the strange coincidences relating to the poor little monkey which continues its pitiful efforts to escape from its living tomb, is that the family motto of the Martyns was 'He who looks at Martyn's ape, Martyn's ape shall look at him'. The family crest is that of a chained ape or, in heraldic terms, 'a martin sejant on a treestump holding in the dexter paw a mirror'.

A last word of warning is offered by Mr Cooke, 'I have no wish to interfere with the ghosts, they do not worry me. I expect they would turn out in force to frighten off the idly curious however'.

Corfe Castle

Dorset
Open to the public during normal hours
On A351
6 miles from Wareham station

This ancient village with its stone-roofed cottages and an attractive character of its own, clusters like a brood of chicks round an eagle's feet, for it is dominated by the crumbling ruins of a castle of treachery.

It was here that the young King Edward was murdered in 978 by his stepmother, Elfrida, in order that her own son should wear the crown of England. King John used the castle as a royal residence and a prison. Twenty-two French noblemen were starved to death in its dungeons and it became known as the 'Royal Prison of Purbeck'.

Queen Elizabeth sold the castle and in 1635 Sir John Bankes bought it from Sir Christopher Halton. Lady Bankes defended the fortress against Cromwell's troops until Prince Maurice brought help, but it was to be attacked again by Sir Walter Erle and finally in 1646, due to a further example of treachery, the castle fell to the Parliamentarians.

On the road leading to the main gateway a vague spectre of a headless woman has been seen over a period of many years. Who she is or why her mutilated figure stands silently by the decaying stones, no-one can tell. One of the local residents who witnessed her appearance in 1967 said that she may be connected with the ghost of the nearby Manor house.

The Crown Hotel*

Market Street, Poole, Dorset
Open to the public during normal hours
On A350
Nearest station—Poole

What was once a thatched cottage built in the 17th century but later to become a coaching inn, this attractive little pub was reputed to be a regular stopping place for Judge Jeffries before holding Court in Christchurch.

In 1966, after a lot of conversion work had been carried out in one of the old stables to turn it into a discotheque called the Malibou Club, a series of hauntings were experienced in the pub. So impressive were they that an Australian sceptic stayed at the inn intending to disprove them. But the sounds and phenomena continued.

An old piano was heard tinkling in an empty room, sounds of 'something' being dragged over the floor of an upstairs room, a misty figure was seen gliding down the stairs and locked doors would open.

When Mrs Marie Hughes, the new licensee, took over in 1966 she decided to dispose of the old piano and obtain a new one, but before this transfer was completed her 20-year-old son heard the sounds of the instrument being played. The room was completely empty at the time for the piano was being stored in the basement of the Club.

Mrs Hughes told me that she had seen nothing but often found doors that she had personally locked wide open. She has also heard the 'dragging noises' but now pays little attention to the phenomena.

Shortly after arriving at the Crown she had been clearing up in one of the old out-buildings and was returning to the house when she heard a distinct voice say 'hello'. Thinking it was her nephew who had arrived unexpectedly she turned to greet him with 'Oh, hello', but no one was there.

Godlingston Manor

Near Herston, Dorset
Road only open to the public
Off A351
10 miles from Wareham station

Only a few yards away from this Manor at a forked junction in the road is 'Burnham's Corner' named after a man who hanged himself many years ago when the custom was to bury suicides at cross-roads with a stake through the body. Marking the site of his burial is a large oak tree under which a 'phantom-like' figure has occasionally been seen.

Near here, on the top of Windmill Hill, King John had three hunting lodges and a Romano-British site lies about a mile from the front of the manor.

The earliest parts of the ancient farmhouse itself, which is unconnected with the suicide, are reputed to be 1000 years old but a portion of it, together with an adjoining chapel and most of the farm out-buildings, were destroyed in a disastrous fire about 130 years ago.

The haunting is confined to the west wing which houses the kitchen and a tower with three feet thick walls.

Mrs Jean Bowerman, owner of the farm in 1968, described an oft repeated phenomenon she has personally experienced. 'At the eastern end of an upstairs corridor leading from the north corner of the old tower lies the guest room. Unfortunately, because of the atmosphere people are reluctant to sleep there. I have often felt the presence of something on the landing at the head of the stairs and when in the kitchen have heard footsteps walking along the corridor in that area.'

Early one morning at 2am in 1959, Mrs Bowerman was in the kitchen and was convinced that she was being watched through the window which overlooks a part of the secluded garden.

In 1964 a previous owner said that she had experienced a similar incident and had, in fact, seen a woman's face at the same window though on going outside 'no one was visible'. Within a couple of weeks her husband and two sons had also seen the face of a woman peering at them through the glass.

Mrs Bowerman feels that this phantom may well be that of a legendary 'grey lady' mentioned in *Under the Blue Flag* by Palgrave.

A guest staying in the Manor in 1966 was nervous of going upstairs after hearing footsteps of an unseen phantom following him to the bedroom. After discovering a Tudor fireplace in the east wing and an unusual niche outside the tower door during alterations in 1967, a series of 'lights on and off' incidents occurred. Once Mrs Bowerman had to switch on one light in 'the dark corridor' three times in succession.

The Manor House*

Sandford Orcas, Near Sherbourne, Dorset
Open to the public during normal hours
On B3145
Nearest station—Sherbourne

Advertised as 'The most haunted Manor in the County', this building was constructed about 1540 though it is claimed to have 11th century origins.

Reports of ghosts here have been made over a long period one of which, according to local residents, is that of a tenant farmer who committed suicide in the 18th century. A figure matching his description has been seen fairly recently on several afternoons.

Other unusual occurrences inside the house have also been witnessed. A phantom in a red dress is believed to haunt the main staircase and weird music has been heard issuing from an empty room.

Monmouth Ash Tree

Horton and Woodlands, Dorset
Open to the public during normal hours
Off B3078
7 miles from Wimborne station

Between the two villages of Horton and Woodlands, a mere two miles apart, stands the ancient Monmouth Ash identifiable by the brass plate attached to its trunk. It was at this spot that the Duke of Monmouth was captured after his escape from Sedgemoor in the last major battle in Britain in 1685.

The Duke's phantom, gaunt and ragged, has occasionally been seen in the immediate locality. He is easily recognisable for he appears carrying his dishevelled head. Difficult to believe?

There are locals who will swear to have seen the apparition, especially on the night of July 16th the day on which the rebel met his death and few dare to pass the tree without the safety of a charm.

The Rectory

Pimperne, Dorset
Private property, please respect

A few miles north of Blandford Forum lies the small hamlet of Pimperne, once with a Tudor mansion. In the 17th century what was left of the ruined house was incorporated into a new building and is now an interesting combination of two distinct periods.

Some years ago when the vicar and his wife moved into their new home, for the old mansion is now the rectory, they began to hear stories from their parishioners of a collection of ghosts which used to inhabit the garden. An apparition of an old gardener and his dog who moved across the lawn and then disappeared, a woman dressed in a deep purple 'Tudor style dress' who glided over the grass and even a pair of slippers which moved up and down some steps.

No one has been able to identify these phantoms and it is many years since any of them have been seen by human eyes.

In March 1971, however, the vicar's wife, Mrs Farquharson-Roberts, stated that at one particular spot on the lawn both her dog and her cat, if carried to it, will 'bristle and fight to get away'. She had been puzzled by their flat refusal to walk anywhere near the place and had occasionally seen the dog, 'snarling and with hackles raised', obviously watching something 'we couldn't see' moving towards the area.

Visitors have also remarked on the 'sudden feeling of intense cold' when walking over the spot.

Durham

Founders of Washington came from here

Open to the public during normal hours or by appointment	4
Private houses	3

Clubs, cinemas	1
Historic buildings, museums, ruins	1
Inns, hotels	1
Private houses, offices, factories	3
Open spaces, roads	1

Phenomena	
Noises	2

Apparitions	
Females	2
Males	3

Darlington and Simpson Rolling Mills

Longfield Road, Durham, County Durham
Private property, please respect

Early in the 1920's an overhead cable railway belonging to these huge steel mills broke, killing five men working beneath it. Since then numerous workers have seen vague shapes in the locality of the disaster, but in July 1970 a group of men saw a 'vaguely transparent shape' in the finishing mill of the works. It glided swiftly across the huge floor and vanished through a wall leading to the Dripping Factory on the adjoining site.

Pursuing the ghost outside into Longfield Road, the workers spotted the apparition on top of the wall where it appeared to lose its balance and, on falling, vanished. Several of the men thought they were mistaken and that the shape was of some smoke from a nearby chimney, but realised later that it was first seen inside the factory.

One report of some years ago suggests that the ghost was one of the younger workers killed in the cable railway crash. Apparently, during refreshment breaks, he occasionally scrambled on to the wall to give youthful gymnastic displays to his amused colleagues until during one performance he fell breaking a leg.

East House Farm

Washington, County Durham
Private property, please respect

It must be a little disturbing for any man having a bath to find himself being watched by a complete stranger—even more so if the visitor is a ghost of a woman.

This is merely one of the incidents that Ian Lowrie has experienced in his home in the last few years. So tangible was the figure in the bathroom that Ian thought it was his wife and asked her what she wanted. Perhaps embarrassed, the apparition promptly vanished through the wall.

A few days earlier a friend, visiting the house and getting no reply to his knocking, asked a woman he saw crossing the farmyard whether she knew when the owners would be returning. As she continued walking towards the pig house without answering the visitor followed her, assuming she hadn't heard him. On reaching the small byre he was puzzled to find the woman had vanished and yet there was no exit from the building.

Although the Lowries have lived in East House Farm only four years they have already learnt much about their mysterious female lodger. She used to be seen frequently during the first world war and, according to Mr Boyle who is a neighbour, was known as 'The White Lady' because of her flowing white dress. Her identity remains a mystery, but in some quarters locals believe she was the former owner of the farm whose soldier son was killed in the war. So distraught was she on learning the news that she committed suicide.

W H Smith and Sons Ltd★

Mirk Lane, Gateshead, County Durham
Private property, please respect

What must be rather an unusual site for a well recorded ghost is a warehouse of the country's best known booksellers. Originally this Victorian building was a well frequented public house, but during a depression period it was closed down and in 1912 purchased and converted by Smith's to hold stocks of the thousands of publications they distribute.

The current manager of the depot, Arthur Rayburn, is one of the numerous employees who has heard the mysterious footsteps of a regular customer of the pub walking through the building. 'They are heard at varying times,' he said, 'sometimes when the men are having their lunch break and also in the evenings. I suppose the sounds could be associated with the opening times of a pub'.

Although nothing has ever been seen and nothing moved, the footfalls have been experienced over many years and as recently as March 1972.

It is believed that the unseen visitor is that of a former regular customer to the building when it was a pub who collapsed and died in a toilet.

Social Club

Greatham, County Durham
Open to the public during normal hours
On A689
5 miles from Hartlepool station

Practically every village in the country has some legend attached to it. Black dogs, white ladies, giants, dwarfs, pixies all figure in the ancient tales now rapidly being forgotten with the advent of other attractions and knowledge. Many legends, however, had some basis in fact.

The legend of Greatham is that 'a lady in grey' haunts the village and it may well be that a long time ago a phantom was seen here, but details have become fogged with time.

Members of the Social Club in this little village reported in 1968, however, that inexplicable bangings, 'footsteps and unknown voices' were being experienced with increasing frequency. Older residents nodded their heads and murmured 'it's the grey lady again'.

Spring Lane

Consett, County Durham
Open to the public
On A68
15 miles from Newcastle-on-Tyne station

In 1896 when the whole area was a thriving industrial complex, one of the big employers in Consett was a paper mill sited at the end of Spring Lane. Among the many enthusiastic young lads who regularly walked from his lodgings in Snows Green to start work at 7.30 in the morning was Jack Arthur.

His 'landlord' was the local postman who found the arrangement ideal. Both left the house at the same time and on finishing his rounds he was able to get back home to prepare the evening meal for Jack and himself.

The young mill worker often accompanied him for a few yards down the road before they parted, each to his own work. The situation seemed satisfactory to both men, but after a few months the age difference began to influence their attitudes. Jack was anxious to 'enjoy himself' in his spare time whilst the postman, rather a staid character it seems, was unable to join in the 'frivolous outlook of the young lad'.

Neighbours began to hear rows and arguments between the two. Jack would want to go out to the pub with the lads and the older man preferred to remain with his pigeons.

The atmosphere worsened and one evening in November 1896 a loud 'shouting match' was heard. It seemed that the postman was threatening to kick Jack out of the house if he didn't stop his drinking sprees and continuing to 'throw his money down the drain'. Locals were convinced at the time that the lad had more money than he revealed for it was known he was a card gambler and could easily have paid more rent for his keep.

The morning following the row, the postman was seen on his rounds but his lodger was never seen again. Numerous enquiries and investigations were made but, despite strong suspicion, no action was taken. Jack Arthur had vanished.

Occasionally reports would be received by the police of a figure resembling the mill worker being seen in Spring Lane, but further searches in the area revealed nothing and the incident was gradually forgotten.

In December 1970 Mrs Nora Conroy, a local postal worker, reported that when delivering letters at the Snows Green end of Spring Lane at 7.30 in the morning she had a 'strong feeling of being watched'. The morning was dark and the lonely stretch of road was terrifying. She had been delivering letters on this route for many weeks and had never had this experience before. To placate her, the authorities transferred her to another route.

Four days later the new postman for the area, Joe Patterson, rushed into the sorting office to report he had seen the ghostly figure of a 'young chap' standing six feet away watching him. The location was identical to that described by Mrs Conroy and the clothes of the apparition matched those of a young mill worker of the 1890's.

Joe had no knowledge of Mrs Conroy's earlier experience and neither had heard of the facts concerning Jack Arthur's disappearance 75 years previously.

A few weeks later a milkman reported a similar incident and claimed that he had seen the figure several times.

The Vestry

Fawcett Street, Sunderland, County Durham
Open to the public during normal hours
Off A19
Nearest station—Sunderland

Many of the pubs in the North cater for men only, a slightly Edwardian attitude which implies that women restrict the enjoyment of the male drinker. One of these establishments recently crashed into the 20th century by opening a discotheque in the basement to cater for the younger element of the heavily industrial town.

Obviously this action has shaken the shades of the past for in the early hours, when the staff are clearing up, the ghost of an 'elderly bearded man dressed in a perfect Edwardian suit' has been seen to 'shuffle along the bar and vanish at a wall of an adjoining cellar'.

Benny Wilson, the manager of the discotheque, was the first to experience the visit in 1970. 'I was standing with my back to the bar when the barman pointed behind me and gasped "What's that?" I turned to see the ghost with a King Edward VII beard vanish through the wall.'

Several weeks later an anguished waitress rushed upstairs to the main bar and exclaimed 'There's a ghost down there with a forked beard'.

The figure has also been seen by the bar manager and Bruno, one of the guard dogs which howled with fear and now refuses to patrol anywhere near the cellar.

Washington Old Hall

Washington, County Durham
Open to the public during normal hours
Off A182
7½ miles from Newcastle-on-Tyne station

It is perhaps a pity that most American visitors to Britain seldom explore more than London and Stratford-on-Avon, for there is a veritable store of associations with the new world scattered around our counties. In Buckinghamshire one finds the Mayflower Barn, believed by some to have been constructed from the timbers of the pilgrims' ship.

Northamptonshire boasts of Sulgrave Manor where a branch of the Washington family lived from 1538 to the 17th century. Nottinghamshire has Scrooby where one of the Pilgrim Fathers discussed and planned the famous voyage.

Another branch of the Washingtons, however, was here at Washington Old Hall where they resided from 1183 to 1613. It became the property of the National Trust in 1956.

Over the course of the last few years, with more tourists visiting the house, reports of the witnessing of a ghost here have increased in number. The phantom is seen as 'a lady in a long grey dress' gently gliding along an upstairs corridor.

Our overseas cousins, no doubt, would welcome the thought that she is indeed one of the Washingtons and of course she may well be for, so far, no one has been able to identify her. One witness said that the figure looks like that shown in one of the family portraits, but this could easily be wishful thinking.

Essex

The county with a history of witchcraft which houses the famous village of Borley

Open to the public during normal hours or by appointment	16
Private houses	4

Clubs, cinemas	2
Historic buildings, museums, ruins	3
Churches, abbeys, rectories	2
Shops, stores	1
Inns, hotels	7
Private houses, offices, factories	4
Open spaces, roads	1

Phenomena	
Smells	2
Noises	7
Moving objects	8

Apparitions	
Females	5
Monks	4
Males	6
Dogs	1

Ambassador Bowling Club

Basildon, Essex
Open to the public during normal hours
On B1007 (off A127)
2 miles from Laindon station

Sited practically in the centre of the new town of Basildon is this modern offering to leisure time enthusiasts. Although built in recent years the hall, or rather one of the bowling lanes, No. 17, is known to have a ghost.

History shows that in the early part of the 20th century a double murder was committed in a farm building which stood on the site and in 1940 a young man committed suicide there.

But the ghost has been unidentified. He has appeared dressed in workman's overalls on several occasions leaning over a bench in front of the affected lane. Numerous unaccountable incidents have also been recorded. A ball rolled down the lane, bowled by unseen hands, and one evening the pin-setting machinery started up on its own despite the fact that the power had been shut off for a couple of hours.

Investigators have also noticed the smell of a farmyard swirling round the lane end and a drop in temperature, normally associated with a genuine haunt.

Beeleigh Abbey*

Maldon, Essex
Open to the public during normal hours
On A414
10 miles from Chelmsford station

Henry VIII seems to have been the cause of creating several ghosts—those in Hampton Court, the ghostly footsteps in Ewell and the phantom of Sir John Gate of High Easter here at Beeleigh Abbey.

The building itself was constructed in the 12th century for the order of White Canons, better known as the Premonstratensian order, who owned 33 other houses in England including two nunneries. But, like many such religious establishments, it became involved in intrigue and conspiracy.

Abbot Thomas Cok with the abbots of Colchester and St Osyth's and the Countess of Oxford were accused of a plot against Henry IV arising from a rumour that Richard II had escaped death. After the enquiry in 1403 into the allegations, Cok received a pardon from the Queen, but two years later he was found dead by poisoning. His murderer was Canon Ultyng, a fellow priest.

On July 15, 1540 Henry VIII entered the scene by granting the Abbey and a portion of land to Sir John Gate who, although holding numerous high positions of rank including Chancellor of the Duchy of Lancaster and High Sheriff of Essex in 1549, lost his head at Tower Hill in 1553. He had somewhat foolishly promoted the cause of Lady Jane Grey.

This property, however, had already passed into the hands of Thomas Francke who is believed to have constructed the brick wall which surrounds the premises.

The picturesque portions of a once important abbey are so admirably preserved that, it is claimed, few places in the county can equal it.

Miss Christina Foyle, the owner of the Abbey, tells me that people who sleep in a particular wing of the premises 'have all noticed a haunting wailing around the house' on August 11 each year. This date is eleven days before Sir John Gate was beheaded and the noise is assumed to be the poor man's fearful cries of misery at his forthcoming death.

Another haunting is that of a four-poster bed in the James's bedroom where the impression of a body has been seen on occasions, though the room is not used.

Bell Hotel*

High Street, Thorpe-le-Soken, Near Clacton, Essex
Open to the public during normal hours
Junction of A136/B1027
Nearest station—Thorpe-le-Soken

Following a report in the *Morning Advertiser* in 1971, I contacted Mr Eaton, manager of this inn, to find out whether the details given were still current. He assured me that they were, 'but many more people have experienced the sensation of a presence in the guests' bedroom since then'.

The initial article in August 1971 stated that when the Eatons moved in they ignored the local legends that the hotel was haunted, but because of numerous incidents had to change their attitude.

Mr Eaton after cleaning one of the bedrooms locked the door but next morning 'found a heavy wardrobe moved away from the wall'. It is this wall which faces the Parish church which adjoins the Bell.

An apparition of 'a female figure, rather shadowy' was seen by Mrs Eaton's mother at the foot of her bed. It moved slowly towards the door and 'seemed to slide right through it, leaving a sort of white glow behind'.

Bedroom windows have often been heard banging at night, though when inspected in the morning they are found to be as firmly latched as on the previous day.

In August 1972 a guest in room 6 found on waking that a heavy wardrobe had been moved and from the state of the clothes on a spare bed in the room someone had slept there during the night, but no one had entered it whilst he was there—at least, no one he could see.

Mr Eaton told me that he quite accepts that the phenomenon is probably associated with Kitty Canham who is buried in the churchyard, 'next door'. It seems that Catherine, born at Beaumont Hall, married the Rev Henry Gough, vicar of Thorpe-le-Soken in the 1700's, but was bored or dissatisfied with the life in a small parish and married Lord Dalmeny. Her new husband, unaware that she was already a wife, took his bride to Verona where they lived together for three years enjoying the social rounds of high society.

Kitty fell ill and was obviously dying. Realising that she had only a few hours before meeting 'her maker', she confessed her bigamous action and asked to be buried in her own village.

Forgiving his 'wife' her selfish action, Lord Dalmeny brought her body back to England. Both 'husbands' helped carry the coffin to its final resting place in a magnificent tomb, which unfortunately was pillaged 'fairly recently' by hooligans. At least, it was assumed so.

I am grateful to Mr WH Downes of Clacton for the following story concerning the return of Kitty's body.

Not wishing to be associated with the shame of being a second and illegal 'husband', Lord Dalmeny hired a boat in the name of Williams, a merchant from Hamburg, had Catherine's body embalmed and placed in a chest on the ship and set sail for Harwich.

Bad weather caused the captain to pull in at Colchester and it was here that Customs Officers boarded the vessel thinking she was smuggling contraband. When the Customs men found the chest they felt convinced that they had caught the free-traders red-handed.

Despite 'Mr Williams' protests and documents including a letter from 'The King of France' which proved that his wife's body was inside, the officials opened up the crate and exposed the body of a 32-year-old woman. Still suspicious, they took the 'merchant' and Kitty to the parish church at Hythe Hill, Colchester, pending verification and identification of the parties involved.

A few days passed before a local gentleman, after a discussion with 'Mr Williams', announced the true identity of the couple and the vicar of Thorpe-le-Soken was advised of his wife's death. The Rev Gough was at first outraged and threatened to run through Lord Dalmeny with his sword, but when the men eventually met they realised that they both really had deeply loved the same woman and were forced to accept the situation.

The final act of reconciliation was when both 'widowers' walked hand in hand to the grave-side.

Borley*

Near Long Melford, Essex
Open to the public
Off A134
3 miles from Sudbury station

So much has been written, filmed and televised about Borley Rectory, which was gutted by fire in 1939, that it would be unwise to detail here the complete history of what became known as 'The Most Haunted House in England'.

Basically the legend was that the rectory of Borley was built on the site of a 13th century monastery and was linked with a nunnery a few miles away at Bures. A monk fell in love with one of the nuns but both were caught before they eloped and were killed. Phantoms of the nun, the coach which the couple used and a headless driver of the vehicle were all current in the 19th century.

Practically the whole of basic tale was discredited in 1938, though by that time Harry Price, who died in 1948, had rented the property for a year. He was instrumental in publicising the ghosts and phenomena which he claimed existed there, through broadcasts, lectures and more especially his books, *The Confessions of a Ghost Hunter* (1936), *The Most Haunted House in England* (1940) and *The End of Borley Rectory* (1946). He claimed at one time that some 200 different ghosts existed in the old building.

The method of his investigation was severely criticised in *The Haunting of Borley Rectory* (1956) published by three leading members of the Society for Psychical Research following an enquiry carried out at the invitation of the Council of the SPR. The book suggested in fact that Price had been guilty of considerable misrepresentation and that some of the 'phenomena' had been produced by him, but the majority, albeit unconsciously, by Marianne Foyster, one of the residents.

Another examination of the evidence in 1969 appeared to clear Price's name, but grave doubts about the whole series of incidents remain in many people's minds and much more has yet to be written about Borley Rectory.

The building itself is no longer there and all that remains of the original haunted area is the coach-house and the parish church opposite the site. Council houses are now rapidly being built on the former garden of the rectory, but stories continue to be published of the phantom nun still being seen gliding down the 'Nun's Walk' on July 28th or 29th.

James Turner, one time owner of the coach house and author of *Sometimes into England* (1970) told me that he, like many others, had heard the sounds of an organ being played in the empty church and saw the 'apparition of a young woman in grey walking up the path to the church door'.

With three other members of the now defunct Ealing Psychical Research Society I spent a weekend on the site in August 1951 and from our own experiences I am convinced that Borley is haunted. Most tourists and casual visitors to the village however, find that the majority of locals, perhaps naturally are 'absolutely fed up with the stories about the Rectory and the Church'. The only people who continue to welcome the perpetuation of the reports are the licensees of the local hostelries.

Having walked down the road which adjoins the Rectory site and nearly reached the lower-gate-way, one of the Society members grabbed my arm and, although obviously terrified, proceeded to describe a phantom that he could see some 30ft in front of him, standing at the end of 'The Nun's Walk'. It was of 'a woman in a long white gown' and moved slowly down towards the end of the neglected garden and on reaching the boundary hedge, in front of a garage, 'just vanished'.

The time was approximately 1.45am on the first morning of our stay and, although August, it was bitterly cold. The witness however was perspiring profusely with fear and later with annoyance that I had failed to see the ghost. I had nevertheless heard the steady rustle of grass and bushes as if something was walking through the undergrowth.

Some 15 minutes later we both heard a hefty rustling in the roadside hedge and called to our two companions to join us. They had been trying to sleep in a haystack!

The centre of the disturbance in the bushes was about 2ft 6in from the ground, but nothing could be seen to account for the noise. The movement of leaves and twigs moved down towards the gateway for the whole length of the hedge and only 'faded away' on reaching the gate.

Two other inexplicable incidents, including the sighting of a phantom greyhound, convinced all four of us that we had experienced a small portion of the Borley phenomenon.

Church of the Holy Cross

Basildon New Town, Essex
Open to the public during normal hours
Off A127
2 miles from Laindon station

An expanding shiny new town is hardly the place in which to find a ghost, but it is the oldest building here which serves the new and growing population of Basildon that has a well authenticated phantom of a monk. Frequently reported by night shift workers and local residents, it is seen floating across the road from the graveyard and vanishes at a spot about 500 yards from the old church.

Witnesses claim that its robes are 'reddish in colour' and 'peculiar noises of footsteps and voices' have been heard to come from inside the 600 year old porchway of the church when it is empty at night.

Belief is that the ghost is of a monk who was murdered in the 16th century, but although his identity is rather vague his regular appearances are well established. The last recorded witnessing was in February 1972.

Cold Norton

Near Maldon, Essex
Private property, please respect

Site of the private home of Christina Foyle, owner of the haunted Beeleigh Abbey only a few miles away, Cold Norton is a tiny little village only a stone's throw from the River Crouch known for its coarse fishing. One of the 15th century houses in which the Foyles have lived for some thirty years had a reputation of being haunted even when they purchased it.

Miss Foyle told me in August 1972 that one of the upstairs rooms was never used because of the ghost, but was 'always a maid's sitting room' in early days. Perhaps the servants eventually got used to the atmosphere or just ignored it and retired early.

However, the new owners decided to risk 'the elementals' and converted it into a bedroom although they noticed 'that there was always a very musty smell in the room which lingers to this day in spite of having had it decorated several times'.

Although Miss Foyle has never used the room herself her late brother, alone in the house one night, slept there and on waking at 2am saw a 'small woman in early Victorian dress who seemed to be the embodiment of evil. He was really scared', although not a person who ever believed in ghosts.

Partly due to this the room was not used for some time, but the caretaker who had risked experiencing the haunting asked permission to sleep downstairs for he was disturbed by 'a woman who stood by his bed in the early hours'.

More recently a young Danish girl stayed with them and during a conversation learnt of the haunted bedroom. The young lady was amused at the tale for 'Danes don't believe in phantoms'.

At breakfast next morning the visitor laughingly commented on the joke played on her by her host. 'When I saw you come and stand by the bed in the middle of the night, I just pretended to be asleep.' Miss Foyle had been nowhere near the room.

The house is a very lovely old building, but, as Christina says, 'it's certainly very eerie'.

Fountain's Head

Tilbury Road, Brentwood, Essex
Open to the public during normal hours
On A129
Nearest station—Brentwood

In 1969 reports of the haunting of this pub, built in the latter half of the 17th century, reached the local press but the licensee is convinced that the phenomenon dates back at least until 1967.

The story associated with the ghost is that in 1786 Peter Andover had annoyed his father, a local landowner, by falling in love with Alice Albright, the daughter of a coachman. In a period when class consciousness was more prevalent than today, it must have been a considerable shock for the older man to suddenly discover his son attempting to rape the girl. Peter, alarmed and panicking on the sudden intrusion and discovery of 'his despicable behaviour', grabbed his pistol and fired at his father.

Unfortunately, due to the heat of the moment, it was not Andover senior who was killed, but the girl. A fight had ensued after Peter's shot missed the target and the older man, in defending himself against his son's rage, had picked up a knife and accidentally stabbed Alice.

Both men confused left the scene, but it was Peter who was convinced that he was the murderer of his lover.

Some 200 years later, in 1968, he is believed to have made himself felt by shattering a large number of bottles in the off-licence one night. Police investigated but were unable to find any cause for the destruction.

Since then tables and chairs inexplicably move around. In the summer of 1968 the barman 'felt the presence of someone standing close to him' and saw the smoke of his cigarette wafting about as if something had 'brushed past'.

I am indebted to Mr WH Downes, secretary of the Clacton Ghost and Occult Research Society, for the details of this case.

The Golden Fleece

Brook Street Hill, Brentwood, Essex
Open to the public during normal hours
On A1023
Nearest station—Brentwood

One of the oldest inns in the area, the Golden Fleece is reputed to stand on the site of the 12th century Priory of St Peter's. The hall and wings are 15th century with later additions.

In one wing a room where Nelson is supposed to have slept en route to Harwich has been carefully preserved. The pub was certainly used as a changing point for horses on the London to Harwich stage run, and one of the old traditions associated with the Golden Fleece was that wagoners would pay the landlord a half-penny to keep their food warm in the oven whilst they were at work in the fields.

Mr Downes tells me that the son of the landlord, Richard Langley, said that his grandmother saw a ghost in the pub some years ago and his sister Gillian has also seen the apparition of a monk in the building.

One of the lady guests, whilst in an upstairs room, saw the figure with his arms crossed reflected in a mirror looking at her, but when she turned to face the monk nothing was to be seen. She returned to her former position only to find the man still portrayed in the glass.

Physical phenomena in the pub have also been experienced for some time. Pots, pans and glasses are often inexplicably moved around in the kitchen and in the bars.

133 High Street

Brentwood, Essex
Open to the public during normal hours
Junction of A129/A128
Nearest station—Brentwood

Once an inn called the Seven Stars, this ancient building dates back some five hundred years but reverted to its original use as a private house in 1729.

For some years it has been a newsagent and tobacconists shop with an employment agency operating from the upper floor.

The evil haunting here is rather intangible but intense, especially near the centre fireplace and in the attic, from where on one occasion an unearthly cackle of laughter was heard.

Objects disappeared and keys vanished only to re-appear on the mantleshelf of the fireplace. This ledge would become so hot that it was possible to dry clothing on it, yet at the same time the keys 'were as cold as if they had been buried in deep snow'.

'Many disturbances were recorded from 1953 onwards,' says Mr Downes, 'but one of the most unpleasant was one evening when the lady of the house was alone with her dog and cat'.

The animals suddenly became restless, growling with hackles raised, and made for the door, 'then the noises started, weird sounds of something dropping down the central chimney'.

The noises continued interspersed with shufflings and knockings on corridor doors for some hours. The phenomena 'then followed in cycles, each lasting about three months' and were usually experienced in the spring and autumn.

On one occasion a man visiting the house was frightened by hearing footsteps approach the upstairs sitting room overlooking the street. When the door of the room was opened no one was there, but as soon as it was closed the sounds receded.

In 1968 the shop owner was decorating the inside of the top floor in preparation for the arrival of the employment agency. 'She stepped back to admire her work' and noticed a large brown dog leaning out of an open sash over the yard. Thinking it was one of her helpers' dogs, she called out but discovered that her friend's animal was shut in another room.

What may account for the haunting is one suggestion that a servant girl fell down the well in the cellar and her body left to rot.

One of the owner's sons thought the cellar would make an ideal photographic darkroom, but found the 'atmosphere quite intolerable'. The haunted chimney, centre of the sinister occurrences, has its foundations in the cellar.

One day excavations may uncover the cause of the mysteries.

Larkhill Road

Canewdon, Essex
Open to the public
Off A130
6 miles from Rochford station

Looking at a map of the area surrounding the river Crouch and
reading the names of villages, one could imagine oneself in another
era—Latchingham and Snoreham, south to Ostend and across
the river to Canewdon—sounds like a route to the middle ages.
But this part of Essex will shortly be one of bustling bulldozers,
earth moving equipment and later aircraft, for it is in the locality
of Foulness, planned site for London's third airport.

Yet only a few years ago it was considered as part of the east
that visitors had forgotten, though in Anglo-Saxon days it was a
popular area. Canewdon itself means 'Hill of Cana's people'.

In the small churchyard here one can see a reminder of at least
the middle ages, for sited in one corner is the grave of a crusader.
Locals have believed for some time that the ghost of this ancient
soldier still inhabits the area and incidents in 1969 and 1970, as far
as they were concerned, confirmed it.

A motor-cyclist riding along Larkhill Road towards the junction
with Puelsey Hall Lane had suddenly to swerve and brake in
order to avoid hitting a figure standing in his path. 'It was all in
white and seemed to have a broad red band down his chest.'
The 'white' appeared to be a cloak over the top of which was 'a
faint ball of mist. I suppose it was the head.' Admittedly one would
have expected a red cross and not a 'band' on the 'gleaming body'
however only a few months earlier a gardener working in a house
a few feet from the same spot had been scared at seeing 'a tall
white shape' appear on the lawn near the front wall.

The Marchings

Gravel Lane, Chigwell, Essex
Private property, please respect

Colonel Arthur Noble never believed in ghosts, but in 1951 when
he and his wife moved into an ancient country house in Gravel
Lane his outlook was changed.

During 1969 his wife, a local Magistrate, reported that she had
seen the ghost of a white lady at the bottom of the stairway. 'But
it's very friendly and we are treating it as such.'

The local legend is that 'the friendly lady', who has been seen

92

only a few times in recent years, is associated with King John whose hunting lodge became the home of the Nobles.

The Moat House Motel

Brook Street Hill, Brentwood, Essex
Open to the public during normal hours
On A1023
Nearest station—Brentwood

The oldest section of this timbered property is a private house complete with the original oak beams and doors, but on what was formerly the stabling area this modern motel and restaurant has been constructed using ancient timbers.

The Moat House itself dates from 1512 although a building has been known to have existed there since the 11th century. Many personalities have resided in the old property including King Henry VIII and Catherine of Aragon who lived there for 18 happy years, though they only used it primarily as a hunting lodge. It is believed that Henry composed a number of poems and songs there.

I am indebted to Mr WH Downes of the Clacton Ghost and Occult Research Society for his valuable information concerning this and other Essex cases.

He tells me that a couple of years ago a poltergeist was believed to be active in the house and a former housekeeper often felt the presence of an entity in the upper floors. 'Some people who have known the place for years speak of ghostly happenings with an impressive honesty,' he said.

Mr Downes offers a suggestion as to the reason for the feeling and the phenomena known to have occurred here. 'After Catherine's unhappy departure, the house's history was not always peaceful' for it suffered much in the period of the Great Plague.

Although little is known of any haunting in the adjoining motel, the manageress has stated that one of the bedroom doors 'refuses to close' and has been unable to find any explanation.

The New World Inn

Great Warley, Essex
Open to the public during normal hours
On B186
3 miles from Brentwood station

Up to a couple of years ago this hotel was a large private house known as 'Goldings' probably derived from 'geldings' and the owners' love of horses. It was built as a cottage in 1830 and enlarged by a Mr Heseltine who also built the Pearl Church a few yards away.

For a few years the Goldings had been run as a country club, but when Mr Downes visited the house in 1968 it was still partially furnished though such items as clocks had been removed.

Accompanied by the caretaker he had been looking over the property, then for sale, and had passed from the morning room into the music room.

'Then', he says, 'I heard the clock. Three distinct ticks, like a grandfather's pendulum. Then utter silence.'

His guide told him that several people had heard the same sound but no explanation for it had been discovered despite extensive testing for beetles, mechanics and anything else that could account for the ticking.

More impressive, however, were the sounds of a large party in progress 'which ceased as soon as the housekeeper approached the hall. And there were the more sinister mutterings and movements of trunks as if the former occupants were carrying on a frantic, futile search for something they had left behind.'

Some years earlier a beneficiary of the owner's will had seen the ghost of 'old Aunt Minnie, Mrs Heseltine, glaring down at her from the bedside'.

On the first floor landing 'an icy atmosphere' was experienced and the same sort of feeling of a 'presence' in the bedroom where the owner, Mrs De Rougemont, died. This room has now been divided and includes a room 14 'where no one seems to want to sleep more than one night'.

In October 1972 Mr Downes asked the current landlord about the hauntings and was told nothing was known though a member of the staff admitted that there was 'something eerie in one of the bedrooms', but refused to divulge which one.

Oil Refinery *

Coryton, Essex
Private property, please respect

Situated on the north bank of the river Thames, only a few miles from the popular resort of Southend-on-Sea, a cluster of oil and chemical refineries pierce the skyline. One of these, owned by Mobil Oil Co, is haunted.

About 20 years ago the site was owned by Cory Brothers, the

fuel distributors, who used the area for oil storage in a collection of huge circular tanks.

The most recent report of the ghost being seen was by George Poole, a maintenance assistant in the production services department, who was scared by the 'visiting spirit'.

One evening in December 1969, George was sheltering from the cold in the cab of a fuel bowser parked near the 'tank farm' when he heard someone walking along the roadway towards a separator unit. This equipment is used to clean the water used in the varying processes before returning it to the river. It is so effective that the water is cleaner than when taken from the Thames.

George, wondering who could be strolling around at 'that time of night'—it was about 8 o'clock—called out asking who it was. There was no reply, but the footsteps moved nearer and he saw, in the glare from one of the standard road lamps, the figure of a stout man, 5ft 9in tall, wearing a boiler suit and a 'safety hat' (a white steel helmet). The man continued to walk on beside 'the moat' (the gulley surrounding certain equipment sites) until he was only 7 yards from George.

Mr Poole, jumping out from the vehicle, began to run towards the figure calling out as he moved. As the figure reached a cross-road 'it just vanished'.

So frightened was he by the experience that George, risking ridicule, reported the incident to the security guards and his supervisor.

It is believed that the ghost, which has been seen several times, is that of a man who, when the site was owned by Cory Bros, accidentally fell to his death in the oily sludge of a separator tank during his nightly tour of inspection.

Prittlewell Priory*

Priory Crescent, Near Southend-on-Sea, Essex
Open to the public during normal hours
Just off A127
Nearest station—Prittlewell

Actually within the boundary of the ever popular Borough of Southend can be found this ancient 12th century priory. Unfortunately most of the remains of the monastery, founded by Robert of Essex in 1100 AD, are at first sight hidden by early 19th century additions and there is little to be found of the vast estate of varied outbuildings which formed the priory in its heyday.

Being a house subject to the Priory of St Pancras at Lewes it was also responsible to the Abbey of Cluny in Burgundy, but after a more or less peaceful existence for more than 400 years it was dissolved like many others in 1536. It housed some 18 monks for most of its life and formed a self-contained community comprising a church, a laundry, a brewhouse, bakery, butlers' and porters' chambers, together with extensive buildings for cattle, sheep and pigs.

After the dissolution Thomas Audley bought the buildings from the King for £400 and, 'gazumping' was known even then, 10 years later sold it to Lord Riche for £800. By 1678 Daniel Finch, second Earl of Nottingham was the owner and at the end of the 17th century Daniel Scratton bought it.

At the end of the first world war a Mr RA Jones purchased the property and presented it to the Corporation.

The ghost of the priory is a bit of a mystery appearing as it does, it seems, in a 20th century restoration area known incorrectly as the 'Minstrels' Gallery'. It cannot be stated, however, that the original building did not include some similar viewpoint to the Refectory, but the current gallery is more suited to provide a view of the roof timbers.

One of the interesting exhibits in the Prior's Chamber, and perhaps relevant, is a wooden chest which belonged to Cunning Murrel, a 19th century white witch of Hadleigh.

It was in 1952 that I first heard of the ghost here, but of what and where I had no knowledge. I visited the priory that year and experienced a strong and distinct mental impression of a monk walking along the corridor to the controversial 'Minstrels' Gallery', after pausing for a moment to look through a window on the left hand wall. On checking this with one of the Council's staff I was told that my impressions were correct and several visitors had reported similar incidents: one couple had actually seen the monk a fortnight earlier.

The current curator however tells me that he has 'during 20 years detailed knowledge of the building . . . not heard of any suggestion whatsoever of the building being haunted. Nor have any of the 19th century histories, articles or press comments relating to this area given even the merest hint towards supernatural visitations'.

But late in 1972, a couple of visitors reported seeing 'a ghostly monk' near the Minstrels' Gallery.

16 Montpelier Road, Ealing, in 1944—the scene of 20 suicides and a murder. Could it be a ghost at the upper left-hand window of this building (empty when the photograph was taken)? Perhaps the image is that of a 12-year-old girl who committed suicide in the 19th century. The building was replaced by a new block of flats in 1970.

63 Wycliffe Road
Battersea S.W.11
London

17½ Green

Thank you very much for your
last letter, I have spoken to daddy
and he said I may go with you
and your friend's to the house in
Ewling. but first we must know when
it is, Perhaps you can let me know.
Well I can not think of no more to say
So I will sign off we hope to hear
from you again

Yours Sincerely,
Shirley Hitchings

Letter received by the author from the poltergeist girl of
Battersea.

Letter from 'Donald the poltergeist', written in a style identical to that of Shirley Hitchings, proves that the girl was responsible for the phenomena.

Castle Restaurant, Sunbury-on-Thames, Surrey, where you might see the ghost of a girl murdered by the Roundheads.

St Osyth's Priory

Clacton, Essex
Open to the public during normal hours
Junction of A120/B1072
4 miles from Clacton station

Attractively situated beside a mill stream in this former lace-making town are the ruins of the 12th century priory and its renovated 15th century gatehouse.

Fairly recently reports have indicated that the phantom of a monk has returned here. It was better known before the war when it was seen in a white robe and black scapula. The face was furrowed with anxiety. In 1969 and early 1970 witnesses saw the figure resembling that of a monk carrying a candle in the vicinity of the ruins 'at about half past eleven at night'. He was seen to glide down to the waterside where after a few seconds he 'just vanished'.

Other buildings in the vicinity have also been haunted at times by 'mysterious lights' and 'peculiar forms', one of the latest incidents being at 47 Church Street where in 1966 the occupants saw an 'eerie mist at the bottom of the stairs'.

The Swan

High Street, Brentwood, Essex
Open to the public during normal hours
Junction of A129/A128
Nearest station—Brentwood

The current building was originally called 'The Argent' and later 'The Gun'. By 1781 mention of the latter had ceased and it was not until 1783 that 'The Swan' first made its appearance in local records.

It originally stood on both sides of a coach yard, now the saloon, and possessed a large paddock which was sold in 1913 to the council. Because of these facts there exists some considerable doubt as to the identity of the ghost which continues to haunt the pub.

Popular belief is that the unseen phantom is that of William Hunter, a young Protestant martyr who was held here for two days pending his execution at the Butts on Shenfield Common on March 26, 1555.

Typical poltergeist phenomena were experienced for some seven months in 1963 during the Harling's licence, though in addition the daughter of the landlord said she saw a 'shadowy male figure wearing a hat' follow her mother across the landing one night.

At the height of the activity police were called twice because doors unlocked themselves and a telephone in a locked room 'fell' off its hook. 'Cold spots' were experienced in the corridors and a dog refused to enter the saloon.

Just before they left, the Harlings were given one final demonstration. A clock left in an empty room began to strike at half-past twelve one morning and continued to do so until taken down from the wall. Yet the strike had been put out of action several months before.

Nevertheless, the new landlord reports that 'unaccountable things still happen', papers vanish only to re-appear in peculiar places and gas taps have been 'tampered with in the cellar'.

Upminster Golf Club★

114 Hall Lane, Upminster, Essex
Open to the public by appointment only
Off A124
Nearest station—Upminster

What must be one of the oldest inhabited buildings in Essex is the 900 year old club house of this rather exclusive golf club. Originally it was built as a monastery but often changed its use during the ensuing years.

In the 17th century a local man, then the owner of what had become a manor house, was intensely jealous of attentions being paid to one of the young and beautiful ladies of Havering. For years, it seems, he had nursed a strong and passionate love for her and when he saw her attractions being shared, his mental stability failed.

He kidnapped the girl, took her back to the manor and buried her alive in one of the walls of what is now the lounge overlooking the car park. But something may well have taken place upstairs before the 'foul deed was done', for the ghost that haunts the house has been witnessed in two particular areas.

The more popular site where the figure of a young girl in a long white dress has been seen by several members of the club is in the first floor hallway. The other is in what is known as the Secretary's flat, though now occupied by other tenants.

Members interested in the continuing appearance of 'Mary' recently measured the structure and found discrepancies in the walls which, they believe, may well indicate a hidden cavity where perhaps one day the bones of a young female will be discovered.

Warley Lea Farm

Near Brentwood, Essex
Private property, please respect

Once part of a 1,000 acre estate owned by Lord Headley, Warley Lea Farm has been standing in its quiet pastures for over 200 years. Now consisting of only 22 acres the building has a long history of having passed through numerous hands and of being haunted.

It was once owned by Lord McPherson, but more recently formed part of the agricultural estate of a Miss Wilmott and it was during her ownership that a farm bailiff hanged himself. From then on the stories of strange happenings commenced though in 1970 the owner, Mr Frederick Scannell of Romford, ridiculed the idea of a ghost.

In August of that year, however, a team from the *Brentwood Argus,* the local newspaper, went to investigate. Journalists are normally hard-bitten sceptics, but after some five hours in what was then a derelict structure they are not so sure. A drop in temperature was recorded at 12.50am, three inexplicable crashes in one of the empty rooms downstairs at 2 o'clock and footsteps heard at 2.16am and 2.56am. These were 'firm steady steps' which, when they approached the stairs, caused the group of five to investigate. Nothing was found. This 'shattered' the team. Then at 3.20am Tony Woolnough saw a figure on the veranda outside the back door. It was about 5ft 5in tall but was unfortunately indistinguishable and even the resultant photograph failed to clarify the figure.

Some 20 minutes later 'all hell seemed to break loose'. The doors crashed, terrific banging was heard and the footsteps resumed their invisible treading of stairs. At 4.30am the group, by now slightly scared but mystified, departed.

Although now renovated, the farm still suffers from the sounds of an occasional unseen stairwalker, but whether he is the bailiff no one has been able to discover.

White Hart

High Street, Brentwood, Essex
Open to the public during normal hours
Junction of A129/A128
Nearest station—Brentwood

A mere 60 yards from the haunted Swan Inn is this other pub with a ghost.

In his researches into the history of the building, Mr Downes discovered that according to Nikolaus Pevsner the inn is pre-1500 and on November 19, 1392 Richard II is believed to have been a guest here.

One of the most striking features of the establishment is the galleried yard used 'until recently as a stage for Shakespearian plays'. Unfortunately for the purist, the gallery is now covered in, but the basic structure remains unchanged since the days when stage-coaches drove in to change horses.

The oldest internal part of the building is the Steak Bar which, in the former days, used to be a kitchen 'with a linen cupboard where the actual bar is now'. One visitor with psychic faculties stated that it is this area that was the scene of 'something dreadful— rape or murder'. Locals connect this with the ghost of a servant girl who haunts the pub, even though one manager felt that the phantom was male. There may very well be two, of course.

Tables move, doors open and close of their own volition, and a door giving access to the water tank eight feet over the Steak Bar is often found open.

Mysterious footsteps are also heard going up the stairway near the Steak Bar and the ballroom, built only a few years ago after a fire, seems to be the site of another haunting.

Here a waitress was tapped on her shoulder and a former manageress was 'held back from walking across the room by an unseen barrier' on more than one occasion.

Gloucestershire

Has a haunted jail

Open to the public during normal hours or by appointment	8
Private houses	5
Historic buildings, museums, ruins	1
Churches, abbeys, rectories	2
Inns, hotels	2
Open spaces, roads	3
Phenomena	
Noises	5
Apparitions	
Females	5
Monks	2
Males	3
Dogs	1
Horses	2

Berkeley Arms

Tewkesbury, Gloucestershire
Open to the public during normal hours
On A438
9 miles from Cheltenham Spa station

Among the many ancient buildings in Tewkesbury is this attractive, comfortable pub with a reputation of being haunted for such a long time that the top floor, the affected area, was completely boarded up several years ago. The building was constructed in 1430.

Although the ghost has been sealed off from customers and

residents it seems that it is still active. Numerous visitors to the bathroom, situated immediately over an alley and below the 'centre of phenomena' in the upper floor, have reported unusual tapping noises which the owners have been unable to locate, though on occasions it appears that the sounds are coming from the aperture below the floor.

'No, it isn't dripping, it's definitely tapping like someone, or something, is trying to attract attention'.

Blackfriars Priory*

Gloucester, Gloucestershire
Private property, please respect

One of the few ancient and historical ruins part-owned by the Department of the Environment which is not open to the public is Blackfriars Priory. The reason for forbidding visitors in this instance is due to its 'ruinous and dangerous state'.

When the extensive work of preserving and repairing the structure is completed, 'we do not renovate' said a Department spokesman, the priory will be opened but 'it will take some time'.

It is a handsome ruin of a 13th century Dominican Priory complete with the phantom of a former resident. Whilst working on the massive project, labourers have reported seeing the figure of a monk in a particular part of the ruins and hut doors have 'mysteriously locked themselves'. In order to ensure absolute safety for future tourists, cavities beneath the old floors have to be strengthened or, in some cases, completely filled in.

In 1969 a previously unknown 'dungeon' was discovered which contained the ancient skeleton of a young child, which some members of the work team feel may be associated with the appearance of the monk.

Gloucester Jail

Gloucester
Open to the public by appointment
Junction of A40/A38
Nearest station—Gloucester

One of the oldest prisons in Britain, this formidable building was constructed by Sir George Onesithorus in 1874, although inspired by prison reformer John Howard. Situated next to the beautiful Benedictine Cathedral which was once the Abbey church of the city, the grim establishment is one of the few haunted jails of the country.

What is perhaps unusual is that the inmates are mainly males, but the ghost is that of a woman, Jenny Godfrey, who was murdered in the 15th century in one of the cells by a drunken Irishman.

Reports of furniture being moved around by unseen hands in cell 25 on A3 landing had been made over a period of some years, but during a seance at Christmas 1969, held by a prisoner Robert Gore, Jenny 'communicated' through an upturned glass.

Having 'resurrected' the murdered girl the inmates of the cell were disturbed at what followed. Pots, pans, books, in fact anything moveable would be hurled around and scratching noises were heard by all the three prisoners.

A few days later, one of them saw a disembodied hand with its index finger pointing at Mr Gore.

Incidents of odd noises and movements continue to be reported from the cell.

Prestbury

Gloucestershire
On A46
2 miles from Cheltenham station

Running as a good second to the village of Pluckley as the most haunted village in England, this small town of Prestbury, a couple of miles north of Cheltenham, has no less than six haunted sites.

(1) Private property, please respect
(2) Open to the public
(3) Open to the public during normal hours

(1) At Cleve Corner, a 17th century farmhouse, the unseen ghost of a murderer has been felt in one of the bedrooms. The phenomenon has been described as 'a dim mysterious light, cold clamminess and a feeling of diabolical evil'. Some people who have slept in the room have felt strong fingers grasping their throat on waking in the early hours. Tradition is that the phantom is of a murderer who killed a newly wed bride in the bedroom and then stole the wedding gifts.

(1) In the 16th century Reform Cottage in Deep Street footsteps of 'The Black Abbot' have regularly been heard at Easter, Christmas and All Saints Day. The sounds come to the front door, then move round the cottage to the side door of the barn and stop.

Shortly afterwards, footsteps are heard walking over part of the floor of the attic over one of the bedrooms. Former occupants, the Misses Sudlow, have often heard him.

(2) At Crossways a phantom horse rider has been witnessed so frequently that the locals accept his appearance as 'commonplace', and he also frequents Shaw Green Lane and Bow Bridge Lane before vanishing. His identity is accepted as that of a Royalist despatch rider carrying news of Cromwell's victory at Worcester, but who was killed before reaching his final destination at Cheltenham.

(3) The hooded figure of the monk known as 'The Black Abbot' not only haunts Reform Cottage, but also St Mary's Parish Church. He has been seen walking slowly down the centre aisle towards the west door. With his head bowed in prayer and hands well tucked into the wide sleeves of his càpe, he continues past the priory to the High Street.

(1) At the turn of the century the figure of a young girl was sometimes seen in the garden of Sundial Cottage apparently playing a spinet. Since the wars, however, she is no longer seen but the sound of her music-making continues to haunt the immediate locality during warm summer evenings.

(1) Completing the collection, one of the latest sightings of 'Old Moses' of Walnut Cottage was during 1961 when the owner and some local residents saw the wraith of the old trainer with his horse in a converted stable near Cheltenham Racecourse.

What is so pleasant about these hauntings is that not only are they accepted as 'just something that happens' by the villagers, but they hold no terror for the occasional visitor who encounters them.

St Mary's Vicarage

Kempsford, Gloucestershire
Private property, please respect
Off A419(T)
20 miles from Swindon station

On the banks of the Isis, or River Thames, whichever one prefers, lies the small Gloucestershire village of Kempsford with an attractive but rather dark Norman church of St Mary the Virgin which has a magnificent central tower constructed by John of Gaunt.

A few yards away one finds the 16th/17th century vicarage. It is a large building with several rooms once used as servants' quarters for, like many current priests' houses, it has housed numerous varied characters and has seen a lot of changes. It is believed it was once a school, but whether this is connected with the three apparitions that have been seen here is not yet known.

The vicar here in 1968, the Rev David Watson, admitted that a visitor heard 'an unusual noise' coming from the stairway leading to the servants rooms and saw the figure of a woman wearing a 17th century dress and carrying a baby, 'gliding down the stairs'.

A young boy in a blue suit has also been seen on the stairs. He was also witnessed by the previous occupiers.

Shaw Green Lane

Prestbury, Gloucestershire
Open to the public
On A46
2 miles from Cheltenham station

Seven miles away at Tewkesbury was what has been claimed as the last conflict in the Wars of the Roses. Others, however, claim that the Battle of Bosworth brought down the House of York, but it was the former that affected Prestbury and the surrounding area.

On May 4, 1471 Edward IV with the Duke of Hastings protecting his right flank and the Duke of Gloucester on his left faced the opposing strength of Prince Edward, the Duke of Devon and the Duke of Somerset.

Among the men delighted at last to see the results of their preparations were the local supporters, the farriers who must have spent a long and tiring night repairing the damage caused by the long march. Some of the horses' shoes discarded after the repairs were found at the camp site early in the 19th century during drain laying operations.

One can imagine the furious activity in both camps as the hour approached. Men rushing hither and thither, tightening horses' girths here, sharpening spears and swords there. An occasional messenger with urgent reports of the enemies' operations would ride in, horse steaming and breathless.

To the King would come vital despatches from other quarters, the messengers dressed in the finery attributed to the Royal Court.

One such courier, perhaps with a message more important than others, must have come in from the east through Shaw Green Lane galloping with as much speed as he could get from his mount.

His thoughts wavered to the attractive village and, failing to notice a solitary archer, he rode on.

A moment later an arrow pierced the emblazoned cloth of his doublet and he fell. Occasionally on spring mornings over the last few years the sound of a galloping horse has been heard by early travellers down the lane, and a few reports of the faint outline of a rider 'looking like a cavalier on a white horse' having been witnessed.

It was earlier this century during road repairs that the partial skeleton of a man was found and, between his ribs, a rusting triangular blade of the fatal arrow provided evidence for the haunting.

Swan Pool

Newland Road, Redbrook, Gloucestershire
Open to the public
On A446
10 miles from Chepstow station

Nearly on the county border of Monmouthshire and Gloucestershire and six miles north of Whitebrook, which lies in the western county, is this tiny hamlet tucked in the side of the magnificent Wye Valley.

Situated on the right-hand side of Newland Road just above the village is a large pond, known as the Swan Pool, home of many legendary spectres. But three that are not so mythical, having been witnessed fairly recently by the occasional wanderer, are the ghosts of a woman with a child and a black dog.

The cries of the baby have been often heard some distance away, but what is rather unnerving is the sight of a tall woman in a white dress holding the tiny infant in her arms slowly rising from the limpid waters. Some reports make her appearance even more awesome by describing the green slimy weed that hangs from her shoulders and is gathered like a shroud over the moaning baby.

Few people, it seems, have waited to see the final act of the apparition, but it is supposed the couple 'just vanish'. Connected with this phenomenon is the appearance of a black dog which trots out from an old lime kiln in the adjoining woods, walks round the pool and returns to its lair.

Some locals claim that the hound is headless and that he was killed at the same time as the woman and her child were murdered, though by whom and when is impossible to say.

Tudor House Hotel*

Tewkesbury, Gloucestershire
Open to the public during normal hours
Junction of A438/A38
9 miles from Cheltenham Spa station

This magnificent and attractive hotel, built in 1540, became the Court of Justice during the reign of James I and some years later the Rev Samuel Jones, who was connected with the Pilgrim Fathers, formed his academy here.

It is sometimes known as 'the house of the fourteen windows' and, according to the Society for the Preservation of Ancient Buildings, is 'probably the best building in Tewkesbury'.

As well as boasting its oak panelling, the Jacobean staircase and its priests' hiding hole in the Coffee Room chimney, it has a couple of ghosts.

One of these, a black labrador, has been seen a couple of times by guests standing on the landing of the main stairway, but the other entity is that of an unknown lady 'in white'. She inhabits one of the bedrooms on the first floor.

The owner, Mr Bigland, was kind enough to allow my sleeping in the haunted room, but although I experienced no unusual phenomena some guests have woken in the early hours to see 'the vague figure of a woman, dressed in white' gliding slowly towards the door where she vanishes. Apparently there is no unpleasant atmosphere on her arrival, but merely 'slight sorrow'.

Vicarage and Parish Church

Arlingham, Gloucestershire
Open to the public by appointment only—church open to the public
during normal hours
On B4071 (off A38 T)
8 miles from Gloucester station

This was first reported in 1953 by Mrs Ellen Hayward of Bermuda Villa who saw 'the little old lady dressed in black, save for a white lace mob-cap; hair black and done in a bun at the back. I had a sensation of feeling very cold', she told the *Gloucester Citizen*.

The figure has been seen in one of the bedrooms of the vicarage so frequently that it is now just accepted as 'a guest'.

Mrs Edith Penny is another local resident who witnessed in 1965 what sounds like an old house-keeper from Victorian times.

Hampshire

Where phantoms can be found in Lord Montagu's home

Open to the public during normal hours or by appointment	12
Private houses	2
Clubs, cinemas	1
Historic buildings, museums, ruins	3
Churches, abbeys, rectories	1
Inns, hotels	4
Private houses, offices, factories	3
Open spaces, roads	2
Phenomena	
Smells	1
Noises	7
Apparitions	
Nuns	1
Females	7
Monks	1
Males	5
Dogs	2

Bagwell Lane

Winchfield, Fleet, Hampshire
Open to the public
Off A30
Nearest station—Winchfield

For some years the 'White Lady of Bagwell Lane' had been unseen and was moving into the realms of myth and legend, though it is known that a woman committed suicide in a pond not far from the canal here in the 1800's.

In May 1968, however, she made her re-appearance with a vengeance for one evening a motorcyclist returning home to Fleet, perhaps rather too quickly, saw the figure of a young woman 'draped in a white gown or dress' glide in front of him. Too late to take any action, he squealled to a stop and turned round only to see the phantom still silently standing in the centre of the road.

'I really did hit her,' he said, 'or rather, drive through her. I went off home in rather a greater hurry after that'.

Two days later, three lads walking down Bagwell Lane saw the ghost again moving from the roadway across a field and into a pond. One of them said 'it looked as if she were trying to get up the side of the pond at one time. But we know it wasn't a real person, the water hadn't moved'.

Beaulieu Abbey*

Beaulieu, Hampshire
Open to the public during normal hours
Junction of B3056/B3054
5 miles from Brockenhurst station

So many people have seen the phantom monks here, usually in the area of the Domus Conversorum, that another report of a sighting draws little response from the owner, Lord Montagu. What is perhaps a little surprising is that he has never witnessed any of the ghosts, though he fully accepts that his home is haunted.

The general attitude of acceptance is verified in Diana Norman's *The Stately Ghosts of England* (Muller, 1972 edn). Lord Montagu told her that 'in the village their attitude is "yes, we see the monks; so what?" But the ghosts here have never been evil,' he pointed out.

One of the most recent incidents was in 1965 when a lady visitor in the Domus apartment saw the shadowy figure of a monk 'in a brown habit seated in a recess just west of the magnolia, reading what looked like a scroll of parchment'.

Thirty Cistercian monks and an Abbot arrived in 1204 and continued in residence until the Dissolution in 1538 when they surrendered to Henry VIII. They must have worked extremely hard at sheep farming and with agricultural pursuits, and during their occupation created a general atmosphere of well being. But in 1209 a certain amount of irritation was caused by the bloodless battle waged by their founder against the Pope because of an appointment of a non-acceptable Archbishop.

Although they survived this and the numerous problems associated with the Wars of the Roses, they were unable to continue under Henry.

However, because of the general peace and tranquility of Beaulieu it is not really surprising that some of the early inhabitants remain, even though they are mere phantoms.

Other incidents that have occurred at the Abbey in recent years include the experience of smelling incense, and phantom footsteps heard at night walking down the staircase.

Church of all Saints

Crondall, Hampshire
Open to the public during normal hours
Off A287
Nearest station—Aldershot
This building with Norman origins, of which some parts remain, has been considerably altered over the years. A central tower that once existed was pulled down in the 17th century when the present tower was added.

To confuse the design even further, the whole church was 'restored' in the late 19th century.

Throughout the years, however, reports by the workmen involved, by visitors and local residents indicate that there are most certainly Cromwellian associations with the site.

On moonlit nights the semi-transparent figure of a Roundhead soldier in full uniform has been seen emerging from a private drive immediately opposite the church and fades away after taking only a few steps.

A local belief is that he was killed when attacking the church during the Civil War.

Ebenezer Lane

Ringwood, Hampshire
Private property, please respect

Should one dismiss everything a child claims to see as 'imagination'? In 1947 I carried out a survey of 125 youngsters aged between 7 and 12 years old to find out what they could experience visually that their parents and other adults could not. From the total answers I found that 65 described recognisable human figures they had seen and sometimes 'played with' or 'spoke to', but which their parents termed as 'imagination'. On further investigation I was able to ascertain that at least 27 of the 65 descriptions matched those of people who had at one time lived in the house occupied by the children. This figure may have been higher

110

if I had been able to spend more time on the work, but of those 27 'fictional characters' nine had been dead for at least 12 months. Remember *The Turn of the Screw*?

This does suggest surely that children, like domestic animals, are often more perceptive and can see apparitions more often and more clearly than grown adults.

In 1967 Mr and Mrs Donald Rumens reported to *The Sun* that their 250 year old cottage in Ebenezer Lane is haunted by a pair of friendly ghosts seen only by their children and other youngsters in the neighbourhood. The descriptions given suggest that the apparitions unseen by the adults are of a Georgian gentleman and 'his lady'.

Fort Wallington

Fareham, Hampshire
Open to the public during normal hours
A27/A32
Nearest station—Fareham

In 1840 Lord Palmerston's actions in connections with Egypt and Turkey had so affected relations with France that for some months war appeared to be imminent. As usual in such a predicament, Britain prepared and small fortresses reminiscent of Martello Towers were hastily constructed to defend vital ports and naval bases. Known as 'Palmerston's Follies', a few of these still exist and one, Fort Wallington, continues to serve the nation's interest as a teenagers' club.

Owned by a vehicle company it was decided in June 1971 to convert one of the dark, dank, dismal dungeons into a discotheque. But the owners failed to realise that although 'pop' music would perhaps shatter the gloomy atmosphere, it would have no effect on phantoms of the past.

During the conversion work the team of four workmen frequently heard footsteps coming towards them from an old sealed corridor leading to the cells. Initially they thought it was the foreman approaching, but only when the sounds had reached within a few feet of them did they realise they were of some unseen phantom.

As soon as they re-commenced work the footsteps would begin again from the end wall. As the building was never used as a military establishment and the dungeons remained empty except for the occasional delivery of goods from the day they were built, who the ghostly walker is can only be conjecture.

Whether he continues his perambulations since the 'poppers'

moved in is not known, but late night cleaners have reported the occasional rhythmic 'bump' which may well be the phantom of the fort.

Marriage Guidance Council

1 St Michael's Road, Southsea, Hampshire
Open to the public during normal hours
On A288
Nearest station—Portsmouth and Southsea

Offices of a marriage guidance council are hardly a suitable home for a ghost, but, as we know, phantoms just don't care.

For many years up to March 1971 this old building housed the Corporation's Welfare Department, but before then was the administrative centre of the original workhouse for the locality.

Reputations are not gained without some basic facts so folk believe. This old brick building has for a long time had a reputation of being haunted and the facts associated with the tale are that numerous council staff have not only heard but seen an old man 'drifting round' the walls. He has been witnessed wearing 'a top hat, a long grey coat and carries an old carved stick with which he frequently taps the ground'.

Mr NE Tallack, director of Welfare Services of the Portsmouth Corporation, stated in an interview with the local paper in January 1971 that a number of his staff had heard the tapping of the old man's stick as he walked round the building.

There seems to be strong evidence for the belief that the old character is, in fact, the original beadle who used to run the workhouse over 150 years ago. The description given certainly matches that of the gentleman concerned.

Moyles Court*

Near Ringwood, Hampshire
Open to the public by appointment only
Off A338
Nearest station—Lyndhurst Road

A famous ghost, that of Dame Alice Lisle who was beheaded for high treason by order of Judge Jeffreys, has been seen walking the courtyard of this 17th century manor house and also, it is claimed, in the vicinity of Dibden Church nearly 15 miles away with her head under her arm. Her connection with the church, it seems, is

112

that her son lived and died at Dibden and she often visited him, one such call being made shortly before her arrest.

Moyles Court is in fact a small forest village named after the manor which was the ancestral home of the Lisle's. Alice's crime was that she sheltered two fugitives from the Monmouth rebellion of 1685.

The building was completely restored after being allowed to fall into ruin and is now a school owned by the Manor House School Trust. Although the ghost has not been experienced by any of the staff in recent years, sounds of the Dame's carriage has been heard fairly frequently on the driveway.

Poplar Farm Inn*

Abbotts Ann, Near Andover, Hampshire
Open to the public during normal hours
Just off A343
Nearest station—Andover

Originally a farm cottage built 450 years ago complete with inglenook fireplaces and a wealth of old oak beams opened its doors as an extremely attractive pub in November 1970. Extending the authentic cottage atmosphere, the owner, Charles Bowyer, a retired director of his own building firm, used ancient timbers and materials from Littleton Manor at Fyfield to create the 'Cottage bar' and the 'Barn bar'.

It was in 1965 that he purchased what was then a derelict cottage and converted it into a six-bedroomed house for himself and his family. On his retirement he felt that an inn for Andover was needed and proceeded to effect the change.

What he had not counted on was that the building had a ghost.

In 1967 footsteps were heard walking up the stairs and doors would close inexplicably. The following year at the same time, 'during the Christmas period', similar incidents occurred but the doors were 'now being slammed shut'.

Each year the haunting seems to be gaining in strength and is now 'rather regular'. Mrs Bowyer told me in July 1972 that the footsteps were heard several times in the evenings now and in June the barman had seen 'the vague shape of a female figure glide up the stairs'.

One explanation offered by the locals is that the ghost could be associated with a 'lady of society who used to hold wild orgies in the cottage some 200 years ago'. Connected with this tale, perhaps, is the fact that a tunnel runs from the cellars of the building to the nearby River Anton, though the entrance was blocked up fairly recently.

Some years ago the ghost of a black dog resumed its ancient haunt in the area and was seen on a farm road near here linking the Salisbury road with Abbotts Ann, only a few yards from the inn. It was witnessed a couple of times, once so close to a farm worker that he 'took a swipe at it with his stick' and the cane passed right through the animal.

The Royal Oak*

Langstone Village, Havant, Hampshire
Open to the public during normal hours
On B2149
Nearest station—Havant

I had the pleasure of speaking to Mrs J Spring, the owner's wife of this attractive waterside pub in September 1972, when she told me of her experiences of meeting a ghost.

'It was in 1969 when I thought I heard someone moving around in my bedroom. I presumed it was my young daughter who has been known to sleep-walk and got up from the bed to lead her back to her own room. I then saw the figure of a woman in white standing in a corner and as I looked she slowly vanished—just faded into the wall.'

Over a period of several years phantom footsteps have been heard in the bar and, Mrs Spring said, 'sounds of chairs being moved, just like the sound of someone pushing it aside when getting up or sitting down. A sort of scraping noise'.

A neighbour in the Boat House, a few yards from the pub, told the owner that she had also seen the apparition some years previously, but the most recent incident was that of a male guest who left after one night after booking in for a week. 'He said the room was haunted. It was the room in which I saw the ghost of the woman. That was in the summer of 1970.

'Perhaps my conviction would have waned a little under the scepticism of some people had it not been for my dog which refused to be alone in the bar. She was obviously badly affected by the atmosphere there.'

When I enquired about the history of the building, Mrs Spring told me 'we have never been able to establish its real age, but it seems that it is about 450 years old'.

Who the lady in white is, is another puzzle. Perhaps she is connected with the bakery that existed on the site before it became an inn.

Rumasa (Williams & Hubert)*

Testwood House, Millbrook Road, Totton, Southampton, Hampshire
Private property, please respect

Although appearing to be a Georgian building, the facade of this old house covers what was an old hunting lodge used by Henry VIII and Edward VI, and is the site of a murder which was committed some 200 years ago. The situation which resulted in the killing was the 'love of a woman by two of the servants.' The passion of a coachman was so strong and he was so desperate to win the heart of the girl that one Wednesday night he killed his rival, the butler, in a fight in a room at the back of the house.

One would perhaps expect that the victim would haunt what is now this sherry shippers' office, but it is the apparition of the coachman that is frequently experienced.

The latest witnessing was about 6.30 in the evening on February 23, 1972 when Mr AW Ranger, director and secretary of the company, having worked late, came down the stairs into what was then the reception room in the main hall and saw a 'tall dark cloaked figure wearing a top hat standing near the desk'. He was so disturbed that he 'went hot and cold' and hurried past the spectre, through the front door to his car where, whilst recovering from the shock, he made a quick sketch of the 'phantom coachman'.

This was not the first occasion the apparition has been witnessed in recent years for the caretaker, Geoff Tebbut, has also seen the ghost at the back of the premises and his Alsatian dog flatly refuses to enter the 'murder room'. On one occasion when Geoff tried to force the animal forward it cowered, turned and bit him in protest.

Selborne

Near Petersfield, Hampshire
Open to the public during normal hours
On B3006
7 miles from Petersfield station

About four miles from Jane Austen's House is the quiet little village of Selborne complete with a 15th century farm, a stream and the ghost of a black dog.

The farm itself, which is privately owned and not open to the public, originally formed part of the old Priory estate which probably stretched as far as the village of Monkwood nearly five miles away. But the cause of the phantom dog is a mystery.

Many years ago several human skeletons were dug up in the locality, but all indicated natural causes of death. The dog is not often seen, but when it is the appearance is always in the original entrance to the Priory Farm, adjoining the stream that trickles beside one of the buildings. The owners have not seen the ghost, but former occupants and local residents have witnessed the haunting, one of them, a Mr Edwards Lucas, on two occasions.

'It was about 9pm,' he said, 'and I was leading a horse to the old harness room. Then this strange black dog suddenly appeared. It had long hair and was about the size of a collie and walked with me and the horse for about 100 yards, but vanished completely when it reached the old farm entrance—just melted away.'

What is surprising is that neither horses nor other dogs appear to be disturbed by the ghost even if they see it.

One idea of its history is that the dog was a companion of one of the race horses accidentally killed at the farm in the 19th century.

Tudor Rose Inn*

Burgate, Near Fordingbridge, Hampshire
Open to the public during normal hours
On A338
11 miles from Salisbury station

Lying on the main road to Salisbury, just two miles north of Fordingbridge, is this 14th century inn which for some years up to 1968 was known as La Chaumière. Probably it owes its origin to coaching days but now to some extent it relies on a different type of coach for some of its business.

In early 1967 Mr and Mrs Hardin, the owners at that time, reported that for many months they had heard inexplicable footsteps both on the stairway and in 'the immediate locality of the stairs'. An unidentifiable apparition, 'just a vague shape', had also been seen on numerous occasions by members of the staff.

A team of investigators from the Paraphysical Laboratory who stayed at the Inn for some hours were unable to find an answer to the noises.

I spoke to the new owner in September 1972 when he told me that the name was changed to the Tudor Rose a couple of years previously and as he had only moved in days before he had not yet had time to get settled in. Mr Brian Cross did say that he had heard some 'weird noises' and would be interested to 'see if anything develops'.

Wherwell Priory

Wherwell, Near Andover, Hampshire
Open to the public by appointment only
On B3049
3 miles from Andover station

The village of Wherwell has been described as one of the most picturesque in the county and with its attractive timbered cottages, neat with their old thatched roofs; the claim is not unjustified. The main traces of the Saxon occupation here are the ruins of the priory founded by Queen Elfrida as a penance for her crimes.

Much of the Queen's history is known. She was King Edgar's wife, she mothered Ethelred II, and attempted to arrange the murder of Edmund, her stepson, so that her son, Ethelred the Unready, could take the throne. She eventually died at Wherwell after reaching the position of Abbess.

The priory was believed to have been used as a type of training establishment for some years after her death, but the reason for the occasional haunting that occurs there is not known.

A few reports of a couple of phantom nuns carrying candles have been made in the last few years, but they are only seen in the churchyard which adjoins the ruins and at dusk late in the year.

White Hart Hotel*

Bridge Street, Andover, Hampshire
Open to the public during normal hours
On A303
Nearest station—Andover

Mr Parsons, manager of this pleasant establishment, has only been there since April 1972 and has had no experience of the phantoms that were reported four years previously. 'It's certainly a very old building,' he told me, 'in fact Charles I is supposed to have stayed here'.

One of the phantoms, seen by numerous visitors, is that of a 'tall lady in a dark green cloak or dress' gliding along an upstairs corridor. On the ground floor, however, several incidents have been recorded by the bar staff of witnessing 'vague shapes moving in the rooms'. One barman said, 'it was as if a couple of people had literally drifted through. Not quite white, but semi-transparent. They had no definite outline but resembled a man and a woman.'

Inexplicable footsteps are also heard sometimes in the evenings. One employee barricaded her bedroom door against the sounds which stopped on the landing outside.

Herefordshire

With beautiful scenery of the Wye Valley, cider apples and a
haunted castle

Open to the public during normal hours or by appointment   1

Historic buildings, museums, ruins   1

Apparitions
Females   1
Males   1
Horses   1

Goodrich Castle

Open to the public during normal hours
Off A40 (T)
22 miles from Gloucester station

One of the most magnificent buildings owned by the Department
of the Environment, Goodrich Castle set on the banks of the river
Wye is now merely an attractive relic of the days when it formed a
vital defensive position as a Welsh Border castle.

Although mentioned as 'Godric's' Castle in 1102 the current
remains are slightly later. The Crown took possession of it in the
12th century, but during the wars with Wales by Edward I,
William de Valence, half brother to Henry VIII, carried out many
additions to the fortress by building living rooms, a chapel and
a kitchen.

Since the 16th century, however, it has been uninhabited and is
now just an attraction for the tourist, the archaeologist, the
historian or even the lover of ancient beauty. Ownership had
passed through several hands until in 1920 Mrs Edmund Bosan-
quet placed the ruins in the guardianship of the Ministry of Works,

now the Department of the Environment by whom preservation is carried out.

One of the romantic tales connected with this imposing battle site is that of Alice Birch and her lover Clifford. The castle in 1646 was under siege by Colonel Birch of the Cromwellians and his niece, anxious to be with 'her man', escaped from her puritanical relative and joined Clifford within the castle walls.

The Colonel, despite the presence of the young girl, attacked the castle with increased force to crush the defenders using huge mortars of 200 lb in weight. Realising their predicament the lovers felt it wise to escape and, breaking through the attacking force, attempted to cross the nearby river. Unfortunately they had failed to realise the power of the flooded waters and were swept away. Their bodies were never found, but a triple phantom has been seen on the river bank near the ancient towers re-living that awful moment.

The occasional witness has seen during stormy nights 'a horseman with a lady mounted behind him' trying to force the animal down into the river. Both figures are described as wearing 'mediaeval type clothes'.

Hertfordshire

Has the Great North Road as a backbone and ten phantoms as an attraction

Open to the public during normal hours or by appointment	10
Private houses	3
Clubs, cinemas	1
Inns, hotels	4
Private houses, offices, factories	3
Open spaces, roads	4
Others	1
Phenomena	
Smells	1
Noises	6
Moving objects	2
Apparitions	
Females	3
Monks	1
Males	2
Horses	2
Others	2

Bramfield Road/Whitehorse Lane

Datchworth, Hertfordshire
Open to the public
Off A602
2 miles from Knebworth station

In the 18th century a regular visitor to the local fairs and markets was a renowned Hertford pieman by the name of Clibbon. He appeared to be an affable character, always showing a keen interest in the movements and activities of the local farmers. After talking to him, however, residents in the area were disturbed at reports of a highwayman's successful exploits in robbing farmers and their workers returning from the sales. The increasing number of co-incidental incidents stopped when the robber of the road was finally caught and revealed as the pieman.

Site of his capture was in the Bull's Green area of the Bramfield/ Datchworth road. The farmers were so incensed with rage at Clibbon's deceit, a friend to them in the morning and their robber at night, that after severely beating him they tied his body to a horse and allowed it to drag the semi-conscious man for many yards to Woolmer Green before finally killing him.

In recent years a few evening travellers have seen the vague shape of a horse pulling 'a black writhing body' along the lanes and heard the moans of the ghostly wreck of Clibbon as he continues to plead for mercy. Some have only heard the sounds of the incident, the horses' hooves and the scattering of gravel accompanied by the unearthly groans of the highwayman.

Whichever experience is witnessed it must be a bit disturbing to those not knowing the cause of the weird noises.

Brocket Arms*

Ayot St Lawrence, Hertfordshire
Open to the public during normal hours
Off A600
Nearest station—St Albans

This small and attractive village renowned for Shaw's Corner, the home of George Bernard Shaw from 1906 to 1950 which has been preserved as he left it, also boasts of an Abbey built in 1200 and this haunted pub constructed in 1378.

Shaw's home, incidentally, is rumoured to be haunted by Lawrence of Arabia who used to visit the family when on leave, but there seems little evidence to support the idea.

The ghost of the Brocket Arms, however, is well substantiated having been seen at least twice in the last four years by Mrs Teresa Sweeney, who works there during weekends, and heard on numerous occasions by visitors and the Allards—the licensees.

The apparition was first witnessed about 9pm early in 1969 when Mrs Sweeney was carrying some sandwiches through the dining room. On her left she saw 'a man dressed all in brown in a monk's outfit with a cowl and everything. His head was bent over so I couldn't see his face, but as I turned to face him he vanished.'

Some nine months later, on a cold winter morning, he was seen again—'an old emaciated face in a sort of smokey haze in the doorway of the dining room'.

The sounds heard by several people are of indistinct voices muttering quietly and noisy thumps and footsteps on the first floor. The apparition is strongly believed to be that of a monk who hung himself in the bar, not, I hasten to add in recent years, but when the building was a hostelry for pilgrims—as was the original use of many current inns and old hotels in the country.

It is not known why a 'man of the cloth' should commit suicide in such an establishment, but there could be many reasons such as over-indulgence in the grape, for example.

Confirming that the monk is still active Mr Allard told me in July 1972 that he had heard the footsteps 'quite recently', but was not worried. 'There's nothing to be frightened of,' he said.

Hawkins Hall Lane

Datchworth, Hertfordshire
Open to the public
Off A602
2 miles from Knebworth station

The Hall here has nothing to do with the ghost of the area, being a private house built in the 1930's.

The apparition, seen fairly frequently in the last 25 years, nearly always appears in the evening, but who she is and why she haunts this quiet country lane is unknown. She has been described as that of a 'little old lady in a long black dress, shuffling along the road in quite a purposeful manner. From the back she appears to be slightly bent with age, but when seen from the front it is obvious that her head is missing.'

One idea is that she is the ghost of an old woman who, in the 1800's, hung herself with a piece of wire in her cottage in Knebworth after the sudden death of her husband. Unfortunately, there is no record of such a suicide, but this does not of course preclude the possibility.

Mardleybury Manor*

Woolmer Green, Near Welwyn Garden City, Hertfordshire
Private property, please respect

This ancient house which was mentioned in the Domesday Book

has a long history of phenomena. One of the famous Godwins originally lived there and, coincidentally, some few years ago a direct descendant of the first inhabitant, the Rev George Watts, moved in.

His arrival caused an immediate reduction in the strength of the incidents here and it was assumed that this provided some evidence that the phenomena were caused by Godwin himself.

Described by local writer, Wynn Hughes of the *Luton Evening Post*, as 'a noisy ghost', the trouble experienced here has been heard as crunching sounds, 'heavy breathing' and the usual inexplicable bangs, crashes and thuds.

Recent occupants, Mr and Mrs Stack, smelt incense in one area, but Mrs Hughes told me that this may have been caused by an Indian student who stayed in the manor during their occupation. However, it wasn't the student who laid the wooden floor of a shed with such precision.

Mr Stack was erecting the new building and had asked that the floor unit, so heavy that two men had to carry it, be propped up against a wall some feet away whilst he prepared the foundation. Returning only minutes later he found that the floor was complete yet no one had been near it, and I repeat the weight needed two men to shift it.

Another rather disturbing incident experienced by the Stacks was that a knotted headscarf was thrown on their bed when Mrs Stack was about to enter the room. They never found the owner of it or where it came from.

There are new owners there now, but Mrs Jean Beard writing a thesis on the Manor recently spent a night in one of the haunted rooms adjoining a priest hole. She heard and experienced nothing other than an unusual and inexplicable ticking noise. There are no clocks in the vicinity of the room and the building does not suffer from death watch beetle.

Shortly after twelve o'clock one April night in 1968 a Mr Newton of a nearby village was driving home and had just reached Mardleybury when a 'figure of a woman in old-fashioned style clothing, grey in colour' dashed in front of his car. Too late to take evasive action, he felt the impact and skidded. Yet when he went to see what happened there was nothing to be seen.

Old Pest House

Rabley Heath, Near Knebworth, Hertfordshire
Private property, please respect

The appetising smell of frying eggs and bacon can usually titillate

123

any Englishman's palate. How frustrating it must be for the owners and visitors to this old building to experience this tasty odour, only to find that nothing is being cooked in the kitchen at all.

This unusual 'haunt', if that is the right word, has been 'witnessed' for many years, even when the building has lain empty for some months. Obviously ghostly smells exist as strongly as apparitions for another 'bacon and egg' haunt can be experienced in Chiswick House.

Palace Theatre

Watford, Hertfordshire
Open to the public during normal hours
On A412
Nearest station—Watford

This major town of Hertfordshire has unfortunately lost most of its interesting buildings through development and expansion plans effected in the 20th century, but the Church of St Mary with a 17th century pulpit and many brasses remains as one of the worthwhile remnants of an earlier and more peaceful age.

Built in 1908 as a music hall the Palace Theatre also remains as a souvenir of the popular days of Victorian theatricals. One of the leading stars of the time, Marie Lloyd, graced the theatre with her presence, but plans are now being mooted for the removal of the old building to make way for further less interesting concrete jungles.

Many theatres have ghosts most of which are pleasant, friendly characters as is 'Aggie', the unseen but often heard spectre of the Palace.

Tony Barnfield, assistant house manager, and many of the backstage staff have not only felt the presence of someone but heard footsteps, once in a dressing room over the scenery dock. Another incident was when curtains covering a door 'fluttered to one side as though someone was walking through them'. This was at 3 o'clock in the morning when a new set was being erected. The team working on the set watched the route of the footsteps in the gallery and were disturbed to see the curtains on the facing door move as the unseen ghost passed through.

One idea is that the haunt is associated with a burial ground on which the theatre is supposed to have been constructed, but the bodies were those of French prisoners of the Napoleonic wars. Perhaps Aggie only enjoys French farces or, and what is more likely, is one of the former stage hands checking that all is well.

Rectory Lane

Datchworth, Near Knebworth, Hertfordshire
Open to the public
Off A602
2 miles from Knebworth station

Datchworth is a quiet little old village, typical of its type, and pleasant in its character. In such a closely knit community which has existed for hundreds of years, one can imagine the affection held for the hamlet and the families that have grown up and died there.

One of the groups were the Eaves who, despite every effort to rid themselves of their increasing debts, found themselves in the mid 1700's thrown into the local poor house where in 1769 they perished. The sight of the cart taking their bodies through the village to the church must have created an everlasting picture of horror and pity in many people's minds at the time.

The unhappy scene of a horseless farm cart trundling silently along Rectory Lane from the village green towards the graveyard has been witnessed by several residents and the occasional visitor in recent years. One of the unusual aspects of this is that not only is the horse invisible but also the bodies of the victims—that is, all except their feet which dangle in a gruesome fashion from the end of the cart.

Watford Rail Tunnel

Watford, Hertfordshire
Private property, please respect

When many years ago the London and North Eastern Railway Company were constructing the rail line to the north, the builders found it necessary to bore a tunnel through part of a churchyard near Watford. Many times coffins were exposed and human remains fell on to the rail workers.

Once the line was constructed the steam engines roared through unhindered, but the locomotive plate men realised that they had a problem.

Every time they fired their boilers, found to be necessary at one spot in the tunnel, there would be a vicious 'blow-back' and several engine drivers were badly burnt by the flames.

On investigation it was found that this occurrence always happened when the engine was immediately below the graveyard and the drivers associated the peculiar effect with the 'ghosts of the dead protesting at the invasion of their privacy'.

Mathews

Market Place, St Albans, Hertfordshire
Open to the public during normal hours
Junction of A5/A6/A414
Nearest station—St Albans

Up to August 1972 this establishment was known as 'The Wellington', one of the many pubs of St Albans. Recent licensees, Mr and Mrs Tew, often heard 'loud bumping noises' in the room over the saloon bar when it was empty except for furniture. After closing time the cause of the noises was discovered but never the method. Most of the furniture had been moved around.

Ghostly footsteps were occasionally heard in a corridor and up the stairs, but when they left the inn, somewhat naturally, no mention was made of their phantom guest.

In November 1971 *The Herts Advertiser* published a report that the new licencees, the Jupps, were experiencing phenomena practically identical to that of the Tews, but the activities of the unseen ghost became more obvious.

'Bottles, jugs and glasses fly from shelves and smash on the floor' and, on one occasion, the pumping gas had been 'mysteriously turned off'.

One of the barmaids, Mrs Bacon, employed at the inn, was rather flattered by the attentions of the phantom for, apparently, sometimes doors were 'opened for her'.

In September 1972, after the pub had been demolished, except for its basement, the Mathews group of companies opened it as the latest addition to their chain of butchers' shops.

The first indication that the ghost had not been demolished occurred when 'a shadowy figure' was witnessed in the cellar by a young apprentice. Continuing the series of phenomena, the manager of the new shop suffered eight punctures to his parked car in the first few months, and the assistant manager complained of seven. The new manager appointed in 1973 ridiculed the stories, but found all four tyres of his car punctured within a week!

Westminster Bank

High Street, Stevenage, Hertfordshire
Open to the public during normal hours
Nearest station—Stevenage

Formerly the Old Castle Inn, these premises have rather grisly associations.

Some 200 years ago Henry Trigg, a local grocer, on leaving the Black Swan saw a group of body snatchers at work in a nearby churchyard. So alarmed was he at the thought of his own body being stolen that he added a codicil to his will requesting that his coffin should be lined with lead and placed in the loft of his home. He died in 1724.

Years later, about 1850, the building was converted into the Old Castle and when the new proprietor carried out an inspection he found the coffin still in its orginal situation among the rafters. Intrigued, he opened it and found the body 'well preserved, still with hair on the skull'.

Henry, however, was not allowed to rest in peace for, during the First World War, some raucous soldiers broke open the coffin and took away the bones of the old grocer as souvenirs.

Betty Puttick, in her *Hertfordshire Countryside*, says that the bones were also used to supplement the soldiers' pay, being sold to other troops anxious to obtain souvenirs of their visit to England. The number required exceeded the supply, so the local butcher was called upon to assist.

In May 1970 a workman on the site was astounded to see the apparition of a man, 5ft 8in in height and wearing a striped apron, glide into an adjoining barn and vanish on reaching a solid brick wall. A few visitors to the area have also seen a similar shape—now assumed to be the ghost of poor old Henry.

White Hart*

High Street, Hemel Hempstead, Hertfordshire
Open to the public during normal hours
Junction of A41/A4147

Parts of this delightful old pub go back as far as 1530 and at one time it was a private house. The haunting here has been known for about 30 years and this knowledge was confirmed only recently by the visit of a Canadian whose father used to frequent the bar 'fairly regularly'. His first comments when entering the pub were, 'have you still got the ghost?'

Numerous customers have experienced the feeling of terror when approaching the stairs and for some months one barmaid refused to go anywhere near them despite having no knowledge of the haunting associated with the spot.

The ghost itself has only been reported on two occasions during the last 22 years—since the current landlord took over, in fact. It is described by both witnesses, one of them Mrs Vasey, the wife of the licensee, as 'a face of a man who looks overwrought with fear, but it was black and white like a photographic negative'.

He was also seen as 'a disembodied face' in 1968 by a guest in a bedroom over the bar, and about a year later by Mrs Vasey 'behind a regular customer standing at the counter'. Mrs Vasey told me she was not worried about the phantom, 'but I am still not keen on going up the stairs'.

In the 18th century one of the methods used to obtain recruits for the Army was similar to that of the Royal Navy. Men were 'press-ganged' into service. Any young man found apparently unattached was grabbed and shipped off to the nearest camp to be provided, compulsorily, with the Queen's shilling.

One of these victims it seems was a tall young man who, in about 1770, was quietly supping his ale at the bar of the White Hart when he was suddenly confronted with 'a group of redcoats', anxious to increase the strength of the Regiment.

In the ensuing fight the intended recruit was killed at the base of the stairway and the half-drunken soldiers were thrown out by the outraged customers. One can imagine with what intensity the lad had fought for his independence and freedom, leaving behind an acute sense of horror and misery as he died.

These few moments of hatred and bitterness have been indelibly fixed into the area. Mrs Vasey said that once one night, when in the bedroom over the stairs, she distinctly heard sounds of raised voices coming from below. But, as expected for that time of night, the bar was empty.

Whitehorse Lane

Datchworth, Hertfordshire
Open to the public
Off A602
2 miles from Knebworth station

Two ghostly incidents have been witnessed here, that of a headless horse galloping along the road and a carriage slowly sinking into a pond opposite Mardleybury Manor.

The first, that of a white horse, is believed to be that of an animal found to be unsympathetic to Cromwell's cause. His owner, a loyal royalist living in Welches Farm in Whitehorse Lane, was caught by the Roundheads and decapitated. His head, it is claimed, was placed on a spike in the stable yard and the soldiers then turned their attentions to the fine stallion. Probably because of the rough handling, the creature refused to co-operate, and therefore also lost his head.

At Burnham Green the White Horse Inn perpetuates the existence of the fine animal.

The carriage haunt is caused, it is thought, by an accident that occurred in the 18th century. Following a party at the Manor one of the carriage drivers, who had perhaps imbibed too much of the grape, lost control of the horses and although he jumped clear as the coach swung over into the pond his lady passenger, a woman in a grey dress, was unable to escape and drowned. So clear is the phantom of the woman at this spot that several travelling motorists have braked hard to avoid hitting her.

The Wicked Lady

Normansland Common, St Albans, Hertfordshire
Open to the public during normal hours
On A5/A6/A414
Nearest station—St Albans

One of the highly popular films made in the 1940's and still remembered by fans of Margaret Lockwood was *The Wicked Lady*. The story was based on the exploits of Lady Katherine Ferrers who, in the late 18th century, carried out an effective double life. During the day, often accompanied by her husband, she would enjoy the normal social activities of a titled lady.

At night, however, she would don the clothes and character of a highwayman. For only a few years she successfully robbed night travellers often selecting her victims from dinners she had attended earlier the same day.

It seemed obvious, at least from the story, that she was more vicious towards her own sex than the handsome young gentry who probably took her fancy. On a couple of her exploits she was accompanied by a 'fellow' highwayman, played by James Mason in the film.

Eventually she was shot in a running battle with some vigilantes, but was able to reach her bedroom before collapsing. It was here that her secret was revealed and a few hours later she died.

This pub, The Wicked Lady, is named after Lady Ferrers and is believed to have been used by her for illicit meetings with her nightly companions.

Whether the unseen ghost who inhabits the inn is connected with her Ladyship is not known, but most certainly the sobbing cries and weeping often heard by customers are that of a woman.

An isolated incident which may also be associated with the female robber was experienced by the manager, Douglas Payne. The *Herts Advertiser* reported that he was exercising his dog on the nearby common at about 11.30pm in December 1970 when he heard the sound of a horse galloping at high speed through the shrubland. It came so close he could have touched it, but nothing was to be seen, not even a movement of the bushes. I understand it took much soothing to quieten his dog which had obviously been badly frightened by the phantom horse.

Huntingdonshire

Centre of the Fenland country and birthplace of Oliver Cromwell

Open to the public during normal hours or by appointment   1

Inns, hotels   1

Phenomena
Moving objects   1

Apparitions
Males   1

Golden Lion Hotel

Market Place, St Ives, Huntingdonshire
Open to the public during normal hours
On A1123
6 miles from Huntingdon station

The landlord of this historical old pub, Mr Ron Woods, was so interested in the phenomena that has been experienced here for so many years that, during 1970, he called upon the Cambridge University Society for Psychical Research to investigate. Spotlighting the need for some serious thought to be given to the continuing reports of ghosts in the establishment was the incident reported by Michael Samuels who was woken at 2am to find a door, normally fixed with a heavy bolt, was wide open and blankets on his bed had been pulled away.

This was no isolated incident for during his stay identical phenomena were experienced three times, and on one occasion when he was out for the day a member of the staff saw the ghostly figure of a 'woman in green' standing in the room. The door, although locked by the maid, was found open and the bed disturbed when Mr Samuels returned.

All this happened in room 12, one of three that have been affected for a long period. Room 15, adjoining, and known as 'Cromwell's Room' because of the belief that 'The Protector' and his officers used it during the Civil War as area headquarters, houses the apparition of a cavalier.

According to the *Hunts Post* in 1970 a chambermaid saw the figure of the royalist outside the room and a few months later a guest reported 'a cavalier just glided into room 15'. Blankets are affected in the same way as in room 12 and two glazed portraits continually fall to the floor, not vertically but diagonally.

As is usual when professional researchers arrive, nothing happened during the team's three-day visit, but only a few weeks later phenomena re-commenced—bell ringing, doors opening and bedclothes being moved from sleeping guests.

Ireland

The emerald isle, full of tales of leprechauns and ancient legend

Open to the public during normal hours or by appointment	2
Private houses	1
Historic buildings, museums, ruins	1
Shops, stores	1
Inns, hotels	1
Phenomena	
Noises	2
Moving objects	1
Apparitions	
Nuns	2
Males	1
Others	1

Castlegard

Near Pallasgreen, County Limerick, Ireland
Private property, please respect

Owned by the Thompson family this really ancient building said to be of the 14th century, is reputed to be the oldest inhabited house in Ireland, but who the ghost is that frequents the stairway, no one knows.

The clear sounds of a lady's gown gently rustling up the main staircase, brushing against the balustrades until reaching the top, have been heard for many years. In earlier days the noises were accompanied by footsteps but these have not been experienced for some time.

Kilkea Castle Hotel*

Castledermot, County Kildare, Ireland
Open to the public during normal hours
On T51
8 miles from Athy station

The oldest inhabited castle in Ireland has, despite the fact it is now one of the most luxurious 55 roomed hotels in the country, retained its magnificent exterior of an 11th century fortress set in 110 acres of lush countryside.

It was built in 1180 for Sir Walter de Riddleford by Hugh de Lacy, chief Governor of Ireland. The first resident died in 1244 and when his grand-daughter Emelina married Maurice Fitzgerald it started a family line that continued for hundreds of years producing such eminent personalities as the late President John Fitzgerald Kennedy of America.

Descended from Lord Otho, an honorary baron of England in 1057, the forefathers of the Fitzgeralds are said to have originated from the Gherdarini family of Florence. The castle itself remained the family seat through the centuries of violence, torture and bloody battles created by the wars between the native Irish, Catholic Royalists and the Puritans.

But the legend of the ghosts is such an ancient one that there must be doubts of it being connected with the 20th century hauntings experienced as recently as July 1970.

It is accepted that room 222 in the original tower of the fortress was where Garrett Og, the 11th Earl of Kildare, practised witchcraft and sorcery in the 16th century but, and this is where credulity is stretched he is also said to have acquired the art of metamorphosis, form changing.

A complicated myth is told of the Earl's activities as a serpent, a flood, a 'small black bird' and finally a cat. Because of his wife's fear of the last transformation the Earl revisits his castle every seven years and will finally rid Erin of all its enemies.

An amusing tale but one that hardly explains the incidents that have occurred in the room in the last few years. Bedclothes have been thrown around and footsteps and female voices have been heard on the roof over the room, where only the wind and the rafters join company.

Confirming that there is little connection between the current hauntings and the 'Wizard Earl' is the fact, discovered by the current owner of the hotel William Cade, that Garrett Og's death is safely and unquestionably registered at Somerset House in London.

'But,' Mr Cade tells me 'since July 1970 the ghost though

benevolent and given more to perfectly harmless pranks, has not manifested himself, at least to the best of my knowledge'.

One wonders if we shall hear of something happening in 1977.

Killakee Art Centre

Dower House, Killakee, Ballyborden Road, Dublin 14, Ireland
Open to the public during normal hours
Nearest station—Dublin

Despite numerous tales of ghostly gunmen resulting from the troubles of the 1920's and the fascinating and delightful stories told by any Irishman of the 'wee folk', the leprechauns, there are some factual cases of hauntings in the Emerald Isle.

One of these originally reported in 1968 by Mrs O'Brien, the owner of this Arts Centre, where amateurs learn the basic techniques of drawing and professionals display their work.

The workmen converting what had been almost derelict premises into the new centre were disturbed by strange sounds, doors opening by themselves and, the most frightening of all, the appearance of a huge black cat.

Mrs O'Brien ignored the stories until she saw the creature herself and was appalled at its size, 'about that of an Airedale'. It was squatting on the flagstones in the hallway, yet all doors were locked before and after its sudden appearance and departure.

A painter who had been helping with the decorations was scared when with two colleagues, he felt the room in which they were working suddenly grow cold. 'A shadowy figure stood in the darkness', he said, 'we heard a deep growl and ran in panic, slamming the door behind us. On turning I saw the door open again and a huge black cat with red-flecked eyes crouching in the half light.' His painting of the creature now hangs in the hallway.

On another occasion he challenged the misty figure of a man standing in the hall and received a reply, 'you don't know who I am. You cannot see me'.

Mrs O'Brien had the house exorcised and until Autumn 1969 it remained peaceful. However, in October some friends jokingly held a seance at a coffee table and the disturbances started again. 'Paintings were torn, crockery smashed and the sound of bells being rung were heard.'

A few minutes before Radio Telefis Eireann sent a camera team to the premises in 1970 Mrs O'Brien had seen the figures of two nuns and 'a tall Eurasian man' walk through the gallery of the centre and then vanish.

A local medium claimed that they were the ghosts of two women who had helped at 'black masses' during meetings of the notorious Hell Fire Club on Montpelier Hill behind the Centre.

The house itself was originally built as the Dower House for the Massey family, a branch of landowners who ruled the area for several hundreds of years.

A legend of the area that members of the Club had once tormented and then suffocated a deformed youngster for sport seems confirmed. During the building alterations in 1968 a grave was discovered in the garden which contained a small human skeleton with a huge skull.

Below the flagstones of the room in which the youth had been murdered a metal statue of a devil was found and has now been placed in the garden as a decoration.

The house was also used as a refuge for Republican forces in the 1920's and a man was shot there.

It was exorcised again in July 1970, but 'weird noises' have been heard since then.

Isle of Man

A minute, sovereign country within the United Kingdom, famous for its cats

Open to the public during normal hours or by appointment	4
Private houses	–
Historic buildings, museums, ruins	2
Inns, hotels	1
Open spaces, roads	1
Phenomena	
Moving objects	1
Apparitions	
Females	2
Males	3

Castle Rushen★

Castletown, Isle of Man
Open to the public during normal hours
Junction of A4/A25/A7

One of the most superb examples of mediaeval castles in Britain is in the centre of the island's former capital, which also contains a fascinating 'Witches' Mill' and the renowned Witchcraft Museum.

The Castle was originally a typical 12th century fortress with a central square tower and walls of some ten feet thick. Additions and modifications were made right through the Middle Ages and up to the 19th century, but in this excellently preserved reminder of the past the chain of authority remains unbroken. Court sittings are still held here and each Governor of the Island has to take the oath of office within the Castle walls before assuming complete control.

Partly because of the variety of rulers of the island it is difficult to accurately identify the ghosts that inhabit the ancient walls. It must be remembered that Man was under the Norwegian suzerainty of Godred II when the castle was originally constructed. Margaret, Queen of Scots and Maid of Norway, took over from Alexander and, changing for a period to English rule, Richard de Burgh, Earl of Ulster assumed control in 1290.

Scottish command was resumed only for a brief period under Randolf, Earl of Moray, but the island from 1333 to 1765 was again under English suzerainty. It was in May 1765 the English Crown took possession of Man.

The apparition seen in August 1960 by a group of four youngsters who, the next morning handed the curator a signed statement to the effect, was described as 'a strange figure of a woman dressed in black with a dead white face, black hands (gloves or bloodstains?) and something hanging down from the head-dress'.

Curator of the Castle, Mr Gale, tells me that this incident occurred at 11.30pm when the castle was empty and locked, and he is certain no person was in the castle. 'I was so impressed with their sincerity and their statement that I was inclined to believe them'. The lads were quite certain of what they had seen on the Eagle Tower, 86 feet above the ground.

The fortress had been used for many years as a prison and in the late 18th century convicted felons were lodged in the Keep which, at that time, was becoming 'increasingly dilapidated'. Many executions were carried out within the grim walls and one of them was of a woman who had brutally murdered her child.

The report in 1960 was not the sole witnessing of the woman in black for she had been seen in 1937 by an assistant custodian. On this occasion she was seen 'leading a child from the drawbridge to the dungeon, now believed to have been a mill, but I paid little attention to the figures at the time'. When a visitor enquired the whereabouts of his wife, the curator replied she had just passed him going towards the dungeon. Both men checked the room, but it was empty. The missing wife was found at the top of the castle admiring the view and had been there for some time.

Other earlier witnesses include the wife of the Warden who saw the apparition twice. On the first occasion the ghost disappeared through the castle wall near the drawbridge when spoken to, and a couple of years later she was seen in the passage.

'The story of this mysterious lady', says Mr Gale, 'was going on many years before this and will probably continue for many years to come. Although I have never seen the ghost, I find it hard to disbelieve all the people who claim to have seen her through the years'.

E*

Falcan Cliff Hotel

Douglas, Isle of Man
Open to the public during normal hours
On A1

Ringed by woods, though only a few yards from the busy shopping centre which it overlooks, the Falcan Cliff is one of the older hotels in Douglas and retains its considerable popularity perhaps because of its age.

One end of the building, which strongly resembles a castle complete with tower, was used during the First World War as an internment hospital for German prisoners. It must have been rather a depressing spot for the soldiers at the time, suffering from physical and mental wounds as they were, miles from their fatherland and with no hope of escape.

The atmosphere proved too much for one of them and he succeeded in escaping, not just from the hospital but from life, by jumping from the top of the 100 foot tower.

Shortly after the last war local residents were often puzzled by the appearance of a grey shape falling from the parapet of the hotel, but over the years the frequency of this phenomenon faded and the only evidence of the haunting that still exists is the attitude of the pet dog. He refuses to go up the tower steps past a certain spot, his hackles rise and he 'slinks back down as though beaten'.

Physical phenomena are occasionally experienced however. 'Plates have been seen to rise from the table and crash to the floor', and recently a bucket in the tower basement inexplicably turned upside down scattering its contents all over the floor. Another incident which may indicate the soldier's spare time hobby was when a table tennis ball bounced across the floor. It had been placed in a deep ash-tray to stop it falling from a table.

The present staff are 'not troubled' by the incidents, though they are reluctant to go up the tower after dark.

Hill Fort

Near Castletown, Isle of Man
Open to the public during normal hours
On A7

Only a few miles from Castletown, the island's former capital and Castle Rushen, a magnificent example of a mediaeval castle, lies a veritable collection of archaeological treasures. On the small headland of Lanquet Point visitors can see at Hango Hill the unique site of a Viking boat burial, an ancient hill fort, the remains of an old gibbet and the ruins of a chapel.

Amassed together they certainly suggest the ideal spot for a ghost, or even a collection of spectres. But there are few evening visitors to this old burial ground for the superstitions that surround the area provide numerous tales of noisy creaking chains, horrible skeletons and practically every type of popular ghostly apparition.

Although the director of the National Trust of Manx feels that there are no instances of well authenticated ghosts on the island, I am afraid I must beg to differ.

In February 1970 Joe Mansley, accompanied by a friend, paid a visit to the chapel on Hango Hill after feeling 'something' brush against his legs earlier in the day when he had seen the 'shadowy shape' of a black animal 'like a dog' glide into the undergrowth.

But the evening visit proved more interesting for from the empty Chapel ruins they heard a faltering voice of a man angrily denouncing an unseen person. Seconds later the apparition of a 'thin man in clerical vestments' was seen in a doorway moving its arms and mouthing what sounded like Latin then English oaths. The figure staggered and fell forward on to the grass, only to vanish as soon as the men approached.

Perhaps the particular witnesses involved are unusually perceptive or sensitive for, on a third occasion, the figure of a sailor 'in rough clothing and dripping with water' was seen stumbling around the cliff edge and to disappear when Mr Mansley moved towards it.

Who the two ghosts are (it is felt that the 'dog' incident may well have been a badger) is not known, but years ago a sailing vessel sank off the south coast of the island causing many deaths. One of the crew was believed to have been a local man.

Tantaloo

Glen Auldyn, Near Skye Hill, Ramsey, Isle of Man
Open to the public during normal hours
On B16

Some many years ago youngsters playing around in the locality of the old mill of 'Tantaloo' were frightened by the appearance of 'an old woman in a grey cloak and a white head-dress waving a frying pan' at them. Over the years several people venturing along the steep lane from Skye Hill also saw the ghostly figure and, it seems, were equally scared.

In 1971, after a gap of over a hundred years, the ghost was seen again by a couple of tourists from the mainland. They described the apparition as 'wearing a peculiar head-dress which she took off and waved about'.

It is unfortunately impossible to identify the character herself, but the description of the head gear rather resembles that of an early Scandinavian type regularly used by fishwives. It would be unusual for it to come apart leaving the bottom 'sun bonnet' still on the wearer's head, but it certainly sounds as if a reminder of the old Norse costumes remain on the island, even though it be a ghostly one.

Kent

The Gateway to England which houses one of the most haunted villages in the country

Open to the public during normal hours or by appointment	14
Private houses	6
Clubs, cinemas	2
Historic buildings, museums, ruins	1
Churches, abbeys, rectories	1
Shops, stores	1
Inns, hotels	3
Private houses, offices, factories	6
Open spaces, roads	6
Phenomena	
Smells	1
Noises	8
Moving objects	4
Apparitions	
Nuns	1
Females	4
Monks	1
Males	7
Dogs	2
Others	4

Boys Hall*

Willesborough, Near Ashford, Kent
Private property, please respect

The first Boys Hall, known then as 'The Moat', is stated to have been built in the 16th century about half a mile from its current site, but Thomas Boys of the Bonnington branch of the family pulled it down in 1616 and created the existing building in 1632 from the original materials.

In the grounds an unusual hollow is believed to have been used for smuggling purposes, probably as a cache for illicit goods, but there are a couple of other peculiar stories connected with the house.

At one time, when the property was on the market, a prospective purchaser having examined the rooms with great thoroughness made numerous notes as to the decoration including the panelling of the hall and dining room. On his second visit, however, only a few days later all signs of the panels had vanished. The obvious answer that the wood had been removed in the interim period unfortunately fails to be acceptable for numerous friends had also seen the decorative wall coverings and there is strong evidence that it had existed at one time. Even today some first-time visitors have claimed to have seen the panelling as it was originally.

Late in the 18th century the then owner of Boys Hall arranged a large Christmas party for his friends and relatives and among the guests was a young lieutenant and his fiancée. Unfortunately a local Irishman was also invited to attend the function.

The reason for it being unfortunate was that he took an instant liking to the girl and many hours were spent in her company. Towards the end of the festivities, the couple having been missing for some time, the Army officer went in search of the couple finding them eventually in the stables.

Nothing further was heard of the 'foreigner' whose disappearance remained a mystery for some years. Meanwhile, however, the girl married the soldier and went with him to live in India until his death.

She returned to England and immediately called at Boys Hall where a friend was astonished at her appearance. 'She was pale-faced and obviously distraught. All she kept saying was "he is calling me: that man I love is calling me".' The friend attempted to calm the widow, but she merely demanded a light, ran upstairs to one of the bedrooms and 'with great strength' pulled up three floor boards. Between the timbers was revealed the skeleton of 'the Irishman'. It was easy to establish the identity from the remains of the clothes, and the cause of death from the bullet still lodged in the skull, but what stunned everyone in the area was the information revealed at the coroner's court. The bones were those of a young woman.

The news shattered the composure of the young widow who, on returning from the official hearing, went to the scene of the 'burial', stood silently for some moments at the window and then threw herself on to the stones below.

During 1970-72 a team of workmen were employed to repair and renovate the building and several of them reported being disturbed by the various inexplicable incidents which occurred. Two of them told me in June 1972 of seeing what appeared to them to be a white smock pass along a path on the side of the building. On another occasion one of them saw the figure of 'someone in white standing by the lake' watching him and on turning back, after pointing out the apparition to a colleague, the ghost had vanished.

Footsteps walking through empty bedrooms have been frequently heard, following a path through doorways now sealed and two carpenters' rulers mysteriously vanished for about six weeks.

Legend has it that a tunnel exists from The William Harvey pub several hundred yards away to the walled garden of the property and that Charles II was supposed to have hidden in one of the panelled rooms—the panelling of which came originally from Windsor Castle. But what is fact and not legend is that in 1972 the owner, whilst making a bed, suddenly turned round to see her transistor radio set slowly move through the air from the top of the built in vanity unit towards her a few feet before crashing to the floor a few feet away.

Another incident the owner told me of was that of a huge pair of double doors, despite a massive bolt securing them, opening several times, always 'around midnight', by unseen hands. I found even the catch rather heavy to move, let alone the doors themselves. But there seems no connection between these incidents and the unfortunate case of suicide.

The house, gradually resuming its former beauty under the expert hands of the builders and the guidance of the new owners, is a fascinating example of early 17th century construction with interesting additions and modifications. A minute priests' room on the top floor has become a stairway to a self-contained flat and the magnificent Jacobean staircase is now lovingly restored.

An unseen ghost frequently heard by both the builders and visitors is that of an invisible dog that pads through a couple of upstairs rooms.

Yet, despite the continuing visitations of a bodyless smock or 'white shirt', the regular mysterious incidents and the sight on one occasion outside a corner window of a ground floor room of an elbow in white cloth, the atmosphere is pleasant and friendly.

Bridge Place Country Club*

Canterbury Road, Bridge, Kent
Open to the public by appointment only
On A2
Nearest station—Canterbury

A building constructed in 1638 as a manor, partly destroyed in the Civil War and eventually converted to a popular country club complete with a large dance floor constructed in the original wing must be intriguing in itself. Still with its 17th century oak stairway and carved stone busts peering down from the corners, it creates an unusual mixture of architectural designs and modern planning.

Mr Peter Malkin purchased the club in 1967 and shortly afterwards was astounded to see the figure of a 'chambermaid carrying a basket' across his bedroom floor. 'It was most peculiar', he said. Members of the club also reported hearing unusual footsteps in empty rooms and witnessing doors opening by themselves.

What proved most disturbing, however, were the pitiful cries of a child which could often be heard coming from a chimney in a ground floor room. Mr. Malkin carried out a thorough investigation and found no reason for the sorrowful moans.

But he was able to find a probable explanation for the phenomenon and the apparition now seen twice by himself.

In about 1780 the owner of the manor house—a gentleman by the name of Taylor—had carried out an illicit affair with the chambermaid. On learning that his wife, who had been recovering from a long illness in Scotland, was about to return he decided that he must rid himself of the evidence of his infidelity so both his young lover and their child were murdered.

One presumes the body of the child was hidden in the chimney, but what happened to the remains of the serving girl is not known.

Although the phenomenon 'seems to have died down over the last couple of years', Mr Malkin said that late in 1969 a young French boy, a friend of his, was staying in the club and early one morning came to him in a very nervous state.

He described a 'cavalier-type figure of a man' that he had seen in his bedroom, but after being pacified returned. The following night the same phantom was seen and the lad was accommodated from then on in another room.

Court Mount Hotel*

Canterbury Road, Birchington, Kent
Open to the public during normal hours
On A28
Nearest station—Birchington

Though perhaps it doesn't look very old, parts of this small six-bedroomed hotel were completed in the 14th century. The ghost appears at 3am.

The hotel has a long history of being haunted though the current owner Mr DR Underwood, has so far not experienced or heard of any guests witnessing the apparition which occasionally visits one of the bedrooms. He only took over in September 1972.

Mr Victor Adams, the former proprietor, like his predecessor was told of the phenomenon when he purchased the property. The previous owners have themselves witnessed the 'early caller' in the affected room which overlooks the main road.

In June 1968 two Gas Board executives were staying in the haunted bedroom without knowing it, and were woken at 3am to see the phantom of 'a beautiful woman with long blonde hair and flowing white dress standing in the middle of the room'.

Neither were afraid (who would be at such a vision?) and both stated they were 'quite sorry' when the apparition moved slowly towards the wall and vanished. Nevertheless, at the time of its appearance Mr Taylor admitted he had been 'a little scared. One doesn't see a ghost like that every day of your life.'

Other guests and members of the staff have occasionally heard the sound of footsteps coming from the room when it has been empty.

Rumours of a suicide in the room in the 18th century have been unsubstantiated.

Downe Court Manor*

Bromley, Kent
Private property, please respect

A 17th century manor house near Orpington bought by Mr Brian Thompson (better known as the owner of Puttenden Manor near Lingfield) in November 1962 who planned to completely restore the decaying property to its former glory and open it to the public. But, due to an overbearing atmosphere of evil which seemed to have affected even the local populace, 'four years of effort produced only heart-break, financial loss and despair'.

In a house in the manor grounds Charles Darwin wrote his world-shattering *Origin of the Species of Man* and this must have added strength to the antagonistic atmosphere of the place.

Mr Thompson told me that the whole area suffered from a brooding atmosphere of evil and antipathy, created he believes by black magic carried out many years ago. 'We've been fighting a family curse there', he said. A house nearby is called 'Widder-shins', adding strength to his belief of former withcraft rites. On one occasion a photograph was taken showing no less than seven ghosts.

There appear to be two specific areas that remain haunted, even though the building has been excorcised twice; a bedroom with an adjoining stairway, and the former butler's room.

Several people have experienced an overwhelming feeling of fear at the top of the stairs and it is here that it is believed a troop of Cavaliers hanged a man after bursting into the building in search of Cromwellian supporters. A young lady who slept in the bedroom was woken up one night by a 'thud' and found a ghostly arm, severed at the shoulder, lying on the counterpane beside her. Several others who have stayed the night in the room have seen vague shapes, heard the sounds of fighting and met a man dressed like a cavalier but with only his head and shoulders visible.

The ghosts in the butler's room are of a young girl, seen with water dripping down her long dark hair, and another 'mysterious shape' that stood beside one of the visitors. A young servant girl is known to have been drowned in a nearby lake many years ago and the associated figure may be that of the culprit.

The owner, optimistic of clearing away the pervading evil, is hoping to re-open the house to the public in a few years time, but meanwhile is relieved that the atmosphere is now considerably more friendly than when he first purchased it.

Kings Head*

Staplehurst, Kent
Open to the public during normal hours
On A229
Nearest station—Staplehurst

Foundations of this old pub, situated on the Roman road, are estimated to be about 12th century and part of the building itself dates back to the 1300's. A major portion, however, was not constructed until 1660.

Practically opposite is a 14th century church with a famous south door claimed to be one of the oldest in the country. The church is believed to have been part of a monastery at one time. One suggestion is that the pub was built on part of the original graveyard, for remaining in the garden path of the Kings Head are two tombstones. One of these was 'thrown out on to a rubbish heap in May or June' of 1972 and it was then that mysterious noises started at night in the empty bar.

'Groans, creaks and sounds rather like bottles clinking' was how the temporary landlord, Mr Burrell, described them to me. But the main phenomenon, which started when major alterations commenced, are unusual noises in the guest room upstairs. 'Although I'm not convinced it's a ghost,' he said, 'I've heard these peculiar sounds and cannot explain them. I can't believe it's just coincidence that it started at the time we moved the tombstones. Even though we have brought the one back from the pile of rubble, the noises continue.

'One thing though,' he continued. 'The sounds are perfectly genuine and have often been heard by the landlord himself, Mr David Keighley, and both the cat and dog refuse to enter the bedroom.'

It was unfortunate that the 'guv'nor' himself was away at the time, but no doubt the locals look forward to the Halloween party to be held in anticipation of more startling events. There will certainly be more groans the following morning and genuine ones at that.

Lympne Castle*

Near Hythe, Kent
Open to the public during normal hours
Off B2067
8 miles from Folkestone station

Being described as a 'romantic mediaeval castle with an earlier Roman, Saxon, and Norman history', Lympne Castle more or less demands to be haunted. The castle was rebult about 1360 on foundations of what was believed to be a Roman watch-tower and was once owned by the Archdeacons of Canterbury. Thomas Becket lived there for some years before becoming Archbishop.

In 1905 a lot of restoration work was undertaken and in 1916 Henry Beecham and his wife bought it and lived there until 1947. It was during this period that the first reports of the hauntings were published.

The current owners are Mr and Mrs Margary who purchased the castle in 1962 because of their love of old historic buildings and the fact that the site has one of the finest views in the country.

Their own family too has a strong historical background, for Harry Margary is a direct descendant of Aubyn de Marguery who captured Dover in 1295.

Although no ghosts have been seen recently, there is still heard the tread on the stone steps of the Roman watch tower which Mrs Beecham reported during her occupation. 'The click of the gate below the castle walls heralds his coming, then one hears the sound of his footsteps. After a few minutes silence he is heard inside the building walking up the steps in the tower, but they never come down.'

The sounds are supposed to be those of a Roman soldier who still mounts guard on the tower battlements.

The other ghost witnessed several times by Mrs Beecham was that of a priest 'with grave sad eyes standing in the little room in the West Tower'. She wondered if it was one of the seven Saxon priests who were dispossessed by Lanfranc, the first Norman Archbishop of Canterbury, for some believe they were murdered. But stories of 'bloodstains on the castle stairs', 'dogs refusing to walk past certain areas' and 'people getting hysterical' on entering a certain room have never been substantiated.

Mrs Margary said that despite the rumours and the 'odd noises', 'the family feel very friendly towards the unseen guests'.

Pennis Lane

Fawkham Green, Kent
Open to the public
Off A20
4 miles from Longfield station

Practically a stone's throw from the racing circuit of Brand's Hatch is the small village of Fawkham Green where, during autumn evenings, the wraith of a nun has been seen wafting along Pennis Lane.

Her history is unknown, but local belief is that she was somehow connected with St John's Jerusalem, a few miles to the north. This establishment is the 13th century headquarters of the Knights Hospitallers of St John and became incorporated into a house in the 16th century.

The nun is thought to have been murdered in the 1400's, but why and by whom remains a mystery.

Pluckley*

Kent
On B2077 (off A20)
Nearest station—Pluckley

I was first introduced to this attractive little village by George Hay of the Environmental Consortium who told me that, not only is it one of the most picturesque spots in the south east, but it is historically interesting and haunted. The first thing that intrigued me was to notice that the majority of the older houses and cottages are fitted with round topped windows.

This design is, in fact, a traditional reminder of the days when a Royalist supported by the Derings, the owners of the village, escaped from his pursuers through a window of this type in the original manor house. The manor was unfortunately destroyed by a fire in 1956, having been converted into a school.

Naturally the more people I met, the more I learnt of the hauntings which have established the title of the village. Jack Hallam in *The Ghost Tour* of 1967 (Wolfe) listed no less than 12 ghosts, Desmond Carrington, a local resident, mentioned 10 in an article, and Basil Cowles, another local, made a film recently featuring 11.

Two of the ghosts vanished in the flames which burnt Surrenden Dering—a poltergeist and the White Lady who, when alive, was Lady Dering. Her body had been embalmed by her husband in order that her permanent beauty could comfort the rest of his days. So convincing was her ghostly figure that an American hunter, Walter Winans, fired two rounds from his revolver at it which merely caused some slight damage to the library wall.

Another phantom that was probably destroyed when Smarden, or Dering Woods, were flattened a few years ago was that of an 18th century colonel who hanged himself from one of the trees there.

Spectres that remain however are as follows:

Elvey Farm*

Pluckley, Kent
Private property, please respect

This 500 year old farm house situated on what was once the Dering family estate, was originally a large barn built in the 1400's, but just over a hundred years later had an upper floor fitted and was converted into a comfortable home.

The current owners, Mr and Mrs Ambrose, run a riding school and stable but are obviously very keen on retaining the old world charm of the place.

Over the last few years a smell of burning wool has been very evident in one of the bedrooms. This is situated over the sitting room and contains much of the main chimney breast. More recently, however, incidents of an unnatural character have confirmed that the farm is haunted.

Lights have switched themselves on and off for no apparent reason during the night, bolted doors have been unlatched and bales of straw in out-buildings have been thrown about. And at 11pm one evening in February 1970, Mrs Ambrose saw a 'large illuminated white ball in mid-air, several feet from the floor, move across the bedroom and disappear by the chimney'.

In the next few days other unusual incidents were noted. A large bowl containing nearly three gallons of milk was found on the floor of the dining room, previously the dairy. This had been moved from the top of the main table without any of its contents being spilt. A few minutes earlier, however, a 'loud crash' had been heard and on coming down stairs to investigate the cause Mr Ambrose found that one of the saddles placed on the saddle-horse in the hallway was lying in the middle of the floor. It needed a pair of strong arms to replace it.

At 8 o'clock in the evening of the following month Mrs Ambrose was standing in the main bedroom tidying her hair in front of a wardrobe mirror and she suddenly realised that an apparition of a young man was lying on the bed behind her. Because of the length of the mirror she could only see the upper part of his body. 'His face was pale with a short fair-cropped beard. He was about 23 or 24 years of age and was propped up on one of the pillows.' When she turned round he had vanished.

The following night Alan Ambrose dreamt of the young ghost who appeared standing in front of him in 'a grey coloured home-spun Victorian-type suit and he was trembling as if from palsy'. On waking Mr Ambrose realised somehow that the front door had been unlatched. He went downstairs to find it wide open and the hall light on. 'We never leave lights on,' he told me, 'and obviously we always check on all doors, bolting most of them before going to bed'.

Numerous visitors have been wakened by the sound of doors being opened by unseen hands in the early hours.

It has been established that a tenant farmer shot himself in the old dairy in the 1850's due to an overpowering feeling of depression at losing his wife and failure in his business. But Mr Ambrose feels that the ghostly happenings in the house have no connections with this suicide.

St Nicholas Church

Pluckley, Kent
Open to the public during normal hours

More often seen inside this old building is the Red Lady, though
sometimes her sorrowful figure is witnessed gliding around the
graveyard. It is believed that she is searching for the grave of her
young child who died and was buried in an unidentified tomb.
Because of an increasing number of reports being received, a
group of 'psychic researchers' recently persuaded the vicar to
lock them in the church all night so they could record the appearance of the apparition.

They were disappointed when the rector released them in the
morning, having seen nothing but a white dog, which they had
ignored presuming it was a normal animal. One can imagine their
chagrin on learning that this was another of the village's ghosts.
They realised then that, if they couldn't get out, no normal dog
could get in.

High Street

Pluckley, Kent
Open to the public

Air Commodore Sutcliffe told me that his racing driver son had
twice heard the noises of a coach and horses driving through the
village past his house in the early hours. These were not isolated
incidents for several late night travellers have heard similar noises
and have seen nothing, though in earlier days reports were of a
headless horseman.

Smarden Road

Pluckley, Kent
Open to the public

Within a few yards of the parish church one finds Rose Farm,
once two delightful old houses both of which were haunted. The
Greystones monk, formerly from one of the original cottages, was
a great friend of his neighbour, a young girl who died from eating
ivy. Phantoms of both used to be seen in the immediate vicinity
of the cottages, but only the monk now remains. His 'shadow'
was seen in 1971 gliding down the lane.

Crossroads

Pluckley, Kent
Open to the public

Near to where two roads cross, not far from the Blacksmith's Arms, a small stone bridge over a tiny stream marks the area of where a watercress woman is reputed to have accidentally been burnt alive. She was tired and fell asleep, so the story goes, when smoking an old clay pipe. Although the poor old soul herself has not been seen in recent years, a faint pink glow has been witnessed on occasions at dusk emanating from the stream side.

Near to the site of where the old watercress woman met her painful death, a highwayman was killed in a sword fight with an intended victim and was pinned like a butterfly to a hollow oak tree. This relic of the tale was pulled down some four years ago, but fairly recently a 'dark shadow' has been seen on the verge where the tree and the ghost of the villain were witnessed in the earlier part of the century.

Dicky Buss's Lane

Pluckley, Kent
Open to the public

Close to Cliff Cottage and the home of an author who has witnessed the apparition, is where a schoolmaster hanged himself about 150 years ago. The description of the sighting during an afternoon in 1965 indicates that the suicide wore 'an old frock coat and what looked like dark striped trousers'.

So although the number of apparitions in the village seems to be dwindling, with no less than seven still obviously active Pluckley can still retain its title of being the country's most haunted village.

Rooks Cottage*

Westerham, Kent
Private property, please respect

This delightful cottage, built in 1816 and sited half a mile south of Moorhouse Bank, was purchased by Denis Druitt in 1954 as a pair of farm cottages. Although it had laid derelict for some 20 years, it had a 'friendly feeling' which continued right through the period of their ownership and even in the early days of converting and modernising.

One evening in December 1970, however, when Mrs Druitt was writing Christmas cards she suddenly heard footsteps in the hall and the sounds of doors opening and being slammed shut. Her two dogs leapt to their feet, bristling and growling at the unseen entity which by now, from their appearance, had entered the sitting room.

The dogs watched as the invisible being crossed the room and vanished by the old fireplace. This incident was repeated several times during the following months, but with the addition of the movements of objects. A chair-back cover was found to be missing and was never discovered, and on another occasion Mrs Druitt found on a chair-side table a small brown paper bag with a hair-net inside. She had never used such a thing.

Despite the attitude of the dogs, the owners were not afraid and continued to enjoy a feeling of general well-being towards their unseen guest. Mr Druitt also heard the noises of footsteps and doors being slammed, as did an electrician and several friends who visited the cottage during the ensuing months.

Before they left in June 1971, the couple had discovered that the previous occupier—a man well over 80 years old, whose wife had died many years before—had been found dead at the bottom of the garden in the 1930's. It seems that he had suffered from a sudden fatal heart attack and must have died within seconds of his unconscious fall.

It was established that he was 'a really friendly old character', but often irritated by his wife's habit of leaving doors open and in her last years of forgetting her hair-net. It seems that he still gets 'a bit annoyed'.

Shorne Lodge*

Shorne, Near Gravesend, Kent
Private property, please respect

In 1947 Mr Philip Warner of Camberley stayed in this ancient building which is panelled throughout with Spanish oak, believed to have been taken from wrecked ships of the Armada.

During his eight week stay there, in which he slept in the 'haunted room,' numerous visitors and guests reported that they had seen the figure of 'an old man accompanied by a dark brown dog'. Mr Warner told me that, although he had seen nothing other than 'a peculiar mist seemingly hanging from the ceiling of the corridor outside his room', he was convinced that the witnesses were perfectly genuine in this report.

Another ghost supposed to inhabit the building is that of a young lady who is believed to have died from some form of throat infection during the 17th century.

'Snob' Boutique*

122 High Street, Chatham, Kent
Open to the public during normal hours
On A2
Nearest station—Chatham

When Eamon Andrews first launched the *This is Your Life* series on television it proved somewhat controversial, but extremely interesting for those intrigued by other people's activities. One of the programmes in 1956 featured the novelist, Ida Cook.

During the war Ida and her sister had organised what she calls 'an amateur refugee organisation' for getting people out of Germany aided by Clemens Krauss, a Vienese opera director, and his wife Viorica Ursuleac, a soprano. Clemens had died some two years before the programme, but his widow was brought from Austria to appear in the feature.

Months after the programme had been transmitted, a member of a Surrey W.I. group on chattering to Ida Cook about her appearance said, 'but I cannot forget the couple with the refugee work'. Miss Cook explained that only the widow was in the studio, but was unable to convince the lady.

In March 1957, whilst with friends in Newcastle, the programme was discussed again. One question staggered Ida, 'who was the tall, very good looking foreigner who dominated the programme? He was never introduced.' On the production of a photograph, the questioner confirmed that, 'that's the gentleman—who is he?' Miss Cook had to admit it was Clemens Krauss who had died over four years previously and yet, it seems, had been seen by at least two independent viewers in different parts of the country.

This case tends to confirm that a light frequency outside the visible spectrum can be photographed, whether by an ordinary camera or by a television camera.

A similar case was experienced in the modern surroundings of this popular boutique.

Because of the value and number of 'modern creations', closed circuit television cameras have been fitted over the racks. The viewing set is in the basement and in December 1969 one of the assistants in the 'viewing room' saw what she thought was a customer standing by the dresses brushing her hair. The design of the woman's dress appeared 'really old fashioned—it looked like a crinoline'. On entering the sales area on the ground floor, the assistant was puzzled to find the shop empty. She returned downstairs only to find the woman still showing on the screen.

Her five unbelieving friends returned upstairs and were astonished to find the potential customer was nowhere to be seen. The television system was checked and found to be in perfect order.

But this appearance was apparently only the introduction to a continuing series of phenomena. During a mid-day break, a woman's face was seen at the window of a top floor empty room by two of the sales girls who were sunning themselves on the fire-escape.

At Christmas 1971 on the fitting room floor, once just an open corridor with a door at either end, an assistant who had been called downstairs returned to find the lights off and both doors wide open. One of these doors was partially concealed by the fitting cubicles and is never used by the staff.

'Odd thumps and footsteps are often heard from the empty upstairs room', Marion Horne, the manageress, told me, 'and a couple of weeks ago' (this was in July 1972), 'we all smelt a very strong smell of mothballs. It lasted for several days and then stopped as suddenly as it started. There always seems to be a coolness when the noises start'.

The building was completed, probably as a private house and later as flats, in the early part of the 19th century. The ghost seen on television and known by her footsteps in an empty room is believed to have been an occupant of one of the flats on the 'fitting room' floor.

Another unusual incident which puzzled the staff in 1972 was during a lunchtime break. One of the assistants had poured a drink into a glass and put it on a table beside her whilst she busied herself getting some sandwiches from her snack box. On turning back to the table she found that the glass had vanished and has never been seen since. There were three other witnesses to this incident and all were as puzzled as the thirsty young girl.

The ghost is fully accepted by the staff who are no longer disturbed or worried at her unusual activities. 'We don't mind her,' Marion told me, 'as long as she doesn't interfere with the customers'.

Another boutique that was affected by a ghost for a very short time in 1970 was the Queen's Head boutique in Newark-on-Trent, Nottinghamshire. It rang the shop bell and was seen as a 'maxi-skirted woman' by the assistants in a mirror combing her hair. No separate entry has been made for this case as it was only for such a short duration and the witness appeared to be rather imaginative. The report could not, therefore, be corroborated.

Thanet House

Open to the public by appointment only
On A255
Nearest station—Broadstairs

A few years after the war, Alan Ambrose, owner of Elvey Farm, Pluckley, visited the grounds of this old house with his father to collect some grapes. They walked along the terrace in the front of the building and then down to the greenhouse with its fruit. But before reaching their goal they heard footsteps behind them and both looked back.

Standing on a stone bridge over a small lake they saw the figure of a man bending over the parapet, apparently looking at the goldfish swimming in the pool.

Because there was nothing particularly unusual about his appearance, they continued on their way to complete their work. However, a few days later Mr Ambrose, on discussing the appearance of the stranger to some local friends, learnt that the description was that of one of the gardeners who had died some six months earlier.

The ghost had been seen by several visitors since the funeral walking the paths of the grounds.

The house itself, built by the multi-millionaire Sir Edmund Vestey, is now a children's home.

Theatre Royal*

Adlington Street, Margate, Kent
Open to the public during normal hours
On A28
Nearest station—Margate

Some theatres achieve prominence by their productions, some by their age. This one can justifiably claim renown for both reasons.

It was built in 1787 and must be one of the country's oldest active theatres still in existence. In 1966 it received wide publicity in the national press and on BBC1 and BBC2, the latter due to Alan Whicker's visit, following reports of the haunting that apparently reached a peak at that time.

Two of the staff stated that when alone in the building at night they heard 'shuffling, thuds and wheezes' of someone unseen. This 'performance' would be followed by lights going off and on and a severe icy blast would 'sweep round' them. Scenery props would be found to have been moved and lights in a toilet were frequently found on despite having been switched off after the last performance.

In 1964 a painter had refused to continue working at night in the theatre because of his unnerving experience. For several evenings he had heard definite footsteps, inexplicable 'thumps' and doors banging 'violently and very loudly'. On a few occasions he had also witnessed, moving from left to right across the stage, a 'semi-globular figure, semi-transparent and about ten inches across'. It glided about five feet from 'the boards'.

It was assumed, perhaps rashly, that the phenomena were caused by the former manageress, Sarah Thorne, for the only discernible 'features' of the apparition were two 'dim points where eyes would have been if it had a face'. The Paraphysical Laboratory commented that the idea of a human outline was possibly suggested to the witness at the time, but no such idea was mentioned to the two chorus girls who fainted during a late-night rehearsal in 1964 when they saw a ghost on the stage.

In September 1972 I spoke to Mr Jacobs, the current manager of the theatre, who, whilst admitting that he had never experienced anything unusual himself, was quite prepared to accept the incidents reported by his staff as perfectly genuine. Only two weeks previously another painter had suffered from 'practically an identical experience' to that of the previous decorator. 'He was really scared,' Mr Jacobs told me, 'and in his fright had knocked over a tin of paint all over himself. It wasn't funny. He just ran out of the building shaking with fear'. Perhaps it's a good thing the ghost only performs late at night.

Timerden Bottom

Near Shoreham, Kent
Private property, please respect

One mile from the site of a Roman villa and about three miles from the attractive Lullingstone Castle, lies the little village of Timerden Bottom.

Here in a private house, parts of which date from the 16th century, a Mr Howard, his sister, and numerous visitors, including a cousin, have experienced considerable phenomena over the last few years.

The series seems to have started on December 26, 1968 when Mr Howard awoke to see the figure of a woman standing by the bedroom door. 'She was tall and dressed in a long black dress.' What was really scaring, however, was the sudden appearance of the head and shoulders of an old man whose face resembled that

157

of a clown, bright red with white hair. The head was gently rocking backwards and forwards near the end of the bed. Slowly, as he watched, the ghostly apparition moved back to the wall and 'faded away'.

The female figure was no longer to be seen.

On the 26th of another month, Mr Howard again woke in the early hours to see an apparition moving up and down on the empty bed in the room. Again it resembled a clown with a red coat and a ruff, but this time no head was visible. The figure drifted towards the window where it 'hung there for some minutes and then vanished'.

Although the spectre of the clown has not been seen by anyone else, the woman in black has been seen several times and noises of someone walking around in the empty bedroom have been heard by several people.

Rumour has it that in the 17th century a clown went mad and hung himself from the window of the bedroom. It has been stated that he used piano wire to commit his suicide with unpleasant results, but there is no explanation for the woman in black, unless she is perhaps the sorrowing widow?

Lancashire

A mixture of moors and industry

Open to the public during normal hours or by appointment	10
Private houses	2

Historic buildings, museums, ruins	5
Shops, stores	1
Inns, hotels	2
Private houses, offices, factories	2
Open spaces, roads	2

Phenomena	
Noises	4
Moving objects	1

Apparitions	
Females	3
Monks	1
Males	4

Chingle Hall

Goosnargh, Near Preston, Lancashire
Open to the public during normal hours
On B5269
5 miles from Preston station

Far from the 'typical haunted manorial hall' in outward appearance, it looks just like a pleasant old farmhouse, Chingle Hall in fact is reeking in ancient and fascinating history and is well and truly haunted.

Adam de Singleton built it in about 1260 and it still retains the original studded front door and unique knocker. Although considerable restoration work has been effected through the years, it has obviously been carried out with considerable feeling and sympathy for the period and with the aim of keeping much of the original structure intact.

One of the interesting facts about the house is that it was obviously used as a prayer or mass centre during the Penal period and in recent years more evidence of this has been uncovered. Miss Ann Strickland, the sister of the owner's wife, discovered a pre-Reformation 'Praying Cross' set in a recess and a modern fireplace when removed disclosed a small hiding place which was probably used to secrete religious vestments. In 1961 another hide was found in the chimney of a Norman designed fireplace.

Further evidence of the cunning of hiding-place experts like the renowned Nicholas Owen are some drawers used for storing religious ornaments which are disguised as beams.

Upstairs one finds two very interesting rooms. The Priest's Room with a couple of ambries as proof of it once being used as a chapel was possibly at one time converted to a nursery. Some people have suggested that it was here that St John Wall was born.

The other room is accepted as the 'Haunted Room' inhabited by the phantom of a Franciscan monk often seen by visitors. Mr Howarth, the owner, once saw the figure cross the small stone bridge which replaced an original drawbridge, enter the house, glide up the stairs and vanish in the room over the porch.

Footsteps have frequently been heard tramping the same route, and on one occasion no less than nine people including the Howarths all heard the phantom sounds whilst at supper.

Tappings on walls and furniture have been experienced and odd incidents have occurred such as dogs watching something unseen pass through the downstairs rooms and doors open of their own accord.

Although the identity of the ghost has not been established, there is a case for believing it might be the Saint himself. Philip Meanley, in his guide-book on Chingle Hall, provides some information on this.

John Wall was executed at Worcester in 1679 and his head is believed to have been smuggled to France, but on the outbreak of the Revolution nuns fleeing the terror of the mob returned to England with the head. In 1834 the order returned to France where the head is thought by some to have been buried though, despite considerable investigations, it has never been found.

One suggestion is that it may well be hidden somewhere in a yet undiscovered hidey hole in Chingle Hall—the place where the Saint was born.

In 1967 one guest reported hearing footsteps crossing and re-crossing the floor of the haunted room for 'some hours'. Could it

The haunted darkroom of Chertsey Offset Printers, Chertsey, Surrey. Photographic negatives showed the letterhead of the previous occupiers, though all evidence of their tenancy had been destroyed.

Busheygate, Robertsbridge, Sussex—home of the author who has experienced psychic phenomena there.

Lion Hotel, Nyetimber, near Bognor Regis, Sussex. Footsteps are heard passing through rooms 5 and 6 in the early hours of the morning.

The haunted corridor of the Seven Stars, Robertsbridge, Sussex. At the far end a steep, narrow staircase leads to the loft and the mysterious 70ft deep shaft.

Air Heating Ltd, near Leeds, Yorkshire. This photograph shows evidence of poltergeist activity. Papers are flying around, though no air activity was recorded at the time

be that the monk was searching for something—perhaps the head of a brother?

Two lads who were accommodated in the haunted room in August 1968 not only heard the 'unusual' footsteps and knocking sounds but were frightened when a 'peculiar light the size of a hand' which had appeared in the centre of the room 'disappeared into the wall'. Was this an indication of the site of the skull?

C Claridge & Co Ltd*

Manchester Airport, Ringway Road, Wythenshaw, Manchester 22
Private property, please respect

There are some 4,000 freight forwarders in this country, all actively engaged in handling Britain's exports and generally improving standards of carrying goods. The possibility of exporting a ghostly cargo, however, is a doubtful one and what Customs Declaration form would be needed raises far too many unanswerable questions. Yet in one of the offices of a leading freight forwarding organisation an apparition was seen several times early in 1971.

The building, housing several companies, was originally the barrack block of 613 Manchester Squadron of the RAF and it may be that the ghost is associated with this. But witnesses, mainly cleaners and late working office staff, describe their unknown visitor as 'an old man'.

Police were called when noises were heard coming from the empty offices and equipment was found to have been moved. A scream was heard one morning and later sounds of footsteps in the corridors.

One of the company's import clerks saw the figure of an old man sitting in a storeroom next to his office, but when he opened the link door the ghost vanished. Another sighting was a few days later by one of the night staff who described the 'old man' who walked through the office in bare feet. Yet another witness was a lorry driver who saw the figure and even one of the local policemen admitted having seen the apparition.

Deane Road

Bolton, Lancashire
Open to the public
On M6 and A61
Nearest station—Bolton

One of the most modern buildings in this town, the birthplace of Samuel Crompton, inventor of the 'Spinning Mule', is the Institute of Technology. Before constructing this centre of learning, it was necessary to demolish several small workshops which had occupied the site for many years. With them, locals thought, went an unidentifiable ghost who used to be seen walking along Deane Road, for he had always been associated with one of the local concerns.

However, in the summer of 1970 he was seen again 'wearing a white shirt, dark grey trousers' standing on the lawn of the College. The figure was at first mistaken for a caretaker.

The following evening he appeared again to a Mrs Dennis of George Street. 'He looked just like an ordinary man. He was tall, thin and middle-aged with darkish hair,' but when she asked him to move so that she could pass he 'just disappeared'.

Several other local residents have also seen the figure following his 'rejuvenation'.

Hall-i'-th'-Wood

Bolton, Lancashire
Open to the public during normal hours
On A676 (300 yards north of Compton Bypass)
2 miles from Bolton station

A brilliant example of a half-timbered Manor House and famed as the birthplace of Samuel Crompton's Mule, the revolutionary machine for spinning fine cottons, Hall-i'-th'-Wood dates from the late 15th century and is now owned by the Corporation of Bolton.

Lawrence Brownlow, a great-grandson of the builder of the same name, added several rooms at the north-west corner in 1591, but in doing so became bankrupt and sold up to Christopher Norris. The new owner had to borrow £2,000 from his son Alexander to purchase the property, but as the latter was to inherit the building in 1639 anyway, he probably thought of it as an investment.

Norris had been given the job of administering the estates in the county which had been confiscated from Royalist families and in doing so had amassed considerable wealth and, no doubt, enraged the former occupiers of Hall-i'-th'-Wood.

One, perhaps, was more incensed than the others for he continues to inhabit the Hall. Although the phantom, a cavalier, has not been seen for many years he has been heard running up the 17th century staircase, but only at Christmas time. The sounds continue throughout the festive season, but are never heard after Twelfth Night until the next December.

No one knows the reason for his cavortings, but the assumption is that he is one of the Brownlows returning to retrieve some incriminating papers from one of the bedrooms.

Young Alexander Norris demolished the whole of the west side of the building and constructed a new and more elaborate wing on the south-west.

By the 18th century the house had become tenements, one being taken by the Cromptons in 1758. Samuel, the designer of the Mule wheel actually worked on the machine and produced the first prototype in Hall-i'-th'-Wood. The Cromptons left the Hall in 1782 and the building gradually fell into disrepair. In 1900 the first Viscount Leverhulme restored it and presented it to the Corporation together with a major portion of its furniture so that it could be opened as a folk museum.

The only item that originally came from the building is the cheese press, displayed in the dairy, which, according to an inventory taken by Alexander Norris, was worth three shillings.

Lawrence Gardens

Liverpool, Lancashire
Open to the public
Junction of A562/A580/A59
Nearest station—Liverpool

In the last war well over 1,000 tons of bombs were dropped on to Liverpool during 1940-44 and it was the fourth largest city affected by such destruction—Birmingham, Plymouth and Glasgow receiving a similar treatment. In comparison, London received some 20,000 tons during the same period. It has been suggested that if the industrial cities and major ports had been subjected to the raids that London received, there would have been a different ending to the war.

However, among the thousands of people killed in the Liverpool area during that period was a well liked and respected policeman who, when 'on his beat', would idly tap doors and railings with his truncheon. Whether this was to warn potential criminals of his approach or just to let the old folk know he was around and 'it was safe' is not quite clear.

One of the centre points of his round was Lawrence Gardens and it was here in August 1971 that residents first saw the ghost of the officer of the law. Strolling gently down the road he was clearly visible, swinging his truncheon and tapping it gently against the house walls. One witness, not realising the figure was an apparition, was puzzled by the fact he was wearing a haversack with a 'tin helmet' strapped to it and tried to overtake him. On reaching the corner of the road the apparition vanished, leaving the resident open mouthed.

Peel Hall Farm

Higher Green, Astley Green, Lancashire
Private property, please respect

What must be one of the most intriguing buildings in the area of Higher Green is this old farm building riddled with romantic tales of underground passages, treasure trove of old wine casks and the ghost of a white lady.

So strong were the stories of the apparition being seen during 1970 that a former policeman moved in as a tenant in order to 'get to the bottom of it, once and for all'.

One young lad in 1965, whilst bird-nesting in the grounds, saw a white figure 'float the trees'. He ran.

A previous occupant was scared by paintings and mirrors being pulled from the walls, and another local resident saw the 'lady in white' at 8.30pm float across the road leading to the farm. 'It scared me', he said.

The ghost is believed to be that of a woman murdered in the back room of what was once the manor house of the village in the 18th century.

The efforts to clarify the situation met with little success for Mr Nolan, the ex-policeman, moved out months later leaving the ancient building holding its silent and tragic secrets.

44 Penny Lane

Liverpool, Lancashire
Open to the public during normal hours
Junction of A562/A580/A565
Nearest station—Liverpool

Made famous by the world-acclaimed Beatles, who made no mention of the ghost in their highly popular song, Penny Lane has become one of the tourist attractions of this great city. But few hear of the unseen ghost which inhabits the printing shop at No. 44.

So loud are the sounds of someone pacing the floor at night when the shop is empty that neighbours have complained to the police and to the owners, Mr Chackman and Mr Hampton. The noises have even been tape-recorded after floor-boards were removed and roof, walls, furniture and equipment checked.

The unseen walker is most active, according to the *Liverpool Echo* which published a report in January 1971, on Friday, Saturday and Monday nights—the most popular periods for 'overtime', but not for people like Mrs Jean Bruce, one of the neighbours who has heard the banging and shuffling noises.

Railway Inn

Waterfoot, Lancashire
Open to the public during normal hours
On A6066
10 miles from Rochdale station

What may appear to be a misnomer, for the railway no longer operates here, the Railway Inn is merely a reminder of the days when even some of the smallest places were served by the steam engines.

For some years the pub has been haunted by the ghost of a woman, affectionately termed 'Jane' by the licensees, who walks through the guests' bedroom and passes through the partitioning wall. 'Jane' however also acts in a rather bizarre fashion by removing bedclothes.

In 1966 Mr Cormack stated that 'quite a few people who have stayed with us have had their bedclothes removed during the night. One guest, Mr Robin Crofts of Aberdeen, not only suffered from the attentions of the spectre but, like many others, saw the woman walk through the bedroom.'

The landlord and his wife have also heard what sounds like their name being called on a few occasions when in the tap room.

What may prove to be a clue as to the identity of 'Jane' is the bricked up room in the old building though a glance through the only entrance, a trapdoor in the ceiling, has given no indication of anything untoward in the room.

Samlesbury Hall

Preston New Road, Near Preston, Lancashire
Open to the public during normal hours
On A677
Nearest station—Preston

Sandwiched between Preston and Blackburn on the main road linking the two major towns, is this fine example of a 14th century manor house. Although later additions were made in the 16th century it has only added to the attractiveness of the property. Mainly half-timbered, Samlesbury Hall, standing in six acres of garden, is not just preserved as an historic building but is constantly used for social purposes, official meetings and wedding receptions.

Whether the ghost, Dorothy, the daughter of Sir John Southworth, attends any of the functions is not known, but it would be rather disturbing if she did turn up in the middle of a luncheon party. Actually she only haunts the spot where her lover was murdered and buried in the 1500's adjacent to the outer wall of the building. Her white wraith-like figure has been seen at dusk standing down at the pathway, muttering soft moans of misery.

The story is that she was planning to elope with one of the Hoghtons, but one of her brothers enraged at the thought of breaking a religious feud so intimately, killed the man (a Protestant) and sent her off to a local Catholic convent. Because of this brutal treatment the poor lady sickened and died shortly afterwards.

Offering some proof of the incident is the fact that a few years ago workmen fitting additional drainage found a major part of a male skeleton lying against the foundation wall. Some years ago an apparition of a male figure was also seen in the locality, but he has not been witnessed since.

Smithills Hall

Near Bolton, Lancashire
Open to the public during normal hours
On A675
2 miles from Bolton station

One of the oldest houses in Lancashire, Smithills Hall was first owned by the Knights Hospitallers in the 14th century, but much occurred before it was sold to the Corporation of Bolton in 1938.

The first change was when Richard de Halton, one of the Knights, presented the Manor to William de Radclyffe whose family resided there until 1485. In 1516 Andrew Barton, who had inherited Smithills, enlarged it and fitted some magnificent panelling into a new bedroom. Tradition has it that some of the carved portraits are those of members of the family.

The chapel was rebuilt in 1856 after a fire. The only surviving remnant of the original is an interesting east window featuring 15 heraldic coats of arms including that of Thomas Cranmer, Archbishop of Canterbury.

Further additions were made about 60 years later when the hall was owned by Andrew's son, Robert, and after his death by his widow, Margery, who married Sir Richard Shuttleworth. It was sold in 1723 to Joseph Byron and in 1801 to the Ainsworth family who made the final additions.

The ghost of Smithills Hall is believed to be that of George Marsh who, in the 16th century, became a priest after first trying his hand at farming. His controversial doctrines annoyed Queen Mary, he was accused of heresy and the Earl of Derby sent to arrest him.

The priest, learning of the danger, made immediate plans to escape abroad, but his mother had been arrested as an accomplice and was being held hostage. He capitulated and was arrested and taken for interrogation to the home of the magistrate, Robert Barton. Here in an upper room he was tried and convicted of heresy, but walking through the chapel passage on his way to being burnt at the stake he stamped his foot protesting his innocence. The resulting 'bloody footprint' is preserved on the stone-flagged floor at the entrance to the corridor.

The apparition seen in recent years is most certainly that of a minister of the church, but he is seen gliding through the green room and therefore may be another member of 'the cloth'.

Speke Hall*

The Walk, Speke, Liverpool, Lancashire
Open to the public during normal hours
Off A581
7 miles from Liverpool station

Owned by the National Trust and administered by the Liverpool Corporation, this fine example of a 16th century half-timbered house is sited in a manor dating from the 12th century practically on the edge of Liverpool Airport.

The Hall was constructed by the Norris family in several parts, the first being built between 1490 and 1506 by Sir William Norris. In this portion the great hall and domestic offices are included, but other rooms, such as the kitchens, were demolished during later modifications and additions.

With the exception of a few internal changes and some additions on the eastern side, the house stands now as it did in 1612; a richly decorated timber frame house with much of the infilling plaster of marl and straw still intact.

The ghost of Speke Hall is supposed to be the wife of one of the later owners, the Beauclerks. The house passed to them through a female heiress in 1736 due to the declining fortunes of the Norris's, but because the new purchasers lived in the south the house was allowed to fall into a dilapidated state and was sold in 1797 to Richard Watt.

He and his successors restored it and in 1943, after being administered by a trust, was handed to the National Trust.

There is no evidence that the Beauclerks ever lived at Speke Hall, thus rather disposing of the popular belief as to the identity of the ghost. The tale is that either Lord Sydney or his son, Topham Beauclerk, returned home one day with the distressing news that they were ruined financially. Lady Beauclerk was so overwrought that she threw her baby out of the Tapestry Room window into the moat and then killed herself in the Great Hall.

But, as P W G Lawson, assistant keeper of the Hall, points out, 'an inaccurate story does not reflect on the validity of the room as a haunted site', which has been confirmed as the Tapestry Room. 'A considerable number of people,' he tells me, 'have discerned a presence in the Room'.

According to Alastair MacGregor in *The Golden Lamp*, the late Adelaide Watt was considerably embarrassed by the appearance of the ghost which disappeared into the wall of a bedroom. Investigations at the spot, close to a window, revealed a secret passage leading down through an outer wall.

This passage may well have been formed during the alterations

168

to the construction, but nevertheless the ghost here has been so well attested and its presence felt that few people seem concerned as to who or what it is.

Stork Hotel

Billinge, Lancashire
Open to the public during normal hours
On A57
18 miles from St Helens (Manchester) station

The outstanding building in this Lancashire village between St Helens and Wigan is the rather unusual Church of St Aidan. It was built in 1717 and consists of a great variety of Gothic and Classical styles with Doric columns and panelled walls.

Another building of interest, however, is the ancient Stork Hotel, built in 1640 as a jail and extensively used as such by Cromwellian troops. In the crypt, now part of the cellars, one of the Royalist supporters kept there as a prisoner for many days died from his treatment—or lack of it—and now haunts various parts of the hotel.

Several evening customers at the bar have heard heavy footsteps walking the floor above them and also seen empty glasses move slowly along the counter top.

Later, at night, the tread of the cavalier has been so heavy as to wake some of the overnight guests.

Leicestershire

Once well haunted, but now with only one unseen phantom

Open to the public during normal hours or by appointment	1
Inns, hotels	1
Apparitions	
Others	1

Belper Arms

Newton Burgoland, Leicestershire
Open to the public during normal hours
On A447
12 miles from Atherstone station

This ancient pub dating back to the 12th century had no ghost at all it seems until 1962 when an old spiral staircase was removed. It was this incident that 'started it off', but no one knows who or what it is that haunts the establishment, for it has never been seen, only felt, mainly in the area where the staircase used to be.

Numerous visitors and some regulars have felt a pair of cold hands suddenly clamped over their nose and mouth with such intensity that they have to fight for breath. The room temperature also drops.

These incidents normally occur at about four o'clock in the afternoon, but associated phenomena are also experienced at the same time in the morning.

Lincolnshire

Home of one of the oldest houses in England dating from 1170

Open to the public during normal hours or by appointment   1

Inns, hotels   1

Phenomena
Noises   1

Ye Olde White Swanne*

Eastgate, Louth, Lincolnshire
Open to the public during normal hours
On A16 T
16 miles from Grimsby station

Just in time the Department of the Environment saved the oldest pub in Louth from demolition and classified it in 1970 as a building of historical and architectural interest. What has now also been preserved is the apparition of what appears to be a 'tall man with a white cape and hood' who has been seen fairly frequently, 'nearly always' at about 11.30 at night.

According to the *Lincolnshire Chronicle* Mr and Mrs Booth, landlords of this 500 year old building, heard on one occasion what sounded like a crate of bottles being dropped on the floor of an upstairs room, but could find no explanation of the 'crash' that shook the bar.

'Unfortunately the apparition has not been witnessed for a couple of years,' Mrs Booth told me, 'and we have been unable to find out anything about it. The building itself was first granted its licence as a hostelry in 1612, but it was an ale house as far back as the 14th century so it has a long history of occupants.'

The Booths have been in occupation for over three years and are a little disappointed that 'the man in white' seems to have deserted them after such a short time. But he may be back.

London

The most haunted capital city in the world

Open to the public during normal hours or by appointment	33
Private houses	4
Clubs, cinemas	2
Historic buildings, museums, ruins	6
Churches, abbeys, rectories	5
Shops, stores	3
Inns, hotels	4
Private houses, offices, factories	9
Open spaces, roads	8
Phenomena	
Smells	5
Noises	9
Apparitions	
Females	14
Monks	3
Males	18
Horses	1

Aldgate Station

Aldgate High Street, London, EC3
Open to the public during normal hours

Many people have heard the variety of ghosts in this underground station, in fact so frequent have been the reports that they are now entered in the 'station log'.

In the control room situated in part of the older rail tunnel where it crossed over the existing line, footsteps have been heard walking over the sleepers and stopping where the original door was sited.

A few years ago one unusual incident was reported by an engineer who saw the figure of an old woman gently stroking the hair of an elderly colleague whilst he was bending down working on the control room buzz bar. Apparently the older man felt nothing but a few minutes later he made what normally would have been a fatal error and 22,000 volts surged through his body.

Although he was knocked unconscious by the power he suffered from no ill effects.

More recently inexplicable whistling has been heard in this relic of London's old rail system.

228 Baker Street

London, W1
Private property, please respect

Built on the site of the home of the famous actress Sarah Siddons, a London Transport sub-station here is regularly haunted by the phantom of the lady.

She has been seen to walk through the rooms, and walls, of the modern building on several occasions by the engineers and staff, both in the mornings and afternoons.

Her haunt is the area known as the 'Top Gallery', a floor which would at one time have accommodated the bedroom of the actress.

Bank of England and Bank Station

Princes Street, London, EC2
Open to the public during normal hours

The underground railway station beneath the centre of the country's finances must be one of the busiest within the City.

Although no ghost has been seen here during the peace and quiet of the early hours an overpowering feeling of despondency and fear has affected the rail workers. Several of them have complained of the pungent smell normally associated with an open grave and reference has been made to the close proximity of Liverpool Street station, believed to have been constructed on a plague pit.

The odour and feeling may however also be connected with Sarah Whitehead whose ghost, resembling that of a nun, has been seen in the Bank garden. Sarah was the sister of an employee of the Bank who on being caught forging cheques in 1811 was condemned to death.

So distraught at this family disaster was she that her mind failed and for the rest of her life she visited the area each day searching for her brother.

On her sudden death she was buried in an old graveyard which was later to become the garden of the Bank, a portion of which was destroyed to form one of the entrances of the station.

Barnes Common

Common Road, London, SW13
Open to the public
On A306
Nearest station—Barnes

Although there is not much left of the original common there are still a few acres to remind Londoners of its past history. One of the most famous ghosts of London, 'Spring Heel Jack', frequented the common in the 19th century and in fact 'attacked' a young lady there in 1838 revealing himself as a creature with a 'hideous and frightful appearance vomitting blue and white flame from his mouth'.

Those days have gone, but not the evenings when a current wraith is that of a man in grey prison clothes, 'I even saw the broad arrows' one witness said, who glides round the common as if intent on committing a crime. His movements are those 'of a furtive criminal'.

One rumour is that he is a convict who escaped from Putney Hospital, whilst another tale claims that he is a grave robber after freshly buried bodies from the nearby cemetery.

53 Berkeley Square

London, W1
Private property, please respect

During the 17th century a middle-aged gentleman lived here with his attractive daughter. After a few years she eloped, but in devotion to her father, promised to return after her marriage.

Her father continued to wait for her arrival patiently and more anxiously until he died, more of a broken heart than old age, for his daughter never returned to her former home.

One moonlit night a few years ago the sad figure of the man, wearing a white satin coat and wig, with lace ruffles at his neck and wrists, was seen by a neighbour, Mrs Balfour, looking out of one of the windows on the first floor overlooking the square.

'He seemed so sad,' said Mrs Balfour, 'with such a hopeless expression'. He was seen again the following year one Saturday morning.

Other reports of his sightings have been made by office workers in the area.

Blackheath

Hare and Billet Road, London, SE10
Open to the public
On A2
Nearest station—Blackheath

Seen here only during autumn evenings when the area is wreathed in mist is a shadowy figure of a woman dressed in dark Victorian clothes.

She is thought to be a married woman looking for her lover who had arranged to meet and take her away. Unfortunately, he never arrived and in desperation the poor love-sick female hanged herself from one of the trees.

She was last seen about 8 o'clock in the evening during November 1971 by a bank executive walking home across the heath.

Boston Manor House*

Boston Manor Road, Brentford, London
Open to the public
Off A4
Nearest station—Boston Manor (Underground)

Currently owned by the London Borough of Hounslow and occupied by the National Institute for Housecraft is this Tudor and Jacobean mansion with superb examples of period ceilings.

During the last war the building became derelict and at one stage was thought fit only for demolition, but due to local pressure was saved, restored and an open-air theatre built in the attractive grounds.

Occasionally staff and visitors report seeing the shadowy figure of a woman gliding from one of the doors at the back of the building along the paved path and vanishing beneath a huge cypress tree.

There is a strong belief that she is Lady Boston who was murdered by her husband after being discovered with Lord Fairfax in 'compromising circumstances'.

The tree figures in the tale as the venue for the meeting of the lovers.

Lord Boston is said to have been overwraught at his actions and buried his wife's body in the grounds. The remains were discovered many years later by members of the Roman Catholic Sisterhood who re-buried the bones in an ivy-covered hillock which visitors can still see today.

There is a story of a ghost of another 'Lady in white' haunting the back lawn down to the lake. She is supposed to have drowned herself as a result of a broken love affair, but there has been little evidence of witnesses for many years.

Bruce Castle Museum

Bruce Castle Park, Lordship Lane, Tottenham, London, N17
Open to the public during normal hours
Nearest station—Bruce Grove

One of the very few Tudor buildings left in London this old museum, at one time a Jacobean manor, was converted into a school in 1827. At the turn of the century it was sold and finally became council offices and now houses a fine postal and history museum and library. Little remains of the Tudor fabric for a new wing was added in Victorian times when it became 'castellated'.

Although Mr Murray, the archivist in charge, assured me that neither he nor his staff have experienced any phenomena in the building, it seems that at least four people have witnessed 'a mediaeval party in the grounds'.

In July 1971 a couple were walking past the museum late one night when they saw 'a large number of people in 18th century costume' apparently enjoying a festive occasion. What was so unusual however, despite the 'couple of dozen people present and the obvious frivolity, there was no sound and the figures seemed to glide rather than walk'.

A few days later another couple determined to find out the truth, spent all night in the locality and also 'saw about a dozen apparitions, all in olden dress', close to the original Tudor portion of the building. When approached the crowd just 'melted into the walls'.

Chingford Mount Cemetery

Church Road, Chingford, London, E4
Open to the public during normal hours
Nearest station—Chingford

Although the cemetery grounds are open to the public, the haunted building here, the lodge, is obviously private. Once part of Lady Hamilton's estate which stretched out as far as Epping Forest the cemetery is nearly ¼ mile long and, like many of London's burial grounds, consists mainly of Victorian graves.

Early in 1971 the Superintendent, Mr J Gradley, and his wife reported that they had for several weeks been suffering from 'eerie voices, whining noises and shaking sounds' in and outside the building.

Despite the fact that the cemetery is closed at night, footsteps were heard by friends on numerous occasions walking on the path outside the building. What was even more disturbing to the family was the statement made by Mr Gradley's son that he had seen 'a funny man on a black horse' riding slowly over the grass.

There is no suggestion that this was Nelson, but it could possibly be the ghost of a rider associated with a royal hunting party in years gone by.

Chiswick House*

Burlington Lane, Chiswick, London, W4
Open to the public during normal hours
On A4
Nearest station—Chiswick Park

Owned by the Department of the Environment this villa, designed by the Earl of Burlington in 1725, has suffered a chequered history. It was originally designed more as a monument to the Earl's appreciation of art and was used initially not as a residence but for general meeting of artists, sculptors and influential politicians.

But a monument of this size would not last for ever as an empty masterpiece of architecture derived from Palladio's Villa Capra. It became a home and an entertainment venue for various Dukes of Devonshire, and the house where two Prime Ministers died—Fox in 1806 and Canning in 1827.

Even in the good old days of the 19th century, however, maintenance and staffing costs rose and the building was sold to become a private lunatic asylum. By 1928 it had become derelict and was bought by the Middlesex County Council who opened it to the public for several years, but finally realising the cost to ratepayers transferred it to the then Ministry of Works in 1958.

The Government department, appreciating its exquisite design, spent ten years on extensive restoration reclaiming it almost to its original state.

When I visited the house during its 'restorative period', a strong smell of frying eggs and bacon were noticeable. Enquiring of the workmen as to who was consuming a late breakfast, as it was early in the afternoon, I was told with a laugh that it was 'the ghost of one of the mad cooks'.

In fact the smell of cooking breakfast foods has been noticed by a lot of people over a long period. Michael Digby, head custodian and one-time Mayor of Brentford and Chiswick, told me 'it comes at irregular intervals. Sometimes for two days in a row and then nothing for three or four months. I also have the feeling of being watched occasionally in the evenings.'

This smell has also been experienced by other custodians who at first thought it was the wood preservative, but this idea was ruled out after investigations. It is now only noticed in the north wing as one enters the villa from the 'Link Building'.

What is peculiar about this is that no-one has cooked anything in the building for years and it is completely isolated from other property. Another factor adding to the mystery of the ghostly frying is that the kitchens used to be in the north wing, but over 100 years ago. They no longer exist.

Covent Garden Station

Long Acre, London, WC2
Open to the public during normal hours

The entrance to this small underground station lies inconspicuously among the crates of tomatoes, boxes of oranges and the general accessories of greengrocery. Soon, no doubt, the clutter will have gone to be replaced by the general sounds of the residential area which the authorities plan in their redevelopment of the area.

The station itself was built in the early days of the Piccadilly Line on the site of an old bakery, but this is unconnected with the ghost which regularly haunts the line.

One of the people who has seen the ghost on no less than 40 occasions is Jack Hayden, a travelling inspector. He first witnessed the apparition in the 1950's when making up the daily log in the underground mess room. It was Christmas Eve and on hearing the door rattle he thought it was a late night reveller. He called out 'there's no way through here,' and opened the door to see the

178

figure of a tall man in a grey suit with tight trousers and wearing a homburg type hat drifting down the spiral staircase. Then he suddenly vanished.

A foreman ticket collector saw the figure leave the platform by the exit leading to the stairs, and a West Indian porter was so terrified at his first sighting that he fainted.

The ghost was seen late at night on the 24th and 27th March 1972 by the station foreman and one of the female staff when in the main staff mess room. Mr Clifford, a porter, heard 'phantom' footsteps in the room and Edward Pratt, an engineer, has often felt 'the presence of an unseen person' in the locality.

Partly because he has been seen so frequently and the fact that his identity is known, the station staff now fully accept his visits as part of the job.

The apparition is in fact that of the famous and well-loved Victorian actor William Terris who, in December 1897, was stabbed by a fellow actor as he entered a private door to the Adelphi Theatre. The murderer, Richard Prince, had become insanely jealous of the popularity of Terris and often accused him of 'persecuting him'. At his trial Prince was found guilty but insane and died in Broadmoor, but his victim obviously continues to haunt the site adjoining his well beloved theatre.

Dental Surgery*

7 Park Road, Regents Park, London, NW1
Open to the public by appointment only
Nearest station—Baker Street

The area surrounding Regents Park consisting mainly of neat, smart terraced four-storied houses is one of the more attractive reminders of the Georgian period, which helps to offset the white starkness of the characterless cement jungle of Marylebone Road.

Looking at the gentle lines of the old buildings one can easily conjure up mental images of quiet pleasant tea parties being held behind the walls; of society characters, of Beau Brummel sipping coffee with Lady Dorchester, and of the peaceful tranquility that surrounded the occupants in those early days.

At number 7 Park Road, where a kitchen has been converted into a dining room and the huge black iron range removed, the smell of roasting coffee was frequently experienced by Mrs. Johanna Connolly and her friends. Some visitors also comment on the smell of frying bacon which 'wafts up' to a second floor bedroom from the non-existent kitchen below.

'It's a good thing we all like bacon,' was one comment.

Currently the house is used by two dentists, Mr Church and Mr Wilson, as their surgery and although they have failed to notice any unusual smells, Mrs Gage, their receptionist, confirmed that she has experienced the rather appetising odour. Rather frustrating, I should imagine, for the patients.

Doughty Street*

Off Chancery Lane, London, WC1
Open to the public
Nearest station—Chancery Lane

Here at No. 48 in this quiet backwater away from the busy legal street of Chancery one finds the house once occupied by Charles Dickens and his family. Though he lived there for only three years, from 1837-39, many relics of his, including manuscripts, portraits, letters and furniture, are displayed for the visitor to examine. Although steeped with the atmosphere of the brilliant writer, it is not here that one has to look for an apparition, but further along the road.

In June and July 1971 when workers from D H Dupree & Co Ltd of Leytonstone were constructing a new office building on the site of one of the old houses, an apparition of a 'short slim man in dark clothes wearing a tallish black hat' was seen gliding past the scaffolding and equipment of the contractors. One workman, according to the *Leyton Express* of 16 July, was so frightened that he 'ran off without even collecting his wages'.

Other colleagues, although admitting they saw the figure on the pavement, were not so scared but, one gathers, the building was completed ahead of schedule. Was the ghost seen so clearly one summer afternoon that of Dickens who was known for his inquisitiveness? Was it that of the Rev Smith who was at one time another local resident, or was it perhaps an early solicitor mindfully preparing a brief for his next case—we will never know.

First Floor Flat*

Admiralty House, London, SW1
Private property, please respect

In June 1969 the Ministry of Public Building and Works carried out investigations into complaints about the water system of a flat occupied at that time by Denis Healey, former Defence Secretary.

Gentlemen of reputation have stated that the Ministry wasted their time for the noises are caused by the ghost of Margaret Reay, the Mistress of the Earl of Sandwich, Lord Commissioner of the Admiralty, over 200 years ago. She was shot dead on April 7th 1779 by Rev James Hackman when leaving Covent Garden Theatre.

It was reported that the ghost has been seen by Mr Healey in the flat at the end of the Hall and by several members of his family—the children treating 'the lady' as a relative.

Others who were haunted by 'Mistress Ray', it has been claimed, were Winston Churchill and Harold MacMillan.

Fisheries Inn*

Harefield, Middlesex, London
Open to the public during normal hours

Dozens of people just visiting a pub for the sake of investigating a ghost must, at times, be more than a little irritating to busy landlords, especially if inconsiderate characters create a nuisance.

Mrs Murphy, wife of the licensee, is more than a little frightened by the two ghosts that inhabit one of the private bedrooms and is anxious that visitors do not mention the incidents.

An apparition of a cavalier in doublet and hose was seen by her husband and footsteps have been heard on an empty staircase.

The hooded figure of a monk has been seen in the affected bedroom, which is now kept locked, and the inn's two dogs refuse to walk anywhere near it.

For the sake of retaining peace of mind, perhaps it would be advisable if ghost hunters delete this establishment from their records—at least for some time.

Hall Place

Bourne Road, Bexley, London
Open to the public by appointment only
On A2
Nearest station—Bexley

Owned by the Bexley London Borough Council and described as a 'flint and brick Tudor house built in 1540 with a 17th century addition', Hall Place is also the site of an apparent suicide.

Many people who have heard the pitiful moans coming from the tower accept the story that it is the ghost of Lady Atte Hall who threw herself from the tower having seen her husband killed by a stag in the courtyard.

Partly because the sounds heard also include mysterious foot-steps and tappings, and once in a while a shadowy figure is reported having been witnessed near the tower, I prefer to believe that the phenomenon is caused by the activities of a former owner, that of Sir John Dashwood, the notorious rake.

He is well known to have been associated with his brother, Sir Francis Dashwood, in creating the infamous Hell Fire Club at High Wycombe and may well have used some of the black magic arts at Hall Place.

Perhaps strengthening this idea is that an American visited the house in the 1950's and with the help of a medium established that some of the crying is caused by the phantom of a servant girl in the attic. She has been seen more recently weeping bitterly and wringing her hands in 'great sorrow'.

Hampton Court Palace*

Open to the public during normal hours
Off A308
Nearest station—Hampton Court

Like the Tower of London, this Royal palace built in 1514 has over the years boasted a wide selection of ghosts from Jane Seymour, Mrs Penn, Cardinal Wolsey and Lady Catherine Howard to a couple of cavaliers from the Civil War. The latter were disposed of when their skeletons were discovered during excavations in Fountain Court.

The latest addition to the 'cast list' is that of the original builder of the Palace, Cardinal Wolsey, for he was seen in 1966 standing under an archway during a performance of Son et Lumière. Since then he has been witnessed on two other occasions in the same location.

One of the regular and perhaps most famous apparitions is that of Catherine Howard whose frequent appearances have established a particular portion of the building as 'The Haunted Gallery'. One of the occupants who resides in a 'grace and favour flat' adjoining the corridor told me that she had so often witnessed the shrieking figure of her Ladyship that she took it 'as a matter of course'.

It was in 1540 that Catherine first came to Hampton Court but as time progressed her reputation dwindled. Unable to cope with the ugliness and repulsiveness of her King she had turned her favours elsewhere with the obvious result. She was condemned to the block. Hours before her death was due she escaped from the guards and ran shouting along the corridor pleading with Henry to spare her.

Either the King failed to hear her or, more likely, ignored the pitiful cries of his fifth wife and continued with the religious ceremonies in the chapel.

In desperation she pounded her fists on the door, but to no avail. She was dragged back still crying for mercy.

It is this scene that is re-enacted so frequently that few can deny its authenticity.

Leslie Finch, the actor, is one of the witnesses to the appearance of Mrs Sybil Penn, a one-time nurse and foster mother to Edward VI. The ghost, known as the 'Lady in Grey', was first reported in the 19th century but obviously she is still seen occasionally. What appears to have increased her activities was the discovery of her old spinning wheel in a previously unknown chamber in the wall of the south-west wing only a few years ago.

Highgate Cemetery

Swains Lane, London, N6
Open to the public during normal hours
Nearest station—Highgate (Northern Line)

Housing some 50,000 bodies, the rambling cemetery of Highgate, the older part of which dates from the early 19th century, provides a miserable appearance of dereliction and neglect. Many of the huge vaults have been broken into and mysterious signs and symbols smeared over the masonry. Some of these appear to be Voodoo inscriptions, whilst others are associated with necromancy.

It is hardly surprising that such an area of forlorn ruin has at least one ghost, for there are rumours of a vampire as well that prowls the 'catacombs' and a section of the graveyard stacked with coffins.

The ghost here always appears in the evening standing near the large entrance gates, peering through the iron bars like some melancholy lover waiting for his paramour. One of the most recent incidents recorded was in January 1970 when a gentleman from Milton Park saw it. His car had broken down in Swains Lane and, pulling into the parking space by the cemetery gates, he noticed the apparition peering at him through the gateway. He didn't stay to examine his car.

Ickenham Station

Near Uxbridge, London
Open to the public during normal hours
On A4020

At 2am in March 1951 whilst on a night shift, a London Transport engineer working in the sub-station at the end of the platform, glanced up to see the ghost of a middle-aged woman wearing a red scarf watching him. She beckoned him to the huge switchboard where she indicated he should follow her down the adjoining staircase.

Suffering from no fear at seeing the apparition, he followed her until she suddenly vanished when nearing the last step.

Several railway workers have seen this ghost, understood to be that of a woman who fell on to the conductor rail and was killed many years ago.

16 Montpelier Road*

Ealing, London, W5
Private property, please respect

In 1887 a 12 year old girl, Anne Hinchfield, committed suicide at a house here by jumping from the top of the 70ft high tower which formed part of the building. In 1934 my mother, then a nurse, was called upon to attend a case of murder and suicide at the same house. A nursemaid had thrown a young child from the tower and then jumped to her own death. Whilst waiting for the doctor to finish his examination of the bodies my mother had walked into the back garden and seen footprints appear in the grass, walk to a garden seat and stop. The seat then moved as if 'being sat on'.

Shortly afterwards the house was sold, to remain unoccupied for ten years.

But by then twenty suicides and the murder had occurred—all from the top of the tower.

In 1944 the house was requisitioned by the Ealing Town Council to use as a store for furniture and goods removed from bombed houses and shops. The Rehousing Officer for the area examined the property to confirm it was suitable, but complained of the objectionable smell in a room on the first floor. The team of council workmen employed to carry out repairs to such property refused after only three hours to stay there due to the 'atmosphere' and the fact that a large number of their tools were missing. It was finally necessary to obtain a work team from Greenford for the reputation of the house had spread.

The Council refused to spend any more ratepayers' money on the property, for they had already stripped and re-plastered the walls and relaid all the flooring in an effort to locate the cause of the mysterious smell which was experienced every 28 days.

When I visited the house with my father in September 1944, it was a glorious autumn day with the sun shining on the whole area. My intention was to examine and photograph the property.

The 'room with the smell' measured about 10ft by 12ft and had been fitted out as a small chemical laboratory. A bunsen burner and several other pieces of equipment remained as evidence of its former use.

Scrambling up the ladder on the third floor to the tower roof I had an impression that I was being physically helped, feeling a pair of hands on my waist, but the only other occupant of the building was on the ground floor.

On reaching the top of the tower, I looked over across the roofs towards London and was surprised at the fantastic view. Slowly a mental message entered my mind to 'have a look in the garden. Walk over the parapet, it's only 12in on to the lawn. You won't hurt yourself.'

I was sitting on the low parapet preparing to jump when my father grabbed me by the scruff of the neck and, despite my protests, pulled me back commenting that 'we don't want any suicides in the family'.

At that moment I was convinced I would not be hurt. Later I realised that the suicides may well have suffered from the same impelling command and were not victims of a real death wish. It is also possible that the crazy paving round the base of the tower created some optical illusion giving the peculiar impression of lack of height. Another explanation may be black magic, for various magical symbols were carved in the stone of the wall.

Some time later, at about 2.30pm I took a photograph from the end of the garden, aiming at obtaining the maximum amount of the building in the view finder. The house was completely empty and locked at the time. My father was waiting for me in the front garden.

Several friends had claimed they could see the image of a young girl in the window and for that reason I arranged for an enlargement to be made.

In 1952, by then a member of a local amateur dramatic society, I re-visited the house to attend rehearsals of a play we were intending to produce. The play, *The Poltergeist*, is a little-known production but one in which Gordon Harker made his name.

The director of the group, Ken Yandell, was a BBC producer living in a flat in the reconstructed house. The complete interior had been stripped out and 15 new flats created. He had no knowledge of the building when he moved in during 1950, but his terrier went 'berserk' every 28 days, running to the sitting room window, snarling, slobbering and trying to fight with an unseen object on the glass.

During our first rehearsal one member went into a 'trance' and talked like a young girl called Anne, 'who didn't kill myself. I only wanted to go into the garden'.

Either this was a case of telepathy, I had made no mention of the 12 year old suicide, or some entity speaking through the young actress.

Ken complained bitterly of a 'foul smell in his bathroom' which occurred every four or five weeks. This was on the site of the previous laboratory.

A week later, during our second rehearsal, five of the seven members present heard the sounds of footsteps some 18 inches from the ceiling walk across the room, open and close a door, and continue until reaching the party wall. On the conversion of the property, various ceiling heights had been raised.

Due to numerous accidents (the male lead was killed in a car crash and one of the females was badly hurt in an air disaster) and the fact that the society was in financial difficulties, the production was never staged.

One day some two years later Ken Yandell told me he had spent a night in the local hospital, suffering from 'sulphur poisoning'. He had slept the previous night in his bath as a result of a late night party in which numerous guests had been accommodated in spare beds, divans and chairs. At 2am Ken's wife had heard him moaning and gasping for breath and on rushing into the bathroom realised he was choking.

The Sister at the hospital told me it wasn't sulphur poisoning—'people don't suddenly develop this when lying in a bath'—but the symptoms closely resembled this type of poisoning.

Other flat owners told Ken of ghostly incidents. The couple who owned the flat which incorporated the corridor leading to the tower had heard the sounds of a 'limping man with a walking stick' walk through their sitting room and their bedroom.

Another couple, living in the tower, the roof of which had been sealed off, had watched their front door bell push being operated by an unseen hand whilst they were sitting in the back garden.

Some years later, in 1961, whilst connected with a popular commercial television programme called 'Jim's Inn', I met one of the script writers, a Jack Edwards, who during a casual conversation mentioned he was experiencing trouble with the local Gas Board. He had complained several times of the smell of sulphurous gas in his bathroom and numerous visits had been paid by officials. But all to no avail. The smell continued to pervade the room

'every month'. 'The funny thing is', he told me, 'there are no gas
pipes in the flats'.

I hardly bothered to ask him where he lived. He was still experiencing the trouble in 1963 when I met him again in London.

The house was pulled down in 1970 and an entirely new block
of flats erected on the site. But vague comments of 'unusual noises'
are still heard by neighbours.

Nag's Head*

324, Hackney Road, London, E2
Open to the public during normal hours
100 yards from Cambridge Heath station

'One of the oldest buildings in Hackney Road' is how the landlord
Mr Andreeti described the Nag's Head. He took over the licence
in 1970, but has so far not experienced the ghost that his predecessor witnessed in the cellars in 1968.

The clearer description was given by the barman who saw it
twice and 'was scared stiff'. Whilst getting a crate of whisky for the
bar Tom Foord suddenly looked up and saw the figure of 'an old
woman in a grey shawl and a long black dress standing in a corner'.
A few weeks later the landlord at the time, Terry Hollingsworth,
persuaded Tom, who had flatly refused to go down there again, to
bring up a crate from the store-room.

After waiting for some minutes, Terry went down the stairs to
find his barman 'frozen and staring at something'. The old woman
had obviously returned. Shortly afterwards Tom left.

Now the only phenomenon that occurs is the occasional sound
of footsteps in an upstairs room, but Mr Andreeti said that he had
recently decorated it, and as he has heard nothing since—'perhaps
it has gone away after approving of the new designs'.

There is no clue as to who the old lady is, but one could suggest
that she is the original Nagger.

The Old Palace

Old Palace Road, Croydon, London
Open to the public during normal hours
On A23/A232
Nearest station—Croydon

Here in Surrey's largest town, before it was incorporated into the massive environs of Greater London, one finds a mixture of old buildings overshadowed and in some places virtually hidden by the high rise office blocks which are now a feature of Croydon.

The ancient parish covered an area of over 9,000 acres and was much influenced by the Archbishops of Canterbury, the Lords of the Manor. Their house, the Old Palace, stands adjacent to the old parish church of St John the Baptist and, although owned by the Community of the Sisters of the Church, is open to the public on certain days during the summer.

Many renowned figures have stayed in the Old Palace including Henry III, Henry VIII and Queen Elizabeth I, and James I of Scotland before he became King was held prisoner there.

The Archbishops left the building in 1758 after some 750 years of occupation and in 1780 it was abandoned, later to become a bleaching factory and then a school for lost orphans. It has been established that it was an incident during this period which created the current ghost.

A mother of one of the young children who had been accommodated here in the 19th century is still seen walking the long passages searching, it is thought, for her lost baby. Slightly out of period though she wears a ruff at her neck and appears as 'terribly sad, wringing her hands in grief'.

Plough Inn*

Clapham Common, London, SW4
Open to the public during normal hours
Nearest station—Clapham Junction

Known to thousands of motorists as one of the traffic jam areas of London and one of the original hubs of the railway era, Clapham Common is also the site of this 150 year old haunted pub.

One of the intriguing aspects of the building was the existence of a hidden room. From the outside can be seen three windows on the top floor, though in the rooms upstairs only two can be found. In September 1970 an entrance was found to the mystery room and the additional window was found to be blocked up, yet it has been seen on occasions to be open.

The ghost, known affectionately as 'Sarah' by the licensee and the staff, affected the pub's dog and was often seen by a former resident barman. He woke during one night and saw the figure of a woman with long black hair in a white gown standing in a corner of the room.

In 1970 Mr Williams, the publican, said 'I have experienced "Sarah" myself. While looking round upstairs shortly after moving here in August 1970, I felt a prickling sensation and found that several members of the staff had felt the same thing.'

The current landlord, Mr Lynch, however, told me he had so far experienced nothing.

Ratcliff Wharf

Regents Canal Dock, Stepney, London, E8
Open to the public during normal hours
Nearest station—Stepney

Jutting into the sweep of the Thames from the north, originating at the infamous Limehouse area, is the Isle of Dogs where in ancient time the King used to keep his hounds.

Now forming the complex of Millwall, the West India Docks, and to the south Cubitt Town, the area has a long tradition of violence and murder.

Slightly to the west, a few yards from Stepney East station, lies the Regent's Canal Dock and to the south of it an old mortuary.

During 1971 within the precincts of the dock, a derelict warehouse in Ratcliff Wharf was restored by a small group of contractors, practically all of whom were disturbed to see the ghost of a priest carrying a stick walking round the site.

It was some 150 years ago that the vicar of Ratcliffe Cross organised a lodging house for seamen in the area. But his main source of income was provided by murdering the richer clients and robbing the bodies. 'The corpses were, no doubt, disposed of by throwing them into the handy waters of the river'.

The ghost has regularly been seen in the evening, usually in July and August, and it is for this reason that, according to one lighterman, 'the dock was always closed at five o'clock as no one would work there after dusk'.

One of the most recent sightings, however, was at 8.30 one Sunday morning in July 1971 when the head of the contracting firm saw an 'elderly man with long white hair dressed in black leaning on a cane only 20 yards away'. So positive was the executive of the man's appearance, that he greeted him with a 'good morning' and began to walk towards him, thinking he was ill.

As the vicar was seen again by others of the team only two hours later and the following Sunday mornings he was seen at ten o'clock, it seems that he has changed his schedule to day-time performances.

Roundshaw Estate*

Croydon, London
Open to the public
Junction of A23/A232
4 miles from Purley station

One of the first airfields to be constructed in this county was at Croydon. Originally there were two—Beddington Aerodrome to the east of Plough Lane (now Mollison Drive) and the other, Waddon Aerodrome, to the west.

Even in 1915 land of what was part of New Barn Farm, Beddington, was used as a base for air defence of London during the First World War.

By 1920 the airfields had developed into Croydon (Waddon) Aerodrome, but operations were still centred to the east of Plough Lane, 'planes having to be taxied over a level crossing in the lane which still crossed the site.

Between 1920 and 1930 massive development created Croydon as the most modern airport in the world. It was from here that Amy Johnson left on her historic flight to Australia in 1930 and returned as a passenger aboard an Imperial Airways Argosy.

But when war came in 1939 the RAF returned and Croydon became one of the triple 'star' fighter bases for the Battle of Britain—Kenley and Biggin Hill being the other two. It was attacked many times and during a raid in August 1940 over 60 people were killed and 170 injured.

When hostilities ceased it was obvious that the airport's days were numbered. By 1959, when it was finally closed, the rapid increase in air traffic and the size of aircraft had made Croydon redundant.

Nine years later, after much debate as to its use, the Roundshaw Housing Estate was officially opened on part of the old aerodrome. The huge development, consisting of 1,800 houses, 4 schools, a health centre, library, community building and shopping centre, was one of the most controversial in the country.

Heating of the houses and other buildings is supplied by a massive oil-fired boiler housed in a large glass-fronted establishment on the corner of Mollison Drive. This was the first of the buildings to be completed in March 1968 on the site of one of the previous runways and only a few yards from the former staff. quarters.

During the commissioning of the boilers, one of the construction team sleeping in the building was often awakened by the inexplicable sound of community singing and, according to one of the engineers, various similar noises are still heard.

One of the council work force, late in 1971, whilst removing some rubbish at 6.30 in the morning, was astounded to see a motor-cyclist roaring round beside the boiler house and shoot past him at full speed. What was disturbing about this incident was that the driver had no face.

Legend has it that the unknown cyclist was one of the Battle of Britain pilots who was killed when his 'plane crashed at the end of the runway during the war.

The singing could be that of the ghostly crowd who used to enjoy their 'socials' in one of the staff huts, cheering themselves up during the long hours of worry in the nightly air-raids.

St Giles Church*

Camberwell High Street, Camberwell, London, SE5
Open to the public during normal hours
Nearest station—Denmark Hill

The existing church here is only about 125 years old but it is the fifth religious building on the site. There was mention in the Domesday Book of a church in the locality in Norman times.

Practically adjoining the church is a small and rather narrow footpath, the Churchyard Passage, which leads round the west end of the Church through the old graveyard across what is now Camberwell Grove to the Clergy House, long since vanished.

Some 30-40 years ago a few local residents occasionally witnessed the figure of a priest walking slowly along the footpath and, although accepting it as an apparition, found it 'far from frightening'. The Rev Roger Tamplin told me that he believed it was the wraith of one of the friendly old clergymen who regularly used the passage to return home from the church in years gone by.

The phantom priest must have continued his haunting unnoticed for a long period, slowly weakening in intensity as the years passed. But in November 1970 two young parishioners reported that they had seen a 'shadowy figure' approaching them on the pathway one evening. The Rev Tamplin interviewed them and was greatly impressed with their sincerity and the sober way in which they recounted their experience. Because of the interest aroused Canon Rhymes, vicar of St Giles, agreed to an appeal in the church magazine for any other similar incidents to be reported.

Three letters were received from parishioners, two of which claimed that they too had witnessed the vague figure of a man in the same locality during the early part of 1971.

Since then no further information has been received, but presumably the old character still continues his evening walk in peace.

St Mary's Church*

Neasden Lane/Eric Road, London, NW10
Open to the public during normal hours
Nearest station—Neasden

Although only a few people have seen the vicarage garden ghost, 'a round tubby jovial monk in normal black clothes,' his authenticity is well accredited for he has been witnessed by an engine driver, a fellow priest and the vicar's wife in the last few years.

His main interest in the garden appears to be the site of a well. Possibly, according to the Vicar and Rural Dean of Brent, the Rev George Oakley, 'it was a holy well' associated with the early days of the adjoining church. His appearance has been made at varying times, very early in the morning, mid-day and early evening. Three people, however, saw the black-robed monk in November 1970 'prowling the grounds of the church'.

The Church of St Mary itself has Norman remains and the south aisle and nave are believed to be 13th century. The north aisle is only Victorian. It is in the church that an 'unseen priest creates a bit of a nuisance'. Door handles frequently rattle in the vestry with no cause and a regular but mysterious smell of incense has been remarked upon by numerous parishioners. 'Although I've heard the noises in the church', the vicar told me with a laugh, 'I've never seen the monk in the garden, but they say it's only honest men who see ghosts!'

Second-hand City

North End Road, West Kensington, London, W14
Open to the public during normal hours
Nearest station—West Kensington

Linking London's exhibition hall at Olympia with Fulham Broadway, over a mile away, North End Road has become one of the busiest streets of West London and, incidentally, home of numerous Australian visitors. With the increasing popularity of antiques, marts or markets and 'antique boutiques' are springing up all over London and one of them is this building specialising in furniture.

Originally it was a Methodist Chapel which achieved local 'fame' with the murder of an elderly widow. The building had been empty for some time but in the winter of 1965 Annie Doohan, a much loved old soul who had been missing from her usual haunts for some days, was found brutally murdered on the floor of the derelict chapel. One theory at the time was that her frail body had been 'dumped' here, another that she had disturbed hooligans wrecking the place.

Not much is known of Annie except her extreme and natural fondness for 'Victoriana', the objects with which she had lived for most of her life.

In November 1971 reports were received that the 'City' was haunted. Frank Hastings, who was in charge of the antique section, told the *West London Mail* that he had seen 'a pinkish grey transparent shape with an indefinite outline floating in the air'. On being pressed for a further description of the phantom he said that there 'was a hint of a long robe and a hood', but he could distinguish no face.

This incident certainly seemed unconnected with poor old Annie, but could possibly be linked with the earlier religious history of the building. The wraith was seen several times following this, always near Victorian chairs, whenever they appeared in the storeroom.

An upholsterer who was working alone one night in the basement heard 'unusual noises' and on investigating saw the phantom 'gliding around in a corner by some old chairs that had just come in'. Despite his enthusiasm for the job, the gentleman never worked into the early hours again. No one does, but at 3am one morning a passer-by reported that all the chapel lights were on.

This may have been some peculiar reflection from other buildings for the place was in darkness on 'opening up' the following day.

Sheppeys Restaurant

Shepherd Market, Mayfair, London, W1
Open to the public during normal hours
Nearest station—Green Park

Shepherd Market, named after an 18th century business man who built a cattle market there in 1735, is practically the centre of the intriguing area of Mayfair, the site of an annual rather bawdy affair which dates back to at least 1272—perhaps even earlier. It was eventually suppressed in 1809 as a public scandal being, according to records, 'a nursery of vice and atheism'.

The oldest house in Mayfair is Sheppey's, a combination of chop-house, restaurant and club bar, which has in its three centuries of history been the haven of royalty, footpads, poets and courtesans.

Sheppey's first tenants were characters of 'low standing', people

193

of the stage, and the upper part became part of a theatre—one of the first in London.

During the middle of the 18th century, no doubt to accommodate the needs of the cattle-men, the ground floor became a coffee house. Boswell, who lived a few yards away in Half Moon Street, often brought his friend Dr Johnson here for refreshments, and the upper floors developed into lodgings for young gentlemen, but disreputable characters have lived here too.

One of these was a notorious highwayman who stored his loot in the cellars and the tunnel that led to the old gallows site, Tyburn Tree, at Marble Arch.

The attractive wrought iron gate to the vaults, which extend forty feet, was the original front door of Sheppey's when Beau Brummell lived there, giving elegant parties for the Prince Regent.

The ghost of 'the establishment' is said to be that of the highwayman and has often been seen by lady cleaners when at work at their early morning chores. But he may well be that of the 'beau' for he has a delightful sense of humour (though highwaymen too were seldom lacking in fun).

He is not only seen but, on occasions, has been felt gently moving aside a lady or tugging at a duster. The figure of the man has been described as 'tall and thin, dressed in a long black coat', but his features have never been clearly visible, always 'hidden by the shadows'. His favourite haunts are the two bars and, despite efforts to exorcise him, he continues to revel in his spasmodic visits.

The Temple

Fleet Street, London, EC4
Open to the public
Nearest stations—Temple or Charing Cross

One of the few pleasant spots for peaceful thought left in the sprawling metropolis, the Temple needs little imagination to set one's mind back to the days of Dickens. Through the 17th century gateway in Fleet Street visitors can recapture the atmosphere of shaded alleys, dusty shelves of legal scribblers and the dignity of be-wigged barristers strolling over the cobbled paving, preparing for the next case in the Law Courts over the road.

The beautifully restored 12th century Temple Church offers even greater seclusion as well as its immediate surrounds of moss-covered stones where visitors sit quietly feeding the London sparrows. The rant and roar of 'The Street' is hardly heard and seems unable to penetrate the charm of this veritable haven.

It is hardly surprising that there is a ghost here, especially as it is of a man in a wig and gown carrying a file of papers under his arm. He has been witnessed late at night, usually by newspaper workers hurrying to catch the last train home, or occasionally by other members of the Temple chambers.

No one cares who he is or when he died. He is merely 'a shade from London's past'.

Thamesmead*

Woolwich, London
Open to the public during normal hours
Nearest station—Woolwich Dockyard

London's new suburb which will eventually house some 60,000 people when finished about 1985 is being constructed on reclaimed land of the Erith Marshes some three miles from Woolwich. The first recreational lake of some 65 acres is already completed and work is now being made on a childrens' paddling pool, boating and play area complete with an attractive little island for 'Robinson Crusoe' games.

Leading to this is Tavey Bridge and a few yards away a small number of shops cater for the needs of some of the residents already living in the new town.

Early in 1971 the RAF Museum authorities at Maidstone heard of the remains of a Spitfire that had been found near the proposed site of the pool during excavations. Anxious to obtain this 'valuable' souvenir of the hectic days of the Battle of Britain, arrangements were made to transport the surviving portions, a pair of wings from the aircraft, to the Museum where they are now housed.

Obviously connected with this was the fact that in May of the same year reports were received by the *Kentish Independent* of an apparition having been seen in the area of Tavey Bridge. The first to report the incident was one of the nearby shop owners, Ken Hancock a butcher, who had seen the figure gliding round the cutting room of the shop.

He described the apparition as that of 'a tall dark man in RAF uniform'. Mrs Hancock has 'sensed' the presence of the pilot, but has been rather disturbed by the fact that coats and overalls have been thrown around the premises and banging has been heard up and down the stairs.

Mrs Kearnes, a neighbour, has also witnessed the ghost through her bedroom doorway and her child also mentioned a man standing in one of the rooms 'when it was dark'.

Several other people have also seen what must now be accepted as the phantom of the pilot killed when his aircraft crashed into the marshes in 1941.

Theatre Royal

Drury Lane, Catherine Street, London, WC2
Open to the public during normal hours
Nearest station—Aldwych or Covent Garden

One of the most famous authenticated ghosts of London is that of the 'Man in Grey', the resident spectre of the Theatre Royal, who appears only between 9am and 6pm. So many actors, actresses and theatregoers have seen the good gentleman it is surprising that his appearance is still doubted.

Harry Secombe and his dresser witnessed the ghost during the 1960's when Harry was appearing in *The Four Musketeers*. In describing one incident in his dressing room he said: 'suddenly all the coathangers in my wardrobe started to swing wildly. They just went mad. Everybody else had gone home yet there were fairly loud tappings at the same time on the wall of the room'.

Of witnessing the gentleman, Harry stated, 'the whole ruddy cast saw him once. He always made his appearance before 6pm and then popped off again. Haunting to rule, I suppose'.

Other celebrities who have witnessed the ghost include James Wentworth Day and the late W Macqueen Pope who in 1951 stated, 'on one occasion it was seen by over 150 people—all at the same time, but another 100 who were also present saw nothing at all. This is how it goes'.

Wentworth Day describes the ghost as 'a grey pearly light moving with the uneven action of a man with a limp'.

Stage folk welcome the appearance of the ghost for it is thought to bring them luck, appearing a couple of days before the opening of a success, never for a failure. *The King and I, South Pacific, Oklahoma* and *Carousel* are four of his 'approved' productions giving some indication of his excellent taste. Perhaps theatre 'angels' should hire him as an agent.

Two young actresses who claim 'the man' helped their careers are Doreen Duke, who felt a friendly pat on the back giving her great encouragement when auditioning for *The King and I*, and Betty Jo Jones. Betty, who flew over from America for the comedy role in *Oklahoma*, realised she was not getting the laughs the part deserved. One night, when on stage with two other actors, she felt a tug at her skirt and then was gently pushed downstage to a

196

new position. She played the scene from there and had the audience roaring their heads off with laughter.

The actual identity of 'The Man in Grey' is rather confused. One belief is that he is the ghost of Arnold Woodruffe. If this was the actor killed by Charles Macklin in the Green Room some 200 years ago in a fit of anger, then it may well be that of the apparition who wears 'a long grey riding cloak, knee-breeches, buckled shoes and a three-cornered hat over a powdered wig'.

About 1850 the theatre was rebuilt and during the work a small room was found which contained the skeleton of a man with a dagger in his ribs. At the time the remains were believed to be those of a victim of an irate, jealous manager anxious to retain the favours of one of the girls in the theatre and many think that the ghost is of the unfortunate who had been bricked up after the murder.

Another apparition that used to be seen in the theatre is that of the famous comedian Dan Leno. Both Stanley Lupino and his wife witnessed his appearance in a dressing room.

A ghost with a long white painted face used to be seen sitting behind people in one of the boxes in the theatre and it was thought to be of Joe Grimaldi—the most renowned of all clowns.

Joe is known to have been interested in ghostly subjects, but it would be more likely if he were to haunt Sadlers Wells where he made his first appearance. The ghost in the box may therefore have been that of his father 'Iron Legs' or even Dan Leno. The fact that Joe Grimaldi insisted on his head being cut from his body on his death should perhaps have created a 'headless apparition', but no reports of such a spectre in this connection have been recorded.

However, a theatre with at least two, possibly three, well attested ghosts could be considered as one of the highlights of the ghostly population of the capital.

Tower of London*

Tower Hill, London, EC3
Open to the public during normal hours
Nearest station—Tower Hill

One of the most recent recorded sightings of a ghost here was in August 1970 when a young visitor from Essex was in one of the rooms in the Bloody Tower. The apparition was of a long haired woman dressed in a long black velvet dress with a white cap and a large golden medallion hanging from her neck.

She was standing by one of the open windows and when the visitor walked over to the figure the ghost vanished leaving the young lady experiencing difficulty in breathing. This feeling was repeated on a return visit a few weeks later.

The witness was puzzled as to who the apparition could have been and, in answering the question, the renowned ghost hunter James Wentworth Day put forward a very good case in an article in the *Evening News* that it was probably Lady Jane Grey.

There have been so many reports of ghosts in the Tower over the years that it is sometimes difficult to identify them all, but poor little Lady Jane seems to be the most popular. She was also seen as 'a white shapeless form' on the Salt Tower on January 12th 1957 by two Welsh Guards sentries.

Other ghosts reported in earlier years include Anne Boleyn seen in the White Tower and on Tower Green. In 1933 a sentry saw her headless body floating towards him and because the spot is known to be one of the worst affected he was merely reprimanded for deserting his post.

Margaret, the Countess of Salisbury, has been heard screaming in abject terror near the site of the scaffold. Her death was admittedly one of the most horrific of the beheading ceremonies for, after being led struggling and shouting to the block, she escaped from the guards and ran round demented whilst the formidable masked figure of the tall axeman chased her until she tripped and fell.

The guards dragged her writhing body to the blood-stained block where the axeman aimed his first blow. It missed. The second and third attempts also failed to reach their mark. The Countess by now must have been completely insane, screaming incessantly and struggling to free herself from the men holding her down.

The executioner, no doubt upset by the disturbance, made another attempt only to tear open half his victim's neck. Screams turned to blood-filled gurgles and moans. Only at the fifth blow did the axeman achieve the object and the head fell to the ground.

An unusual spectre reported by some of the military personnel is that of a bear which presumably is the sole survivor of the days when the Tower was used as a menagerie, or perhaps for the occasional bear baiting session.

The Duke of Northumberland used to walk between the Martin and Constable Towers and Sir Walter Raleigh's ghost was, in earlier days, reported near the Bloody Tower.

But the only current ghost still appears to be that of 'the little Lady Jane' who, though one of the youngest, died with the full dignity of a queen.

The Volunteer

247 Baker Street, London, NW1
Open to the public during normal hours
Nearest station—Baker Street

Not far from the fictional site of the famous Sherlock Holmes's apartments in the busy thoroughfare of Baker Street can be found this popular pub run by Mr Joseph Gardiner. Thanks to Mr Gardiner's thorough investigations the ghost that he and several customers have seen at odd times during the day since 1969 has now been identified as Rupert Nevill.

The first time the apparition was seen the licensee was in the cellar when the door to one of the unused alcoves opened to reveal the figure of a man 'wearing a surcoat, breeches and stockings', typical costume of the 17th century period.

Partly because of its age, it was built in 1794, the pub has often been suspected of being haunted, but it was only when considerable alterations were carried out in 1963 that the feeling became more intense. 'Lights were turned on and off and several people heard footsteps around the place.'

On one occasion the power was cut off, depriving the bar of the necessary liquid refreshment for some time.

The Volunteer was built on agricultural land on which two farms, Park and Daget, existed. Whether Rupert Nevill was connected with either of these is not known, but it seems that he and his family were Royalist supporters and had been present at the Battle of Naseby. The entire Nevill family had died in a fire in 1654, presumably in one of the farms, and it is for this reason that the spectre still walks the area. It would make little difference if the building was a block of offices.

Westminster Abbey

London, SW1
Open to the public during normal hours
Nearest station—Westminster or Victoria

The accepted place for the coronation of English royalty since the 11th century and the site of tombs of many mediaeval kings from the time of Henry III, the Abbey stands on what was once Thorney Island in the mouth of the river Tyburn. As with most buildings of this age, it has been considerably altered over the years, one of the last major additions was the construction of Henry VII's chapel in 1503.

During the numerous modifications the floor level has gradually been lowered by some two feet in depth and it is this significant fact that accounts for occasional reports from the night visitors and cleaning staff describing the ghost of a monk seen gliding about with the hem of his cloak some distance from the ground.

Who he is no-one has been able to ascertain, but it is possible he is one of the former inhabitants, or could it perhaps be the re-juvenated ghost of Father Benedictus the last recorded visit of which was in 1934?

In 1932 when he appeared his shoes seemed to be about a couple of inches from the floor. His major performance was in 1900 when he was seen as 'a Benedictine monk standing with his hands hidden in the sleeves of his habit and with the cowl half back from his head'. He walked backwards looking at the people in the south transept and disappeared through a wall after 25 minutes of haunting.

Despite a popular legend concerning this gentleman, there is no record of a monk being killed in the Abbey.

Another ghost of the Abbey is that of a soldier in the uniform of the First World War who has been seen standing with head bowed in sorrow a few feet away from the tomb of the Unknown Warrior. Some believe he is the warrior himself, others that he is the brother of the soldier buried there, but no-one will ever know.

The bodies of four complete unidentified men killed in four areas of France during the war were covered with a Union Jack and one was chosen by the General in charge at the time to be 'The Un-known Warrior'. The body was brought to England on November 11th 1920, given a 'royal funeral' and finally buried in earth from France under a slab quarried in Belgium.

But another spectre of the Abbey has been identified as that of John Bradshaw, president of the Court which condemned Charles I. He has been seen in the last 25 years in the Deanery where the death warrant was signed.

Wig and Pen Club*

230 Strand, London, WC2
Open to the public by appointment only
Nearest station—Aldwych

This club, one of the few surviving buildings from the Great Fire of London in the 1600's, lies opposite the Law Courts and is claimed to be built on Roman remains.

In its varied history it had been a shop, a private house and a cluster of solicitors' offices. Once during its life it was a keeper's cottage and rumour has it that at that time Cromwell's head was spiked on the top of Temple Bar. One night a gale blew it off into the cottage. Now, the Wig and Pen still in its attractive rambling 17th century construction, it is a private club for gentlemen of the law and the press.

The owner, Dick Brennan, and his manager have often found it necessary to sleep on the empty premises, and have been puzzled by the sound at 2.15am of an unseen man walking along a corridor on the ground floor. Immediately below lies the basement, converted some years ago into the club's dining room, whilst above is the television lounge.

Rumour has it that the footsteps are those of a solicitor who was found dead in his office one morning during the Victorian era. But the footsteps have also been heard on Saturday afternoons. In the early days of the profession of course, even lawyers worked during week-ends.

63 Wycliffe Road*

Battersea, London, SW11
Open to the public during normal hours
Nearest station—Wandsworth Town

In 1956 I was asked by the *News Chronicle* to investigate reports of a poltergeist in one of the old early Victorian terraced houses of Battersea.

The case involved Shirley, the daughter of the house, a 15 year old who appeared to be intensely interested in French history and the morbid worship of a young film star, James Dean, who had been killed in a car crash at the height of his career.

Through a series of raps, one for 'no' and two for 'yes', she was able to communicate with the unseen entity which she had affectionately named as 'Donald'. According to her, he was Louis Capet, the illegitimate son of Charles II of France born on 16 July, 1798 and drowned in a ship. Contact had been made with the girl 'because she resembled a Portugese princess Donald knew'.

After several hours of questioning the father, the mother and Shirley, it appeared that 'Donald' controlled the life of the complete household. Mrs Hitchings was reluctant even to go shopping without obtaining approval from the poltergeist, especially as he had often 'put things into the shopping bag that I hadn't purchased'.

It seemed that Shirley, an anaemic young teenager, was able to 'crack her joints' but I was puzzled when, on request, 'Donald' knocked twice on the ceiling and then on a wardrobe.

The case of the 'haunting' had started some two years earlier when the father had found an unidentifiable key lying on his daughter's bed which 'had dropped from the ceiling' early one morning. From then on 'things got worse'. Donald threw ink on to the ceiling, papered one wall of the front bedroom with front covers of a popular weekly film magazine stuck on to the paper with jelly, and had written numerous letters to various personalities asking for help and confirmation that he was genuine.

At one time Mr Hitchings thought that the disturbances were connected with his neighbours, an Indian family, but had finally accepted his daughter's explanation.

The knocks and movement of objects continued for a further two years, decreasing in intensity as the girl grew older and more interested in other matters.

Neighbours, however, continued to complain about the inexplicable knocks and bangs heard in the early hours.

In a massive redevelopment of the area in 1971-72 the entire street was demolished, but it might be interesting to examine the building which eventually replaces the house of 'the poltergeist girl'.

Norfolk

Known for its Broads, providing 200 miles of open water for sailing

Open to the public during normal hours or by appointment	5
Private houses	1
Historic buildings, museums, ruins	1
Private houses, offices, factories	3
Open spaces, roads	2
Phenomena	
Smells	1
Noises	4
Moving objects	1
Apparitions	
Females	1
Males	2

Aylmerton

Sheringham, Norfolk
Open to the public during normal hours
Off A148
3 miles from Sherington station

South of the coastal road to Cromer are a number of prehistoric pit dwellings and it is in one of these ancient sites that a phantom has been experienced so many times at dusk that the name of 'The Shrieking Pits' has been given to the area.

The apparition is of a tall woman, dressed in white, who is obviously searching for something. She walks around weeping and crying, distraught with untold grief and occasionally 'emits terrifying screams of anguish'.

Local belief is that she is looking for her murdered child buried in one of the pits by her husband who killed her and the babe in a fit of jealous insanity sometime in the 19th century.

Bircham Newton Aerodrome

Near Kings Lynn, Norfolk.
Open to the public by appointment only
On B1155, off A1067
4 miles from Kings Lynn station

A case which created a lot of interest early in 1972, through being mentioned on Jack de Manio's radio programme over a three-week period, was that at this desolate aerodrome on the north coast of Norfolk.

It was originally constructed in 1914 and left derelict between the wars only to be re-opened for 'active service' in 1939 when the RAF, Australian and Canadian forces were stationed there.

Some years after the end of hostilities the Officers' Mess was converted into a hotel for use by executives and guests of a construction company which had taken over the site. Part of the building was allocated to an industrial film company for their use as a studio whilst producing a film on the company's activities.

Some distance away, behind the hotel, is a single building converted into a squash court with two playing areas. It is one of these that is haunted.

The first indication of a manifestation was during one evening when a player glanced up at the gallery overlooking the courts and saw a man in RAF uniform gazing down at them. Puzzled he stopped his companion and they both watched the 'pilot' walk along the gallery to the doorway at the end and disappear.

Because of the conviction that they had seen a ghost, the couple arranged for a magnetic tape recorder to be left in the affected court overnight. They had, it seems, intended to stay with the machine, but were too scared at hearing loud footsteps walking along the gallery in the empty building and left. It was pointed out at the time that only one key exists to the building, which was locked after setting the machine going.

Literally thousands of radio listeners have heard the resultant noises that were recorded in the empty building. Sounds similar to those of a busy workshop, a metal bucket being placed on the floor, a loud saw-like buzzing sound, numerous metallic clangs and a peculiar 'pinging' sound. Highlight of the recording, however, is the sound of a woman's voice saying two words, but because of the background noise they are indistinguishable—they could be 'watch out' or even 'stop it'. Another puzzling aspect is the drone of an aeroplane clearly heard, yet no aircraft were flying anywhere in the locality that night.

Determined to find out more of the ghost, a medium, John Sutton, was called in and a seance arranged. In the meantime a letter from a radio listener had been received stating that the ghost was of a man named 'Wiley' who had committed suicide in the Officers' Mess during the war.

The medium, on entering the court, began to sob and told of a plane—'an Anson, that caught fire and crashed on to a local church killing three men'.

Local residents who had stayed in the hotel told of bedclothes and curtains being thrown around, water taps being turned on and off, feeling 'taps' on their shoulders and on a couple of occasions a man in RAF uniform was seen to walk through the wall of the old billiard room.

During the height of the investigations a BBC woman interviewer from the *Nationwide* programme decided she would stay the night in the 'haunted court' with a tape recorder and was, at her request, locked in. She described later the intense feeling of cold, the sounds of banging doors opening and closing and the peculiar fact that the recorder stopped without any reason at 12.30. It was only when she had returned to the studio that she was able to get the machine working again. No fault was found with it.

The hotel was demolished later in 1972 leaving the mystery of the haunted squash court so far unanswered.

Caravan B77

Seashore Camp, Great Yarmouth, Norfolk
Open to the public during normal hours
Junction of A47/A12/A149
Nearest station—Yarmouth

Not far from the Marine Parade a cluster of caravans indicate the popularity of Yarmouth as an ideal resort for adults and children. What must be nearly unique in the annals of ghosts, however, is that one of the caravans on the camp appears to be haunted by a resident ghost.

On June 5, 1971 the *Sun* reported that a Mr and Mrs Dunford and their three children arrived on a Saturday for their holiday with enthusiastic anticipation of a good time. But on the Wednesday night one of the children, David, was prodded twice in the ribs by an unseen entity and the temperature in the caravan dropped. 'It was difficult to breathe', was Mrs Dunford's comment. A few moments later Reg, another son, was prodded.

So upset were the Dunfords that the family went to stay with their grandparents for the night. The incidents were repeated on their return the following day however and so, to ensure a good night's rest, they were provided with another caravan.

Students of parapsychology will not doubt feel that it was poltergeist activity and well it might be, but site manager, Bob Whitworth, said 'nobody will stay in the van and we can't find anything wrong with it'.

Although there is no history of sudden death in the camp, it is known that many caravan site owners purchase the 'mobile houses' second-hand. It is possible, therefore, that a previous owner continues to frolic, albeit unseen, in the confines of caravan B77.

Castle Rising Castle

Castle Rising, Norfolk
Open to the public during normal hours
Off A149
4 miles from Kings Lynn station

The village here was at one time a port but the spectacular Norman castle, standing in impressive ramparts probably constructed by the Romans, is the dominating building.

The castle was built about 1150 by the Earl of Sussex who gained his title on marrying the widow of King Henry I. The only period in which the fortress achieved fame was in about 1330 when Edward III provided accommodation here for his mother Isabella.

Although officially in disgrace because of the part she played in the murder of her husband and her association with Roger Mortimer, she was it seems quite comfortable in the early days of her so-called imprisonment. She was frequently visited by her son and grandson, the Black Prince, but eventually the scheming mind of this old woman failed and she drifted into screaming insanity.

Despite the fact that it is over 600 years since her incarceration, tourists and a few local villagers have sometimes been disturbed to hear issuing from a room in the upper portion of the castle shrieks and hysterical cacklings, 'like some mad old witch'. There is no need to guess who it is that sends shivers down the backs of the visitors.

Happisburgh

Norfolk
Open to the public
On B1159
8 miles from North Walsham station

Although this is only a small village, the name of which is derived
from the Anglo-Saxon 'Haep's Fort', it provides an important
landmark to seamen for both the tower of St Mary's Church and
the striped lighthouse warn them of the nearby sandbanks. Some
of the carvings in the church depict 'wild men of the woods', but
the ghost, one of the most horrifying blood-curdling phantoms in
the country, is not of the forest but of a smuggler.

Early in the 18th century three 'free-traders' had an argument
over sharing out their loot and in the course of the fight one of them
was brutally killed and his body hidden.

In 1765 a ghostly figure was seen 'gliding in from the salt flats',
moving slowly around a field and finally vanishing at Well Corner.
The spine chilling apparition was seen to be without legs and his
head wobbled grotesquely, being joined to the neck only by a
narrow strip of flesh. What added to the horror was that the figure,
dressed in a dark blue jacket, was carrying a weird limp bundle
under one arm.

So impressive was the sighting of this spectre that after several
reports the area of his vanishing was searched and the remains of a
male torso, a blue tunic and a rotting bundle of a man's legs and
head were discovered.

But even today the occasional evening stroller reports seeing a
'column of bluish mist with the round top wobbling grotesquely'
in the region of Well Corner.

Mission Hall Cottage

Briningham, Norfolk
Private property, please respect

In the 19th century an old stable attached to what eventually
became the Mission Hall was converted into a pleasant little
cottage for a member of the staff.

But not only does the original occupant still inhabit the precincts—so do the horses.

In August 1970 Mrs Bird, the owner at the time, reported that
she, her husband and four children, and friends had over many
years heard the sound of a horse 'clopping round the house at

about 10.30 at night'. The internal unseen resident, however, is a walker whose footsteps with a heavy tread are heard on the landing at 5 o'clock in the morning—just about the time that a groom would be getting up to deal with the horses.

Neither Mr or Mrs Bird are worried about the noises for they, like their predecessors, are quite used to them. Visitors are sometimes a little disturbed though when the sitting room 'suddenly goes chilly and an earthy smell can be experienced'.

Northamptonshire

Once the county of squires and spires

Open to the public during normal hours or by appointment	4
Private houses	2

Churches, abbeys, rectories	1
Private houses, offices, factories	3
Open spaces, roads	2

Phenomena	
Noises	3

Apparitions	
Females	3
Males	3
Monks	1
Horses	2

1, Castle Street

Wellingborough, Northamptonshire
Private property, please respect

This case is rather puzzling for there seem to be two manifestations completely unconnected. A previous owner who now lives in Cornwall said recently that she and her family used to hear footsteps in several rooms of the house and often 'what sounded like loads of coal going down the cellar shute' late at night. Her dogs were certainly affected by the atmosphere of the basement for they consistently refused to enter 'the underground rooms'.

In 1971 Mr Wilfrid Franklin, another former occupant, also heard the mysterious footsteps but also suffered from the sudden death of his pet dog. He was carrying it down to the basement one evening when it suddenly became extremely agitated, leapt from his arms through a window and on to the road where a passing car accidentally killed it.

It is possible that the footsteps are those of the phantom of an old lady wearing an 'old-fashioned dress' who has been seen many times over the last thirty years standing in the bathroom.

But the late night delivery of coal remains a mystery.

Great Oxendon

Northamptonshire
Open to the public
On A508
3 miles from Market Harborough station

In 1969 when the old St Helen's church in Great Oxendon was closed pending restorations, reports of seeing a ghost in the vicinity of it reached a peak. Dozens of villagers have witnessed the figure of 'a hooded monk-like shape' gliding along the path towards the church and vanishing through the closed door.

Mrs Betty Judkin was walking home one night with a friend, Mrs Beryl Freeman, when they both saw the phantom 'emerge from the hedgerow. It was dressed in a long habit but we could see no movement of legs or the robes. The cloth just seemed to hang motionless, but the ghost sort of glided over the ground towards the church'.

Another villager and his family living opposite the church, heard the sound of footsteps outside and looking at the window saw a 'hooded figure' glide past, but when he opened the front door to see who it was, the street was empty.

Nene Cottage

Oundle, Northamptonshire
Private property, please respect

As brewers like any other trade become more aware of competition and the need for 'rationalisation' more attractive old inns and pubs will be closed down to revert to their original use as private homes or to make room for development.

This 300 year old cottage, once an inn, was sold a few years ago by Colonel and Mrs McMichael who had during their years of occupation often experienced inexplicable rattling of door handles. Also 'a particular bedroom had an unusual atmosphere', they said.

With the arrival of the new owners, the Hyndman family, incidents increased in number and variety. These were experienced not just by the occupants but also by the workmen carrying out decorations to the property.

The team often reported having seen a 'shadow' on the wall of the affected bedroom and heard footsteps in the room when they knew it to be empty.

Two apparitions have actually been witnessed by Mrs Hyndman. One is of a young girl with long black hair wearing what looks like a night-dress, crouching in front of one of the outhouses. Associated with this phantom is that of a young boy, with long fair hair but wearing Edwardian style clothes, who 'leaps out from the garden and disappears by the wall' of the same building.

Old House

Hind Style, Higham Ferrers, Northamptonshire
Private property, please respect

This is a case of a private house with a long established and often witnessed ghost. The owners of the old house, the Ladds, many of their friends and relatives have frequently seen 'the apparition of a shadowy old housemaid' usually on the path outside the kitchen door.

Victoria Ladd, an 18 year old daughter, says that the figure is about five feet in height but 'one senses its presence more than actually sees it.'

Giving a clue to the identity of 'the dear old soul' or even perhaps of her fate, was when Ann Hale, who was cleaning upstairs, heard footsteps coming down a non-existant stairway. She was determined to find out more about the housemaid and the mysterious noises and discovered an earlier flight of stairs, 'probably those to the servants' quarters', which had been bricked up about 100 years ago.

Pig Lane

Abington, Northampton, Northamptonshire
Open to the public
Off A45
Nearest station—Northampton

A suburb of the county town, Abington boasts of a tiny church with a few early 13th century remains. One of the monuments is by the local sculptor, Samuel Cox, who completed the figure of a robed gentleman in 1730. There is also an 15th century font.

Pig Lane recalls the days when Abington was better known for its market attracting numerous famers and land owners to the village.

It was one evening in about 1780 that a local squire, incensed by the attentions being paid to his young daughter by one of the peasants, drove down Pig Lane filled with uncontrollable rage and intending to storm into the home of the young lover to 'finish the affair for good'.

His anger reached a peak when he saw the man come out of his house and walk into the path of his trundling coach. Spurring the horses on he drove straight at the lad, beating him to the ground and crushing the body beneath the wheels of his vehicle.

It is not the victim who haunts the Lane, but the squire, his coach and two horses. One reason for him being seen headless is explained by one witness. 'Rumour has it that he shot himself in the head afterwards, perhaps through remorse at breaking his daughter's heart'.

St John the Baptist

Boughton Green, Boughton, Northamptonshire
Open to the public during normal hours
Off A43
4 miles from Northampton station

Boughton Green, beside the road from Boughton and Moulton, is the original site of the village gaol which was demolished within living memory. One of the regular inmates of the prison was the leader of a gang of ruffians who used to terrorise stall-holders at the annual horse fair.

Eventually he was hung shortly before Christmas 1825 at Northampton, for it had been established that he was not just a hooligan but a horse thief and a blackmailer as well.

Why he is the one who haunts the immediate locality of the semi-ruined church is a bit of a mystery, but 'spine-chilling moans' have been heard near the old walls and the 'shadowy figure of a large man' whose description matches that given for the ruffian has been seen here at dusk at Christmas time.

Northern Ireland

Has an ancient but troubled history

Open to the public during normal hours and by appointment	5
Private houses	2
Historic buildings, museums, ruins	3
Churches, abbeys, rectories	1
Inns, hotels	1
Private houses, offices, factories	1
Open spaces, roads	1
Phenomena	
Noises	3
Apparitions	
Nuns	1
Females	2
Horses	1

Antrim Castle

Co. Antrim, Northern Ireland
Open to the public during normal hours
Junction of T7/T8
Nearest station—Antrim

The grounds of this ancient ruined castle on Lord O'Neill's estate are open to the public and can be viewed at normal times in the year. The gardens themselves are in fact practically unique for they are one of the very few in the country designed on the French style.

The Fortress was burnt in 1922 but the shell still contains a 17th century period door.

The ghosts of the castle only make an annual appearance here, on May 31, the anniversary of their deaths in the 18th century. They consist of a large coach with four fine horses seen galloping down the highway from the castle straight into the Long Pond where the combined apparition sinks out of sight.

The incident that caused this persistent haunting occurred when a drunken coachman late one night, mistook the moonlit waters for the road surface and plunged himself and his passengers in a cold wet grave.

Ballygally Castle Hotel

Ballygally Head, Co. Antrim, Northern Ireland
Open to the public during normal hours
On A2
22 miles from Belfast station

The resemblance between this ancient building and typical Scottish baronial castles is not unusual for the 17th century design is common to both countries and it was built by James Shaw, one of the Shaws of Greenock.

The clan itself owes its foundations to King MacAlpine and the Royal MacDuffs and can trace its history back to 834. What may confuse historians is that many of the descendants have borne the name of Stewart in addition to the family name.

In 1625 the Crown tenant of the time, the Earl of Antrim, granted land on a sub-lease to various 'freeholders' one being James Shaw who 'bought eighteen score acres' at the yearly rent of £24. Building his new castle from local stone at the head of Ballygally Bay on the coast road, James had copied a basic design which had been introduced a hundred years earlier into his homeland, by the mother of Mary Queen of Scots.

The lines of the fort are those of a French Renaissance chateaux, with small pepper pot like corner turrets, dormer windows and walls five feet thick.

The castle intended to act as a place of defence combined with a home, used to be called 'O'Halloran's' due to M'Henry's novel of the same name, though the hero of the story was purely fictional.

For some 200 years the Shaws occupied the castle, despite the rebellion of 1641 when it suffered a seige, and a threatened massacre in 1689. By the 18th century the then John Shaw and his wife adopted a nephew Henry Shaw, born in 1760, as heir to the estates, but this was strongly resented by a brother-in-law who had been coveting the inheritance for himself. A legal battle ensued and Henry finally died in 1799 suffering from 'a broken heart and an empty pocket'.

His son realising the amount of outstanding debts sold the estate to a neighbour, James Agnew of Kilwaughter Castle, in 1820. Over a hundred years later the Hastings Hotel Group opened the building as a 24 bedroom hotel.

First reports of a ghost in the old building, commenced shortly after the death of a Mrs Nixon of County Fermanagh in the 18th century.

The squire of the period, Henry Shaw, had married a daughter of Sir John Hamilton of Donemana. Two sisters of Mrs Shaw, both childless widows, came to live with them and because of the large Shaw family, it became necessary to build additional accommodation for them and their servants.

This was completed as the west wing with the two buildings being connected by a passage. The new construction became known as 'Madame Nixon's room' but this later became separated and was used as a dwelling house by one of the tenant farmers.

Much of Mrs Nixon's time was spent in the castle and when she died in its precincts her apparition in a silken grey dress, was seen walking the passages at night 'amusing itself by knocking at the doors of the different rooms'.

Although she is no longer seen in the hotel, numerous guests have heard footsteps walking the upstairs corridors and have been puzzled by hearing loud knocks on their bedroom doors for when opened immediately only an empty passageway is revealed.

Crom Castle

Enniskillen, Co. Fermanagh, Northern Ireland
Private property, please respect

Although not the general type of ghost and in a private estate, the 'White Light of Crom' is so well attested that it is felt unwise to omit mention of this unusual apparition, if it can be classed as such.

The historic castle, seat of the Earl of Erne, is situated in a huge estate in the valley of the Upper Lough Erne. The peculiar light is seen rolling over the lake but only days before momentous events affecting the country occur. It was certainly seen in 1939 and in 1971 and, reports suggest, as far back as the 19th century.

This 'warning glow of a large round ball of white light' is believed to have been caused by a family spell, though it has been witnessed by numerous strangers.

Drumbeg

Co. Down, Northern Ireland
Open to the public
On A1
1 mile from Belfast station

In the last few years numerous reports have been made of a mysterious 'ball of light' having been seen 'rolling over the graves' in the churchyard of the small parish church here. Although similar in appearance to the 'White Light of Crom Castle', it seems to have no purpose and is believed to be associated with another more recognisable ghost which has been witnessed gliding slowly along the top of Upper Dunmurry Lane.

This apparition, last seen in the 1970's is that of an old woman dressed in peasant's clothes with a shawl over her head. She appears to be carrying a small child in her arms.

The actual site of her hauntings is what was the coach road to Dublin and one much frequented by highwaymen. Several of these 'knights of the road' on being caught were hanged practically on the spot and the old beggar woman is thought to be the widow of one of these criminals who on realising the desperate state of her own future, killed her child and committed suicide.

Ecclesville

Fintona, Co. Tyrone, Northern Ireland
Private property, please respect

Built in 1610 on the site of an old Abbey, this private house has been the home of the Browne-Lecky family for many generations and has been haunted for nearly as long.

Although unseen, the ghost known affectionately as 'Aunt Hessey' makes her presence heard by the gentle rustling of her silken gown as she moves through the drawing room at even-tide.

One of the latest recorded incidents in the house was in 1962 when a visitor heard the distinct sounds of a piano being played in one of the downstairs rooms. Intrigued by the music he opened the door only to find the room completely empty of any furniture and the sounds of the music faded away.

Lambeg

Co. Antrim, Northern Ireland
Open to the public
On A1
8 miles from Belfast station

Practically part of the town of Lisburn and on the border of County Down lies the small village of Lambeg, which like its larger neighbour suffered severely in the terrorist compaign of 1971-3. One of the victims of the bombings was the interesting old Lambeg House which was completely destroyed in 1972.

It seems however that the internal war has had little effect on the apparition for it has been witnessed since the demolition of the house.

The ghost is that of a nun seen fairly regularly in the evenings, gliding along the road from the site of Lambeg House, to the entrance gate of the local graveyard a few yards away.

The burial ground of the Church of Ireland is a really ancient one, originally being part of a large monastery which was destroyed, it is thought, in the 18th century. The nun was connected with the monastery and has been seen so often in the past few years that a portion of the churchyard is called 'The Nun's Garden'.

Springhill

Moneymore, Co. Londonderry, Northern Ireland
Open to the public during normal hours
On T8/A29
12 miles from Dungannon station

One of the National Trust properties this 17th century house is renowned for its magnificent oak staircase and the interesting examples of early furniture and paintings. But it also houses the ghost of a lady sorrowing, it is said, for her children who died in the house.

It is not known exactly when Springhill was built, but in the marriage articles drawn up in 1680 between Miss Anne Upton of Upton Castle and William Conyngham, son of Colonel William Conyngham, a strong supporter of Cromwell, it was necessary to 'build a convenient house of lime and stone two stories high' for the bride. William supported the Protestant cause and commanded a locally raised regiment which he used to dispute King James II's forces claim to enter Derry. Later he became a member of King William's Council of Six.

Will Conyngham died in 1721 and was replaced at Springhill by his nephew, George Butle Conyngham, who died 44 years later in 1765. His son, William, who had served in the Seven Years War as Colonel of the Black Horse, a regiment officered largely by Irishmen, retired on his father's death and returned to Springhill where he was created Deputy Governor of County Londonderry and later elected as MP for Dundalk.

Local legend has it that the ghost is that of a Mrs Henrietta Hamilton whose three children died of smallpox in the house during the Seven Years War, but there is no mention of a lady of this name in the official history. It is known, however, that in 1775, 12 years after the war, William the MP married a Mrs Jean Hamilton, a widow of a John Hamilton of Castlefin who had at least one daughter, Jane, by her first marriage. George Lenox Conyngham, a nephew of the MP, married Jane then Olivia Irvine of Castle Irvine. Thus William could have become uncle to his stepdaughter if he had been alive at the time.

It all becomes somewhat confusing because of the fondness for the name of William. By 1816 another step-child, that of Jane Hamilton and also named William, succeeded to Springhill and and in 1856 William Fitzwilliam had become the owner only to pass it to his son, William Arbuthnot in 1906.

The apparition, whoever she is, has frequently been heard by visitors walking about the landing half way up the stairs and Mr Butler, the warden, has also heard the sound of firm footsteps when the building has been completely empty in 'broad daylight'. It seems that in the earlier part of the century she was seen 'walking the stairs in a pitiful fashion wringing her hands in sorrow', but perhaps her grief has dissipated somewhat over the years. If the ghost is that of Jean Hamilton, who may also have been named Henrietta, it suggests that her second marriage failed to recompense for the loss of her children.

A relative of Will Conyngham, Lady Conyngham and owner of Balnagown Castle near Ballchraggan in Ross and Cromarty, finds that the ghost haunting her home, 'a grey lady with copper-gold hair and green eyes' is 'very gentle and friendly'. It is perhaps unusual to find two branches of the same family both connected with haunted properties.

Northumberland

A county of varied beauty

Open to the public during normal hours or by appointment   5

Historic buildings, museums, ruins   1
Inns, hotels   1
Open spaces, roads   3

Phenomena
Noises   1
Moving objects   1

Apparitions
Females   2
Monks   1
Males   2
Others   1

Alwinton

Northumberland
Open to the public during normal hours
Off B6341
30 miles from Hexham station

This tiny village is one of many which is practically cuddled by the Cheviot Hills. It can be found at the junction of the rivers Coquet and Alwin and is only about a mile and a half from the site of an old castle.

Few tourists reach this spot for 'it's too much off the map', but it is a popular area for hill walkers and a few archaeologists anxious to examine the Roman road which lies four miles to the south.

Within a 10 mile radius one finds a hoard of unusual names.

Bloodybush Edge, Beefstand Hill, Blindburn, Smitter and an ancient site called Wutty Bell's cairn. Whether any of these are connected with the ghost of Alwinton is not known, but the area of Bloodybush Edge has ominous connections surely and the cairn, although situated over 1,000ft up, is probably that of an old tomb.

The village of Holystone is only 4 miles down the road and with a name like that some religious remains cannot be far away.

The phantom seen on the moors surrounding the village has been witnessed for some years and in 1965 the *Newcastle Journal* reported yet another sighting. 'The figure is of a 6ft tall man walking slowly and rather heavily. It travels about 30 yards and then just fades away.'

Other witnesses who have been nearer to the figure have stated it is that of a cowled monk, and in 1967 a team of psychic researchers carried out an investigation into the appearances but without much success.

Buckton

Northumberland
Open to the public
Off A1
12 miles from Berwick on Tweed station

Running parallel with the main trunk road is the country lane linking the village of Buckton with Fenwick and Detchant. Near Buckton a group of trees is well known for its ghost of a figure in a dark cloak which walks around for some minutes before vanishing.

The most popular explanation is that the phantom is not that of a real highwayman, but is of the daughter of Sir John Cochrane. It seems that in 1685 he was sentenced to death for supporting the Duke of Argyll and his daughter, Grizelle, decided on a bold attempt to stop the execution.

She disguised herself as a 'gentleman of the road' and held up the mail coach carrying the death warrant. She was successful in her scheme, for this action caused sufficient delay to enable Sir John's friends to arrange a pardon for him and his eventual release.

But those few intense moments of waiting for the coach to arrive and the anguish and worry as to the success of her campaign must have impinged themselves on the mind of the girl. The life of her father was in her hands.

The spinney is still called 'Grizzy's Clump' in remembrance of the incident.

Craster Tower*

Craster, Alnwick, Northumberland
Open to the public by appointment only
Off B1399
6 miles from Alnmouth station

An inexplicable mystery surrounds Craster Tower, the former home of Sir John Craster. 'It is supposed to have been built about 1290', he tells me, 'but the modern part dates from 1730'.

The tower, only about 65ft high and 36ft square, holds three rooms and in his own book, *North Country Squire* (Oriel Press), Sir John described the incident that occurred there which puzzles him and everyone else who knows the story.

One autumn morning he came down before breakfast and the maid asked him to go to the dining room 'before she moved anything'. He writes of 'two big and heavy china vases, on each side of the mantlepiece, that on the left as one faced it was broken in half, with the upper part lying horizontally where it had stood, and the other half unbroken in the fender. Behind the fire-screen was an uneven shaped heap of soot.

'The nearest inside window seat was a good five yards distant and there was not a scrap of soot between this and the heap in the fender; and yet, on the window-seat was the perfect outline of a naked human foot in soot, and just the one foot at that.'

This was not the only incident in the tower, but was the only one of its type. Other phenomena heard by both Sir John and his wife when in the front library have been 'strange bangings and things coming from the wall dividing the front from the back libraries'.

The noises are certainly not made by rodents and, having become accustomed to them, the Crasters merely accept them as 'one more unsolved mystery'.

The best known phantom of the Tower is that of the grey lady who has been witnessed by dozens of people over the years. James Wentworth Day in *A Ghost Hunter's Game Book* (Muller) tells of when his young daughter in August 1955 enquired about the woman who 'opened the front door, came upstairs and went into the drawing room'. James himself heard and saw nothing, but 'a presence was definitely there'.

Fairly recently Sir John's sister heard a coach and horses come to the front door and stop. Although the night was perfectly clear and the drive was brilliantly lit by the moon, nothing was to be seen. Yet, after a few minutes, the invisible carriage was heard to move again and drive round to the stables at the back of the house.

The lady is more often heard by the sound of her rustling skirts, but according to one witness 'she comes in by the first floor front

221

landing window, moves slowly towards the pele tower and then vanishes'.

Craster is on a small road running along the edge of the coast and is only two miles from Dunstanburgh Castle, open to the public and owned by the Department of the Environment.

Holy Island*

Northumberland
Open to the public
Across the sands from Beal (Off A1)
10 miles from Berwick-upon-Tweed station

Lindisfarne Castle, the priory and the whole of the surrounding area from the mainland to the small island reek of ancient history. The beach is where the Vikings landed in 793 and many relics of their 'invasion' have been found here.

The monastery founded in the 7th century was destroyed by the Scandinavians, but the Normans re-created it as a priory. Giving some indication of the spine-chilling reputation that the Vikings held, were their names; Eric Bloodaxe, Ivor the Boneless were two of the terrors who ravaged the coast.

The ruins of the priory are now owned by the Department of the Environment and the castle, built from the Priory stones in 1549 as protection against Scottish raids, is administered by the National Trust. For 300 years it was in ruins, but was renovated for habitation by the designer of London's cenotaph, Sir Edwin Lutyens, and still retains the atmosphere conducive to ghost stories.

Walking across the sands to the ancient rocks on which the impressive castle and priory stand can easily fill one's mind with mental pictures of the terror-stricken monks rushing across the beach with their valuables pursued by the bearded men of the North. Swords flashing, battle axes swinging and the cries of victory as the Norsemen capture a monk or kill a fleeing abbot. Most of the treasure from the priory was, in fact, saved but at the cost of many lives.

It is the ghost of only one of the victims who can occasionally be seen drifting rapidly over the narrow causeway to the hopeful security of the mainland. Most witnesses admit that they had little previous knowledge of the historical associations of the area and are surprised to learn that the apparition of the grey clad figure they had seen could well be that of a man who watched the landing of the Vikings. A Worthing couple on holiday in 1962 told me that they thought the monk was real until he just faded into the sand. Some claim that the phantom has been seen in the area of the

222

priory itself. Other stories suggest that the ancient castle too has its permanent reminders of the past in the shape of a Cromwellian soldier.

Lord Crewe Arms

Blanchland, Northumberland
Open to the public during normal hours
Off B6278
23 miles from Newcastle-on-Tyne station

Although the village here was planned only in the 18th century, it must be one of the most attractive in the county and remains completely unspoilt. The cottages were built on, or in some cases just follow the foundation lines of, monastic buildings founded in the 12th century by White Canons.

To ensure that the advent of tourism will not change the atmosphere a modern car park restricts vehicles to an area outside the Blanchland Abbey environs.

On the dissolution the monastic property was sold and the Abbot's guest house and kitchen became a manor house and eventually the Lord Crewe Arms. The remaining monastery buildings clustering around the courtyard were naturally adapted to private houses.

The ghost of the hotel, excellently detailed in Jack Hallam's *Haunted Inns of England* (Wolfe), is understood to be that of Dorothy Forster.

Another phantom accepted by most villagers is that of a ginger-haired monk, one of the victims of a Scottish raid when all the inhabitants of the Abbey were murdered. But a local vicar was not happy at the attentions of the spectre and requested a transfer to another post.

The identity of the hotel's phantom is rather confusing for there are two Dorothy Forsters, one the sister of Tom Forster who plotted the 1715 rebellion, and the other an aunt who married the Bishop of Durham. She was 21 years old when her husband, Lord Crewe, was 79.

Visitors wishing to see the haunted area have to pass through a huge doorway at the top of stone stairs. The massive door itself was found recently to be the original inn sign and it was only after careful cleaning that Lord Crewe's coat of arms was revealed.

One of the many people who have experienced the haunting was Hazel Jones of Ontario who wrote of her stay in the hotel in the December of 1968 issue of *In Britain* published by the British Travel Association. Not only was she conscious of a 'presence in the bedroom', but felt a 'thump at the bottom of the bed' which she described as if 'a heavy cat had silently leapt up and tramped across our feet a few times looking for a place to settle, then decided to jump off'.

One morning shortly afterwards a chambermaid, having completed the tidying up in the affected room, turned round to check she had dealt with everything and was astonished to see that the neat fresh linen on the bed had been pulled apart and was 'now heaped in disarray'. But she had been alone in the room.

Nottinghamshire

Associated with the legendary Robin Hood

Open to the public during normal hours or by appointment	3
Private houses	1
Historic buildings, museums, ruins	1
Inns, hotels	1
Private houses, offices, factories	2
Phenomena	
Noises	1
Moving objects	1
Apparitions	
Males	4

AA Headquarters*

Fanum House, Derby Road, Nottingham, Nottinghamshire
Open to the public during normal hours
On A52
Nearest station—Nottingham

Some motorists see apparitions on roads, others in car parks, so it is rather comforting for drivers to know that the Automobile Association itself has a ghost. They can expect a sympathetic hearing when describing their experience with a spectre during their travels.

The ghost not only affects the headquarters building but also the adjoining store owned by a fruit machine supplier who, a year ago, asked for advice of his neighbour as to what to do to prevent more damage to his 'one-armed bandits'. These units weight between 3 and 4 hundredweight each and yet on a couple of occasions, when opening the store in the morning, he had found them 'tossed around like cardboard boxes'.

Although some 2,000 to 3,000 motorists a week visit the offices in the summer the AA apparition has only been seen twice, once by Ken Glasby, a shift worker, at 1 o'clock in the morning. He thought that the figure standing at the door was a client who had broken down and called for aid, but as soon as he asked the man how he could help, the spectre 'just vanished'. Ken, disturbed at the experience, immediately checked the front door and confirmed it was locked.

Mr Cobley, the office supervisor, told me that incidents had been reported over some ten years. Definite footsteps on the first floor are heard by all the 16 night staff which, he pointed out, are in various age groups from 30 to 60. In 1971 an ambulance driver was so puzzled at the crashing sounds from the upstairs canteen that, despite the timidity of his colleagues, he dashed into the room only to find it empty and nothing moved.

The building was constructed in 1958 on what had been the local council refuse dump, but a year later the area supervisor of the AA suddenly collapsed and died at his desk at 5.30pm in his new office. Coincidence—or is it this work-conscious gentleman who now haunts his previous work place?

Denewood Crescent

Clifton Estate, Nottingham, Nottinghamshire
Private property, please respect

Every year dozens of reports of haunted council houses are received, some by tenants anxious to obtain better accommodation. Other cases involve new occupiers from a completely different environment who are unused to the noises and lights of the surrounding locality.

Even more are of poltergeist phenomena which flair up to a peak and then cease as mysteriously as they started. All these categories have been omitted from this case book.

The phenomenon at Denewood Crescent, however, appears to be a completely genuine case of a haunting which Mr Hill, a bus conductor, described on BBC *Late Night Extra* in February 1968. It was also reported in *The Sun*.

The Hill family of five moved into a house in the Crescent in November 1967 and within days taps were found turned on and gas and coal fires went out for no reason. What sounded like a man singing was heard close to an internal wall.

At 2.20 one morning in February 1968 Mr Hill woke to see a

man moving towards his bedroom window. 'I thought he was a soldier from the Foreign Legion. He had some sort of peaked cap with a white cloth over his neck.' Five nights later a similar incident was witnessed at 'about the same time'. Mr Hill pointed out that he was smoking a cigarette at the time so 'there was no question of my being asleep'.

But the 'soldier' was to be seen again in a few days, this time 'in broad daylight, about nine o'clock in the morning'.

The eldest daughter, 17 year old Sandra, was also to witness the apparition. On February 5, she was alone in the house with the family's dog. 'He suddenly got up and went to the door at the bottom of the stairs and started snarling. I went to see what was wrong and saw a man going upstairs. He was wearing white trousers and a blue jacket.' But just before the upstairs door slammed shut, the figure vanished.

Local residents recall in 1955 a young 19 year old window cleaner killed himself in the front bedroom of the house when he was suffering severe depression. He had been paralysed after an accidental fall at work and a friend of his was fatally injured at the same time.

'He often sat in the garden singing', one neighbour said, 'we used to see him wearing an old blue cap with a white handkerchief hanging down from the back, to protect his neck from the sun I suppose'.

The Hills have now been rehoused.

Hippo Restaurant

Bridlesmith Gate, Nottingham, Nottinghamshire
Open to the public during normal hours
Off A609
Nearest station—Victoria (¼ mile from Nottingham station)

A new building situated on ancient foundations is always likely to be affected by the atmosphere of the previous establishment and this restaurant seems to be such a case.

The local paper, *Guardian Journal*, reported in February 1971 that staff cleaning up between 1.30 and 3am had seen bottles and glasses smashing themselves and experienced 'icy cold zones'. Mr Brian Palmer, the manager, went to lock the basement room at 1.30 and on opening the door to check 'all was well' saw a dark figure sitting at one of the tables. 'It was wearing a Quaker costume with a dark coat and a large hat. But the face was frightening. It was just an oval mist with no features.'

The daily cleaning staff have also heard footsteps when in the basement. This room was only discovered when the building was being renovated in 1969 and was, at the time, believed to have been connected with the ancient caves which honeycomb the area.

Newstead Abbey

Linby, Nottinghamshire
Open to the public during normal hours
On A60
9 miles from Nottingham station

Owned by the Corporation of Nottingham this building is but part of the original 12th century priory which had been built by Henry II. Although originally constructed as a 'peace offering' for the murder of Thomas Becket, it was converted by Sir John Byron into a home for his family in 1540. Another portion of the ancient house was destroyed when it was 'reconstructed' in Gothic style during the 19th century.

Due to Lord Byron's debts, he had to dispose of the Abbey in 1818, but it still contains many of the poet's relics, furniture and manuscripts for visitors to examine, and is admirably sited in nine acres of gardens and lakes.

Many romantic and imaginative stories are associated with this property of pale ladies and black dogs, but the only genuine phantom which is known to exist here is of Sir John Byron himself. The heavily bearded gentleman has been seen many times, usually in the afternoons, sitting in a chair in one of the corridors. Above him is his own portrait to confirm the identification.

Oxfordshire

The beauty of this county hardly ever changes

Open to the public during normal hours or by appointment	3
Private houses	1

Historic buildings, museums, ruins	2
Inns, hotels	1 1
Private houses, offices, factories /	1

Phenomena	
Noises	1
Moving objects	1

Apparitions	
Females	3
Males	2

Blandy House

Hart Street, Henley-on-Thames, Oxfordshire
Private property, please respect

Like many haunted establishments this ancient building is privately owned and is not open to the public, but the ghost is well authenticated.

Over 200 years ago Mary Blandy on realising her father's strong disapproval of her forthcoming marriage eradicated the problem by feeding him with arsenic. She was hanged for the crime at Oxford in 1752.

At the bottom of the long garden of the house is an old mulberry tree under which the ghost, not of the father but of the murderess, has often been witnessed standing silently contemplating on her foul deed. Ocassionally the shadowy figure of her lover accompanies her, but only in the late evening.

Church of St Michael and all Angels

Rycote, Oxfordshire
Open to the public during normal hours
On A1429
9 miles from Oxford station

This is in fact a domestic chapel of the 15th century with two unusual family pews, one being equipped with an organ and is in two storeys. It is one of the few chapels that is administered by the Department of the Environment.

It was originally incorporated into a large mansion, the home of Lord Williams, which was burnt out during the middle of the 18th century. It is believed that a close relative of His Lordship died in the fire which would certainly account for the haunting of the chapel in the last few years by 'The Grey Lady'.

She has been witnessed by several visitors and by the custodian in 1970. Apparently she glides from one of the pews towards an old doorway and disappears through a stone wall. Presumably this spot was where in olden days she walked through into the adjoining house.

Minster Lovell Hall

Minster Lovell, Oxfordshire
Open to the public by appointment only
On A40
5 miles from Shipton-under-Wychwood station

The ruins of this 15th century manor house, the result of partial demolition in 1750, are all that remains of the once magnificent home of the 9th Baron Lovell. Once a wealthy aristocrat he staked his money on the Yorkists in the Wars of the Roses and because of his support became a Viscount in 1483.

However, when Richard III lost the Battle of Bosworth and was defeated in another rebellious attempt in 1487, the Baron was forced into hiding in an underground room of the Manor and 'was seen no more'.

In 1708, when renovations were made to the building, workmen discovered the skeleton of a man sitting at a table with a book, paper and pen in front of him.

The Lovells built a priory on the grounds during their early years here but nothing of this remains and even the site has been lost.

It is perhaps not surprising that the ruins are haunted, only very occasionally, by a 'figure of a tall man in what looks like a cloak' but more frequently by the sounds of 'groans, footsteps and rustling of papers' that issue 'from the ground'. Witnesses assume that the sounds and the phantom are those of the Baron, either bemoaning his losses and foolishness or just 'revisiting the home of his youth'.

White Hart

High Street, Minster Lovell, Oxfordshire
Open to the public during normal hours
On A40
4 miles from Oxford station

Formerly a 15th century coaching house but now a modern pub only a few miles from the home of Witney blankets, this intriguing establishment like so many of Britain's inns, has its own ghost.

For no reason at all the apparition is called 'Rosalind' and she has been seen and her activities experienced over a period of several years. The phantom wearing a veil and apparently crying bitterly has been witnessed in the old brewery room, close to the site of an old spiral staircase leading to the loft.

Among the incidents associated with the sorrowful figure has been the tipping over of a barrel of sherry, a hand-bell being thrown to the floor and numerous glasses being 'mysteriously dropped from the shelves at the back of the bar'.

Rumour has it that the girl suffered from unrequited love and hanged herself from the staircase.

Rutland

The smallest county complete with a ghost

Open to the public during normal hours or by appointment   1

Inns, hotels   1

Phenomena
Smells   1

Apparitions   1

Bluebell Inn

Belmesthorpe, Rutland
Open to the public during normal hours
Off B1176
3 miles from Stamford station

Just within Britain's smallest county border lies this attractive little pub, which, according to tradition, is built on the site of an ancient monastry. Indicating the age of the current hostelry the site of a 30ft deep well, although now bricked up, can still be seen.

For some years the spectre of a hunchback has been seen occasionally by local residents in the area of the well. Mrs Bradbury, wife of the licensee of the Bluebell, reported to the *Lincoln, Rutland and Stamford Mercury* that she too had witnessed the ghost several times gliding towards the water source late at night before locking up.

Not only does the inn possess this hunchback, but also a smell of incense which 'pervades the house during the night', especially noticeable when there is a full moon.

Scotland

A separate nation full of romance, and rugged, beautiful scenery

Open to the public during normal hours or by appointment	13
Private houses	2
Historic buildings, museums, ruins	8
Inns, hotels	3
Private houses, offices, factories	2
Open spaces, roads	2
Phenomena	
Noises	8
Moving objects	3
Apparitions	
Females	4
Males	2
Monks	1
Others	1

Alison Hutchinson & Partners

Craigcrook Castle, Edinburgh, Midlothian, Scotland
Open to the public by appointment only
Junction of A7/A9
Nearest station—Edinburgh

This castle has been inhabited since it was constructed by William Adamson in 1545, not as a major fortress but primarily as a defence and provisioning centre in the event of Edinburgh being besieged. The builder is believed to have been the son of Bailie Adamson, a guardian of the City who was killed at the battle of Pinkie in 1547.

Various owners have altered the building through the years, even though in 1719 John Strachan, clerk of the Signet, left the property to charity. The resultant trust, originally known as the 'Craigcrook Mortification' still handles the testator's wishes.

In 1815 the castle became the summer residence of Lord Jeffrey who not only carried out some alterations and modifications to the structure, but also reconstructed some of the older parts. One of the most personal reminders of this senator of the College of Justice is his small library in the round tower. The ghost of the castle is believed to be Lord Jeffrey though some think it could well be one of his contemporary visitors such as John Player, Thomas Carlyle or even Sir Walter Scott.

The castle is now occupied by a partnership of architects, engineers and planning consultants who have followed the general pattern by renovating and extending the premises, but also restoring a considerable portion of this interesting old building.

Some of the most recent reports of the haunting here were made in 1969 when Mr Charles Cameron, an accountant who stayed two nights in the castle, heard footsteps just outside Lord Jeffrey's library. The noises were accompanied by a slight shuffling 'as if cloth or a heavy object was being dragged across the floor'.

It is in the library that 'an intense feeling of cold' was also experienced and the doorbell had been heard to ring on more than one occasion though no one was in the grounds at the time.

In June of the following year poltergeist activity started. Paper clips and pins struck office girls and one of them was hit and cut by a 2in screw which 'came from nowhere'. Most librarians are 'down to earth' characters and Ronald Adamson, like so many, was a professed sceptic until a paper clip hit his desk. 'I was looking for it,' he told the *Daily Record* 'when something shot straight up past my face from the desk. How could anyone engineer that?'

How indeed?

Bedlay Castle*

Chryston, Glasgow, Lanarkshire, Scotland
Open to the public during normal hours
Junction of A81/A727
Nearest station—Glasgow

Here is the ideal combination for the ghost hunter—an old Scottish castle complete with bats, a fine collection of antiques, and a phantom.

Captain Alex McAdam, proprietor of the thriving antique business, moved into Bedlay Castle in 1969 with his wife and two young daughters, unaware at the time that the ancient walls contained not only bats and wrens but also the ghost of 'a big man'.

He tells me that he personally is not enthusiastic about ghosts, but it was shortly after the family arrived that both the children stated that they had seen a ghostie and his wife felt something un-seen touch her hair. Perculiar noises like footsteps have also occásionally been heard.

Bedlay itself is really ancient. The walls date back to 1175, the date it was built as the country manor house for the Bishop of Glasgow. Captain McAdam says that a new manor and chapel was built at Lochwood, at the Bishops Loch, in 1350, for Bishop Cameron died in suspicious circumstances about that time in a lake that once existed at Bedlay.

This led to the abandonment of Bedlay for ecclesiastical pur-poses, but obviously the Bishop remained for in Hugh Mac-Donald's *Rambles Round Glasgow* published about 1880, 'a good account of the ghost of Bedlay' is contained in a chapter describing Chryston. The haunting about that time was so acute that a local minister was 'called in to exorcise it', but from recent experience it seems that years have softened the effects and the Bishop Cameron merely 'pounds the floors'.

Benalder Cottage

Inverness, Scotland
Open to the public during normal hours
20 miles from A9(T)
12 miles from Corrour station

Twelve miles from the nearest inhabited dwelling in this craggy but beautiful land of deep vales, lochs and forests and the en-chanting Pass of Drumochter, one can find this wee cottage on the shore of Loch Ericht. Not far away a small natural cave, called after Prince Charlie, reminds the rare visitor of the route taken by 'the Young Pretender' in his retreat north.

During 1972 Sydney Scroggie achieved 'Nationwide' fame through two interviews on BBC television. The reason is that this highly popular mountain climber is blind. But he is also one of the hill walkers who has had personal experience of the ghost of Benalder Cottage.

The hut itself is merely a three-roomed building of which there are many in the mountainous areas, although normally of one room, erected as temporary shelters for the mountaineers and hunters. Legend claims that a butler with a shooting party hanged himself here in the Victorian days of high society. But such legends are associated with practically every bothy in the Highlands.

Early in 1970, Sydney with Dennis Fagan, a theatre technician friend, spent a night in the cottage—empty except for an army bed and an old wicker chair. Both men stretched out on the floor in their sleeping bags, idly watched the candles throwing a flickering glow over the dusty walls and heard the blazing wood crackling in the fireplace.

Although it was pitch black and bitterly cold outside, the atmosphere in the cottage was snug and cosy. But then the scratching started. 'It sounded like someone with long nails scrabbling at the door', said Sydney. After a few minutes there was the sound of the clump of heavy boots on the bare boards pacing up and down the floor of the adjoining room.

The regular footsteps continued for some time and then suddenly stopped, leaving the atmosphere pregnant with fear, at least for Denny. Before his companion had time to suggest an investigation, shuffling, bumping and grinding noises of heavy furniture being moved was heard by both men.

This continued for a further short period only to stop and develop into a longer session of very human groans, 'deep and loud'.

There was no explanation. The room was empty and anyone entering it would have had to pass both men lying on the floor.

Minutes later a fellow walker entered through the front door and was more than puzzled to hear their comments. Knowing they were there, he had walked up over the hill to join them but had heard nothing. 'In fact, if it were not for the smoke from the chimney and the candle-light, I would have thought the place was empty, it was so quiet.'

But more was to come. Standing upright on the mantlepiece with other food stocks was an unopened box of cheese biscuits and whilst the two men watched speechless, it 'sailed across the room' finishing its journey on the floor against the far wall. The contents were not even cracked.

In 1971 Sydney paid another visit to the haunted bothy with Angus Carmichael, a minister's son, and no sooner had they closed the door when it burst open as if 'someone had charged at it' and a loud bump was heard on the floor 'like a package being dropped'.

It seems that the mysterious resident of 'the wee hut' will be continuing his activities for many years yet.

Cape Wrath

Sutherland, Scotland
Open to the public during normal hours
Off A838
50 miles (approx) from Lairg station

Should this extreme north-west point of Scotland perhaps be re-named Cape Wraith, for such a figure has been seen many times outside a ruined cottage near the lighthouse by locals from Sheigra and Durness.

The figure is that of a tall man 'about 6ft 6in in height' wearing a three-cornered hat, knee-length boots, and 'a long dark coloured coat'.

Although the cape is isolated, the nearest town is about 12 miles away, it holds a fascination for the occasional hiker or tourist. Two such holiday-makers were Miss Smith of Kingston and Miss Styring of Sheffield who are among the most recent witnesses of the 'auld sea captain' in 1967.

They had been looking out to sea through field-glasses and saw the man standing on the beach by the wall of the cottage. By the time they had started to walk towards the building he had vanished, and it was only when they made enquiries about the owner of the cottage that they learned of the 'ghostie' of an 18th century seaman who's ship had been wrecked on the vicious rocks over 150 years ago.

Careston Castle*

Careston, Near Brechin, Angus, Scotland
Open to the public by appointment only
Off A94
10 miles from Montrose station

In June 1965 this castle, overlooking the South Esk, was opened to the public for charity and in a room two storeys under the room reputed to be haunted by 'Jock Barefoot' one young lady heard the sound of footsteps coming up and down the stairs.

Colonel Campbell Adamson, the owner of the attractive old building, told me that Honor Erle, the artist and niece of Somerset Maugham, after one night's stay refused to sleep there again. 'Apparently she had a ghastly (ghostly) night.'

A similar experience was suffered by a Mr Johnson who felt the ghost of Jock moving over him, though Colonel Adamson offers the suggestion that the feeling was caused by a nightmare.

Further historical details of Jock Barefoot will be found in Warden's *Angus* and Jervase's *Laude of the Lindseys*, but as for the ghost, only personal experience will provide the answers.

Crathes Castle

Near Banchory, Kincardineshire, Scotland
Open to the public during normal hours
On A93
18 miles from Aberdeen station

Stated to be one of the finest examples of early Jacobean castles in Scotland, Crathes dates from late 1553 and, thankfully for visitors and tourists, is in the care of the National Trust for Scotland.

Built in the typical baronial style, it has a magnificent hall with a carved granite fireplace and some superb painted ceilings.

For many years The Green Lady's Room had a reputation of being haunted and one still hears of visitors seeing the wraith of a poor young woman, whose skeleton was found when a modernisation scheme was carried out at the castle. Accompanying the bones of the ghost were the remains of a very young child and it is this that is believed to be the reason for the double murder.

Some time late in the 17th or early 18th centuries, the owner's daughter disgraced her family name by becoming pregnant by a local ghillie. The scandal of this degrading situation could not be withheld except by the disappearance of the girl and her child and the immediate dismissal of the father.

It was only about 150 years later that the truth was discovered by the finding of the pitiful remains, but it seems to have had little effect on the appearance of the 'Lady in Green'. She has been witnessed so many times that it has become accepted that she will continue to haunt for some years yet.

Duntrune Castle*

Lochgilphead, Argyllshire, Scotland
Open to the public by appointment only
On B8025
18 miles from Oban station

Close to the end of the Crinan Canal and slightly north of the lighthouse one can see this excellent example of a 12th century Scottish baronial castle. Built on to solid granite foundations it faces out over the waters of Loch Crinan and beyond to the Sound of Jura on the west coast of Scotland.

Set in the most glorious landscapes of Argyllshire, the fortress stands proudly and even loftily on a small peak in its own huge estate of woodland. Originally it was a lonely fortress guarding the rich mainland from marauders, but in the 16th century a dwelling house was incorporated into its massive stone walls.

Up to 1729 it was the seat of the Campbells of Duntrune but their neighbour, Malcolm of Poltalloch, bought it when the trustees of the last owner offered it to the market.

For such an ancient structure it is unusual that there is so little recorded history: no one has any knowledge of who built it or exactly when it was constructed, but one of the few details known is linked with the ghost that continues to haunt the ancient fort.

In the 17th century Ulster Macdonnel Coll Ciotach, known as 'The Left-handed One', landed in Kintyre and marched north with his forces ravaging the people and property as he went. Intent on destroying everything and everyone associated with the Campbells, he finally reached Duntrune Castle and, in an effort to establish the strength of its defences, sent his piper in as a spy.

The piper gained admittance but was locked in one of the turrets under suspicion. Realising that he had to communicate with his chief somehow to warn him of the impregnable state of the fortress and the strong defences of the Campbells he decided that he would use his pipes to signal to the Ulsterman.

Looking through the window of his cell he saw Coll Ciotach's ship approaching and immediately began to play the pibroch 'The Piper's Warning to his Master'. The action was successful for the ship turned about, sailing back to the Emerald Isle. But the piper must have known he had committed suicide.

The Campbells realised what he had done and cut off his fingers and finally killed him.

For many years the sound of the pibroch haunted the castle and in the 1910's, when some alterations were being carried out to improve the facilities, a fingerless skeleton was found hidden in the old walls.

The tenant at the time, an Episcopal clergyman, was asked to give the remains a Christian burial and to 'lay the spirit'. This rite he carried out and the ghost was thought to have been excorcised, but in 1972 the current owner, Colonel G I Malcolm of Poltalloch, told me that certain evidences of his spirit are still to be seen and heard. 'Strange knockings on doors when nobody is without, pictures falling for no reason' and on one occasion several heavy pewter objects were thrown to the floor by unseen hands.

One reason for continuing his activities is believed by Colonel Malcolm to be due to the fact that the piper was probably a Macdonell or a Macdonald and therefore more than likely to be a member of the Catholic faith. Being buried in the wrong church has, it seems, disturbed the piper's peace of mind.

239

A Former Youth Hostel

Kirkmichael, Perthshire, Scotland
Private property, please respect

Between Blairgowrie and Pitlochry on the Moulin Moor Road a building that strongly resembles a Victorian church manse and which was until a few years ago a Youth Hostel has no visible or noisy ghost as such but an 'area of terror'.

The two-storey house stands a few yards from the main village and suffers from 'a rather gloomy atmosphere even on sunny days'.

In 1970 Mr A Reid, a senior marketing assistant for an internationally known oil company, was with a friend on a touring holiday in the area. Leaving his companion in the house he went to a local farm for milk and, on his return, found his friend standing outside the house obviously in a state of mild shock.

'It transpired that whilst in a bedroom (upstairs, left hand corner front)', he tells me, 'the nape of his neck became extremely cold, his hair seemed to rise and he was overcome by a feeling of abject terror in a matter of seconds . . . Immediately he left the house he was all right and had no more experiences of this nature during the next couple of days, but he was never inside the building on his own and the bedroom was shared dormitory fashion'.

Mr Reid goes on: 'I continued my tour landing eventually at Aviemore. When I was there I got into conversation with a couple of older teenagers from Aberdeen and we talked of the places we had visited. One of them mentioned Kirkmichael and stated he would never go back there. Making no mention of my friend's experience I enquired as to the reason'.

The day prior to meeting with Mr Reid he had visited a bedroom on the same floor of the same building and had experienced the identical feeling of terror, although in a different room. So frightened was he that despite the lateness of the hour and after a hard day's cycling he left immediately and travelled a further 30 miles to the next Hostel.

The area of Kirkmichael is well known for its strong connections with the Covenanters, having witnessed wholesale murder, burning and pillaging of property on at least two occasions during the uprising of the 1700's.

A tank farm of Mobil's Refinery at Coryton, Essex. The ghost of a former worker has been seen walking the road beside the tanks.

The Brocket Arms, Ayot St Lawrence, Hertfordshire. A monk in a brown habit has been seen here quite recently.

The haunted bedroom of Boys Hall, Willesborough, Kent.
A strange story of love, murder and suicide is attached
to this house.

Elvey Farm, Pluckley, Kent. The site of one of the hauntings
in the most haunted village in Britain.

Hall i' th' wood, Bolton, Lancs., where a phantom cavalier runs up a staircase at Christmas-time.

Glamis Castle*

Glamis, Angus, Scotland
Open to the public during normal hours
On A94/9928
9 miles from Dundee station

A picturesque 'fairy' castle with a grim past and a horrible phantom is a reasonable description of one of Scotland's most famous castles. Long celebrated for the legend of the 'dread secret' disclosed only to the heir and his agent, the fortress is claimed to be the oldest inhabited castle in the country but the owner of Duntrune in Argyll challenges this.

Regardless of the claim it is certainly very ancient, though the present appearance is due to considerable re-modelling in the 17th century which gives it a 'French chateau look'.

Although the ghostly spectre which is believed to inhabit a secret room hidden in the massive 15ft thick walls has not been experienced, if ever, for many years, other ghosts have been witnessed and heard on a few occasions within the last two decades.

In 1951 I had the pleasure of being invited to meet a resident of the castle and of having the opportunity of hearing her personal experiences. The strange utter silence of the huge building, standing as it was at that time wreathed in evening mists, created a feeling not of terror but certainly of sinister awe, and I had the unusual feeling of being continually watched by something not of this world. It was probably imagination.

The lady, Mrs Hunter, told me that she had worked and lived there for some years during which time she and her husband had both heard the strange, terrific and inexplicable crashes that are heard on occasions coming from the oldest part of the building. They are always heard at 4am.

A friend of hers has also heard sounds of men stamping and swearing coming from an empty locked room near the top of the western tower.

But as to actually seeing something, 'well', she said, 'I've seen the figure of the Grey Lady in the chapel. I was in there only a fortnight ago, intending to arrange some flowers, and there she was kneeling at one of the pews. We've got quite used to all the happenings here though'.

Unfortunately no one knows who she is or why she always haunts the chapel, but most certainly she must be one of the most frequently witnessed ghosts of the Castle. The Dowager Countess Granville saw her one afternoon, the late Lord Strathmore saw her fairly recently and James Wentworth Day writes 'I walked into the chapel one day to examine a picture and turned round to see the Grey Lady on her knees praying. I just tiptoed away.'

Mrs Hunter, when out in the grounds one evening with her husband and some friends, saw the white face of a woman peering from a window half way up the old tower. Her companions were distressed at the appearance of the woman who 'looked so ill' and even more so when the Hunters tried to ignore it. They had to explain it was merely another apparition of Glamis and a second later, 'we all heard horrible shrieks' and the face vanished. 'I wish we knew who it was', my informant said as she offered me a cup of tea and some delicious scottish pancakes.

Offering strength to the belief of a hideous monster as being the 'Secret of the Castle', a monster born to one of the original owners, is a portrait hung in the drawing room. It depicts the first Earl of Strathmore, his two young sons and an indescribably ugly deformed dwarf.

Hermitage Castle

Near Newcastleton, Roxburghshire, Scotland
Open to the public during normal hours
Off A7
55 miles from Carlisle station

One of the loneliest fortresses in the country, this squat 13th century castle is situated in the bleak, stark moorland some 12 miles north of Langholm in Dumfrieshire. It is even described by the custodians, the Department of the Environment, who have administered it since 1930, as 'a gaunt forbidding solitary ruin amid eerie surroundings'. Despite its age and its desolate site, there is practically no damage to the walls or main structure and one visitor commented, 'it's weird'.

It was built as a Border castle and in 1300 was ordered to be repaired at a cost of £20. The first owners were the de Bolbeck's, then the de Soulis took control, but only for a short time, and it changed hands repeatedly until about 1540. Sir Alexander Ramsey was starved to death in its prison in the north-east tower in 1342. The site is described as 'a frightful pit or dungeon, apparently lightless, airless and devoid of sanitation'. In October 1566 when the Earl of Bothwell was recovering here from wounds gained in a fight, his lover, Queen Mary, rode over from Jedburgh to visit him. The 50 mile journey there and back was accomplished in a single day; an achievement in those days. Later, the Earl was to murder the Queen's husband, Lord Darnley, and marry her.

The castle when the home of Lord Soulis, an enthusiastic black magician, was used by him for numerous horrible deeds. Local belief is that among the horrors he perpetrated was the ghastly murder of young children obtained from nearby farms. The babes were kept in a 'secret dungeon', possibly where Sir Alexander Ramsey died, until required for some foul ceremoney.

Eventually, parents and relatives joined together in an outraged mob, stormed the castle and attacked Soulis. He was captured, bound in iron chains and a 'blanket of lead' and boiled to death. A justifiable end for an atrocious killer.

Farm workers and the very occasional evening traveller have reported that sounds of horrifying and blood-curdling screams have been heard coming from within the ancient walls. For the sceptic who might suggest 'foxes', might I suggest that country-men should be able to distinguish the sounds of animals from those of tortured children.

Inverawe House*

Taynuilt, Argyllshire, Scotland
Private property, please respect

Situated in the magnificent scenery of the Pass of Brander in the rugged solitude of Argyllshire and overlooked only by the 3700 ft high Ben Cruachan, Inverawe House is seen basically as a typical Scottish manor house. Currently owned by Mrs Campbell-Preston who moved there in 1967, Inverawe House boasts one of the well attested ghosts of the country.

The Campbells have been associated with Inverawe for some 400 years and in a history of the family, privately published in 1951, the author writes: 'On the assumption that the first Inverawe was a son of Sir Neil of Lochow who died before 1316 and had married the sister of King Robert Bruce . . . this family would be the oldest branch of Argyll still to hold the name of Campbell'.

An amusing incident relating to the family occurred during the last war when the German radio included the locally known song 'Cruachan Beann' in a programme of Irish music. The answer given by the local residents was to immediately organise the Cruachan Spitfire Fund.

Over many years the ghost of a woman was seen in the Ticonderoga room but who she was no one was able to say, though she was known as 'Green Jean'. Some local workers believe she was the Maid of Collard, but as the historian says 'there appears to be no reliable evidence to support this belief'.

About 30 years ago the captain of Dunstaffnage described his experience. When putting up a fishing rod he glanced upwards at the top of the rod and to his astonishment saw 'a girl in a green dress walking along the gallery that overlooked the hall. The girl had beautiful fair hair and looked to be about 16 years of age.

Having reached the end of the passage, she passed into what is known as the Ticonderoga room and was not seen again'.

The captain also tells of how in 1912, on the night before new owners moved in, loud screams were heard coming from the empty room. The disturbance was believed to have been caused by 'Green Jean' finding the room stripped of all accustomed furnishings.

Robert Ross saw the apparition when driving sheep along the Inverawe road and he was surprised to see the animals stop 'to let her pass through their ranks'. Both he and his wife also experienced Jean's door opening activities.

An earlier ghost associated with the hall in the 18th century was that of Duncan Campbell's murdered foster brother who was seen about 1755. Duncan died near Glasgow in 1760 after receiving wounds in the attack on Ticonderoga in 1758. It was this battle that is commemorated in the name of the haunted room.

Jean has been quiet for some years now but at least one guest has felt her presence in the affected bedroom—in fact she 'turned him over in bed'. This was in August 1967. The legend concerned with the ghost is that it only appears to bona fide Campbells—the guest was one.

Mrs Campbell-Preston tells me that although neither she nor her son-in-law, Alastair Campbell, have experienced anything her 10 year old grandson 'senses things in this house'.

Moncreiffe Arms Hotel

Moncreiffe Hill, Bridge of Earn, Perthshire, Scotland
Open to the public during normal hours
On A90 (T)
4 miles from Perth station

This establishment would probably be an ideal centre from which to explore the delights of the surrounding countryside, rich in historical associations. The Roman fort at Abernathy, the attractive angling village of Blairgowrie, the romantic castle of Blair and the Fair City of Perth itself—all offer themselves within easy reach of this interesting coaching inn.

The pub also has a fairly long history of haunting and one of the regular visitors here for many years has experienced unusual and 'strange noises upstairs'. The Young family took over during the latter half of 1970 and tried to ignore the inexplicable sounds of footsteps and crying which emanated from one of the upper corridors.

However, what must be considered as one of the most peculiar incidents in the following year occurred in the bathroom. Mr Young, wishing to use the room, went upstairs and attempted to open the door but found it locked and heard the sound of splashing water. Nothing unusual about someone having a bath, but five minutes later the licensee found the door open and both the bath and all the towels completely dry and cold.

No one had been near the room for about a quarter of an hour.

Muchalls Castle

Stonehaven, Kincardineshire, Scotland
Open to the public during normal hours
Off A92
Nearest station—Stonehaven

Built by Burnetts of Leys in 1619 Muchalls Castle is said to be haunted by two ghosts and although neither have actually been witnessed by the owners, Mr Simpson tells me that one weekend he and a friend experienced an inexplicable 'frigid atmosphere' in the withdrawing room.

'The chill struck right to our bones,' he said, and yet previously he had always found the atmosphere particularly pleasant and has never found 'the room again as it was that night'.

The story of the haunting is connected with an alleged underground passage from the castle to the 'gin' store. This provided a quick getaway to the sea and was later used for 'a bit of smuggling on the side'. A daughter of the house had a boyfriend on one of the ships and, having sighted the vessel, went down the tunnel to meet her lover. He would be rowing in to the entrance, for the passage opens out into a tidal cave.

Unfortunately, the girl was drowned and it is her phantom known as 'The green lady' that is believed to appear in the withdrawing room, now an upstairs dining room.

About 1906 during Lord Robertson's tenancy the most memorable incident was provided by a guest staying the weekend at the castle.

He arrived late and because 'the dressing bell had sounded' was advised to hurry. 'On my way downstairs to the drawing room', he said later, 'I passed a bedroom door which was slightly ajar'. He glanced in and saw 'a girl in a yellow frock titivating in front of the mirror, so I realised I was not the last to arrive'.

The gentleman was 'unmoved' on reaching the drawing room where the others were apparently waiting to start their dinner, and explained he was not the last. He was astounded to learn, however, that the lady he described did not exist and that she must be the phantom of the castle.

St Andrews Cathedral

St Andrews, Fifeshire, Scotland
Open to the public during normal hours
Junction of A915/A918
6 miles from Leuchars Junction station

Although known more as the Mecca of the Royal and Ancient Game of golf, St Andrews is also the Canterbury of Scotland, even though its massive 12th century cathedral has been a ruin since the Reformation. On part of the huge site is the ruined church and tower of St Regulus (or St Rule's) dating from about 1127. Little of the church remains except toothings on the east face and the tower, 108ft high. It has been heightened at least twice.

In 1948 a visitor from Edinburgh walked up the narrow winding stairs of the tower to see for himself the magnificent panoramic view of country and sea offered from the summit.

About half way up there is a particularly dark area and he found himself slipping on the worn steps and clinging to the hand-rail for dear life.

'As I approached the next small slit window in the stonework,' he said in his report, 'I suddenly became aware of someone standing above me on the twisting staircase. He was wearing what looked like a cassock of some dark material with a girdle round his waist. 'It's all right', he said in a low pitched pleasant voice, 'you can hold on to me if you like'. 'Thank you', I replied, 'but I can manage myself'.

The figure moved to one side as the visitor passed and within a minute he had reached the top. It was when he was standing admiring the glorious view that he realised he had felt nothing when brushing past the monk-like figure on the stairs, and on returning to the ground asked the custodian if anyone had come out since his entrace.

The answer confirmed that he had not only seen but spoken to the ghostly Monk of St Rule's.

Over 250 years ago the monk had been 'foully murdered in the tower' by a jealous rival. Although his appearance has been limited to the time of the full moon, he has always been noted for his pleasant, friendly and helpful manner at any hour of the day or night.

Sandwood Bay

Sutherlandshire, Scotland
On A838
50 miles from Lairg station

Only some ten miles south of Cape Wrath, the northernmost point of west Scotland, is the quiet and peaceful Sandwood Bay. For many years local legend has given the spot a reputation of being haunted by a ghost sailor and most residents of Durness are willing to tell the occasional visitor about the 'wee bay and its ghostie'.

One popular story is that told by a shepherd who lives on a small farm at Keoldale—where the ferry to Cape Wrath starts—of an English lady who, after taking a small piece of wood from an old wreck protruding from the sands, regularly saw an old fashioned sailor pacing up and down across the road from her home. Conscience caused her to return the wood and the ghost never reappeared.

In 1969 a party of ten hikers visited the bay without having heard of the reputation of the spot. There are no houses within a mile of the bay which can only be reached on foot over a track which ends at communal peat beds.

After leaving the track, the route leads through high sand dunes which hide the bay itself from view of the walker. One of the party, more anxious than the rest to 'look at the sea', shouted from the top of one of the dunes that there was someone on the sand already. When the rest of the party reached the bay—a small crescent of about half a mile with flat sand of some 200 yards wide—it was deserted. The figure of 'an old sailor' had vanished.

Once on the flat the party strolled over to the wreck of the old wooden ship, almost completely buried in sand but just above normal high water mark. One of the group spotted a set of bare footprints coming out of the sea, up to the wreck and returning to the water. The surface of the sand surrounding the marks was 'firm and undisturbed'. It could have been possible for someone in a boat or a skin-diver to have stepped ashore to create the prints, but who was the old sailor who vanished without trace?

Shropshire

Wild moors of the Welsh border area

Open to the public during normal hours or by appointment   2

Historic buildings, museums, ruins   1
Inns, hotels   1

Phenomena
Noises   1
Moving objects   1

Apparitions
Males   1

Lilleshall Abbey

Near Newport, Shropshire
Open to the public during normal hours
On A518
10 miles from Wellington station

Administered by the Department of the Environment these impressive ruins are of a house founded in 1148 for Arroasian canons. A magnificent survival of 12th century decoration is the south door from the church to the cloister, but the main quarters are to be found to the east and south of the court.

Some visitors to the Abbey have been alarmed by unusual noises heard during early evenings. Many claim that they resemble the moans and shrieks of 'someone being tortured'. Offered as evidence of a foul deed committed here in ancient days is a dark brown stain to be seen on two stone slabs of one of the floors.

Swan Hotel

Watling Street, Dawley, Shropshire
Open to the public during normal hours
On A442
3 miles from Oakengates station

Standing on the site of an old coaching inn beside Watling Street
this centuries old pub, although completely rebuilt a few years ago,
is still haunted with 'a nice ghost with a real sense of humour'.
Affectionately called 'Humphrey' by the landlord, Jerry Jolliffe,
he is held responsible for moving pictures and making the dog
bark.

The cook at the Swan, Mrs Peggy Sawyer, however is one of the
people who has seen the ghost. He was walking along one of the
landings, wearing a long dark coat and trousers that resembled
untanned leather. Several times footsteps of the ghost have been
heard walking beside one of the bedrooms.

It is believed that the apparition is that of a traveller who was
murdered and robbed in the old building over 150 years ago.

Somerset

Home of King Arthur's Camelot?

Open to the public during normal hours or by appointment	7
Private houses	1
Historic buildings, museums, ruins	1
Shops, stores	2
Inns, hotels	2
Private houses, offices, factories	1
Open spaces, roads	2
Phenomena	
Noises	3
Moving objects	1
Apparitions	
Females	2
Monks	1
Males	3
Others	1

Cashman's D.I.Y. Store*

52 Temple Street, Keynsham, Somerset
Open to the public during normal hours
On A4 (5 miles SW of Bristol)
Nearest station—Keynsham

In this 150 year old building, now a compehensive store for the 'do-it-yourself' enthusiast, several members of the staff, including the manager and a few customers, have over the last few years witnessed some unusual ghostly incidents. Unfortunately the staff refuse to talk about them, but one gathers that among the peculiar occurrences 'a tall thin apparition of a man in a black cloak' was seen to cross the floor just inside the entrance late at night when the premises were closed, and lights have been turned on by unseen hands.

Footsteps have also been heard walking across the floor and upstairs in empty store-rooms.

The answer to these incidents and others is believed to be connected with an earlier occupant who, it is rumoured, was either a highwayman or connected with black magic.

This case is one where exorcism failed to stop the activities of the entity, for a service of this nature was carried out in the 1960's. The ghostie was not seen or heard again until 1970 and from then on has continued his walks unabated.

Cedar Avenue

Butleigh Wootton, Somerset
Open to the public during normal hours
Off B3151
14 miles from Bridgewater station

Described by Suzanne Padfield as 'a half mile long avenue of cedar trees leading from nowhere to the ruins of Butleigh Court, a beautiful mansion now in ruins', Cedar Avenue is the third 'ghostly trousers site' in the country. Although only one is included in this book, there is a case in Surrey and a similar one in Devon.

The building of the mansion itself was cursed because, according to local legend, part of a graveyard had to be dug up to enable the foundations to be laid. The family were warned not to proceed, but despite the threat that the resultant house would fall into ruin they continued with their plans. The lonely, dilapidated structure that the locals now shun is the result.

But to the trousers seen by several different people in the area. One of the most recent occasions when they were witnessed was late at night a couple of years ago by two young men.

They were cycling home on their tandem across the open moor when, in the moonlight, they saw 'an odd shape in the road' moving slowly in front of them.

On drawing level, to their horror and fright, they found it to be a pair of mens' brown trousers and boots 'marching with deliberate intent the way they were going'. The witnesses took off.

The fact that this was most certainly not an isolated incident merely confirms the need for further investigation into the case.

Court Hotel*

Chilcompton, Somerset
Open to the public during normal hours
On B3139
8 miles from Frome station

A country house hotel of the 17th century is nearly always a pleasant place to stay in when one is on a touring holiday, or at any other time for that matter. This one is as comfortable as most and although the owners had moved in only a few months earlier when I visited there in 1971, I was made very welcome and the food was quite enjoyable.

The site is a peaceful one though in its earlier years it must have been one of mental torture for originally it was the Court House of the infamous 'Hanging' Judge Jeffreys. There is little here to remind the visitor of the anguish that must have pervaded the area in past years, except a massive oak tree in the garden and the now sealed doorway through which 'His Honour' used to walk to carry out his judgement.

Both are objects of interest to the ghost-hunter for the apparition of the judge has been seen to walk through the closed door after standing for some minutes, no doubt considering his next case, beneath the spreading branches of the oak.

Several visitors I was told, had seen the spectre and on occasions the sound of the 'front' door opening had been heard by the proprietors.

Forde Abbey*

Near Chard, Somerset
Open to the public during normal hours
Off B3167
7 miles from Axminster station

Administered by trustees of a former relative of mine, Forde Abbey is situated in 15 acres of gardens and lakes on the border line of Somerset and Dorset and is only three miles from Devon. It was founded in 1138 by Cistercian monks and a lot of the 12th century work can still be seen with that of Thomas Chard, the Abbot who in 1500 constructed the Great Hall and tower.

It was not long after these additions were completed that it became the home of Sir Edmund Prideaux, the Attorney General for Thomas Cromwell. In 1680 the Duke of Monmouth was accommodated here whilst gathering support for his rebellion.

When I visited my cousin, Mr G D Roper, owner of the Abbey in the early days of the war, I found the massive hall one of the most impressive rooms I had ever seen, but was appalled to learn that the quarterly window cleaning account totalled over £200.

The apparition, seen only by a few people, is that of a monk coming from the monks' walk who may well be associated with the argument that took place here in the 13th century.

The unorthodox Abbot at the time was William of Crewkerne who, because of his encroaching on the rights of his Abbey, excommunicated the Bishop of Exeter. In retaliation the Bishop excommunicated the Abbot. The quarrel was satisfactorily concluded in 1277, but it was the Bishop who won the day.

Grey House

Batheaston, Near Bath, Somerset
Private property, please respect

One of the larger houses in this small village, the Grey House, is the former home of an old lady who, a keen and ardent horticulturist herself, was 'unable to abide the damned old men who called themselves gardeners'. For years she tended and nurtured her own plot, weeding here, pruning there and was not loathe to 'doing a bit of hefty digging at times'.

Time came for her to join her forefathers and the jobbing gardeners in the area breathed with relief. The lady in purple had gone to rest and one of her favourite dresses, a deep mauve, which was found weeks after her death was 'disposed of'.

Shortly after the war a recently 'demobbed' soldier returned to the village and asked the owner of the Grey House whether there were any odd gardening jobs he could do. He was lucky and was asked to deal with some weeds on a particular plot at the side of the house.

Minutes after starting work he saw the figure of a 'tall, well built woman, wearing a purple dress' coming towards him waving her arms 'apparently in anger'. Although no sound came from her, he assumed she was annoyed and left. Hours later he returned and was only then told of the attitude of the previous owner who had died before he was born.

Most of the other gardeners employed at the Grey House have experienced the same visitation over the years, but 'far less frequently of late'. It is possible that, as one local suggested, the 'old lady in purple' has come to accept that the gardening must be done, even though by someone else.

New Road

Taunton, Somerset
Open to the public
On A38
Nearest station—Taunton

There are only about ten actual reports recorded of witnesses to the haunting of the A38 over the last five years, but there are probably many more motorists who have been so disturbed at hitting a pedestrian that vanished that they have been reluctant to talk about the incident.

On the west side of Taunton the road veers south to Wellington and Exeter passing through the tiny village of Rumwell, and it is here that the apparition of a middle-aged man has been seen standing nearly in the centre of the road. He wears a long grey overcoat and his head is bowed down.

Mrs Swithenbank of North Street, Taunton, was one of the drivers who was returning home from the west one evening in August 1970 when she suddenly spotted the figure standing motionless in the path of her speeding car. She swerved, 'practically into the ditch', braked and stopped. On getting out of her vehicle to tell the man exactly what she thought of 'stupid old characters standing in the middle of the road', there was no one to be seen.

Unfortunately, there are no records of any case of a death on this section of the A38, so who the man is remains a mystery.

Rumbling Tum Restaurant

Chilton Polden, Somerset
Open to the public during normal hours
Off A39
5 miles from Bridgewater station

Restaurants are nearly always popular if situated in an old building and this one is no exception for the construction is believed to be well over 300 years old. Though little history is known about the previous occupiers, one continues to inhabit the building for 'a shadowy figure of a tall lady in a long white dress' has been seen several times near the main fire place and in the kitchen.

Both Mrs Wilson and her nephew, who manage the restaurant have witnessed the phantom, but Mr Mancey has also described the spectre he saw as that of 'a little old man who appears to be crippled with arthritis'.

The *Bridgewater Mercury* reported in 1971 that a coach party were startled when a decorative brass plate, hanging on the wall of the dining room, suddenly hurtled across the room. Lights have frequently and inexplicably been switched off and on.

A friend of Mrs Wilson staying in the building was woken one early morning by an unseen phantom blowing on her face.

Perhaps when ordering a meal customers should ask for 'fish with no phantoms' or should one expect ghouls without goulash?

Youth Club

Peter Street, Shepton Mallet, Somerset
Open to the public by appointment only
On A371
9 miles from Castle Cary station

During September 1967 the phenomenon here which has been experienced for some years was investigated by Suzanne Padfield of the Paraphysical Laboratory.

The building itself is an old one and was previously a grammar school but had been taken over as a Club House and the basement converted into a coffee house.

Miss Padfield reported that at about 10.30pm with three members and the leader of the Club she had 'gone up to the attic room at the top of the building', for the house has only three floors including the basement, 'and went into a small room at the end and shut the door. One of the boys was telling a story when we heard footsteps coming up to the door'. One of the men opened it and 'we all looked into the open room with the light on and heard the sound of little feet, like those of a child, running across the room. Yet there was not a soul to be seen. The room was completely empty except for table tennis tables which were stacked against the wall.

The footsteps were running away from the open door.

This mysterious and rather weird incident has been heard many times. Investigators who have spent the night downstairs with all doors locked have heard the footsteps above them in the empty room.

Staffordshire

Pottery but no poltergeists

Open to the public during normal hours or by appointment	2
Private houses	1
Clubs, cinemas	1
Inns, hotels	1 1
Private houses, offices, factories	1
Phenomena	
Noises	2
Apparitions	
Males	1
Others	1

———————————————

Hills House Farm

Bloxwich, Staffordshire
Private property, please respect

A ghost in a 16th century farmhouse would not be unusual, but
what is slightly out of the ordinary here is that two or three times
a year 'loud cracking noises' are heard in a bedroom. Not just the
creaking of old timbers, but 'sharp cracks like nuts breaking', was
how Mrs Roe described the sounds.

Shuffling footsteps of 'carpet slippered feet' have also been
heard ambling round the bed, even though the room was empty.
Practically every month, always on a Sunday evening, a 'shadow
of a figure' passes the living room window.

This appearance is accompanied by the sounds of a car driving
up to the house, but the dog appears to be deaf to the arrival of this

unseen visitor: being a good guard-dog he always barks at any other car which visits the Roes.

Despite investigations into the history of the property and attempts to identify the unseen callers, nothing so far has been discovered which could account for the noises or the shadowy figure.

Tudor Bingo Hall

Longton, Staffordshire
Open to the public during normal hours
On A50
4 miles from Stoke-on-Trent station

Like many bingo halls this building was probably a cinema in its early days. What is certain though is that some years ago one of the staff fell from the top balcony late one night and broke his neck.

But like so many conscientious characters, and there are few of them left it seems, he continues to return to the building for early in 1971 the caretaker, Mr Newman, was puzzled to see a shadowy figure move across the second balcony.

On moving closer to find out what the intruder wanted, he saw a middle-aged man in dark clothes 'gliding around the front row of seats'. Mr Newman ran up the stairs to the balcony, but found the area empty.

The incident may well have been forgotten had it not been that a few days later, when with his guard dog, the caretaker witnessed the figure again on the top balcony. 'He was bending over the rail and just vanished when I called out. My dog was bristling at the time and was obviously scared. But he is a trained guard dog.'

White Hart Inn

Caldmore Green, Walsall, Staffordshire
Open to the public during normal hours
On A34/A454
Nearest station—Walsall

In the Central Library at Walsall is the mummified arm and hand of a child, but it can only be seen on request. This small relic was found with a 17th century sword in the loft of the White Hart Inn in 1870.

Thought to be connected with witchcraft, the limb is associated with the ghost of a young girl who is known to have killed herself some 150 years ago and who haunts the inn.

In 1955 an impression of a small female hand was found in the dust on a table which was stored in the attic, and a few years later a report was made of an apparition having been seen at the bedside of one of the licensees.

A relief manager told the local paper that on one occasion whilst sitting in the living room immediately below the loft he heard 'someone slowly pacing the floor of the empty attic'. The inn's dog was looking up the stairs, bristling and growling.

Members of a psychical research society spent a night in the haunted area, but although nothing was seen the atmosphere indicated the existence of something paranormal and the temperature was much colder than it should have been.

There is rather a mystery about the arm itself for it has been established that it is a hospital specimen and injected with a preservative.

Suffolk

A combination of industry and farming

Open to the public during normal hours or by appointment	2
Private houses	1
Private houses, offices, factories	1
Open spaces, roads	2
Apparitions	
Monks	1
Males	2

Abbeygate Street

Bury St Edmunds, Suffolk
Open to the public
A134/A45
Nearest station—Bury St Edmunds

The town of Bury St Edmunds is famous as the birthplace of the Magna Carta and the burial place of King Edmund who was murdered by the Danes in 870.

The belfry of the cathedral church of St James was formerly the ceremonial entrance to the Abbey, one of the richest in England. Perhaps it was partly because of the wealth that the abbots were constantly clashing with the town's folk, and during one riot in 1327 the gateway was destroyed.

Exercising their power the Abbots insisted that the people, as a punishment, should build a new Abbey gateway not far from the Norman tower and this was done in 1347. During the fight with the monks many must have been killed, but whether one such victim is the ghost that haunts at least two cellars in Abbeygate Street is not known. However, it is that of a monk.

Mr Peter Hearn, a carpenter, reported in September 1967 that he had seen the 'grey shape' in the wine vaults of a local merchant. This sighting was only six months after Mr E Walton had seen 'an apparition of a monk in brown clothes' in the cellar of his shop, practically opposite that of the wine merchant. It would probably be found that both cellars were at one time joined and connected with the now ruined Abbey.

Adding to the evidence of the haunted area a few local residents over a period of many years have witnessed the phantom of a monk, 'gliding about the gateway itself, only a few yards away'.

Birds Eye Foods

Rantscore, Lowestoft, Suffolk
Private property, please respect

What must be one of the most unghostly sites for a haunting is a factory kitchen yet when repairing an oven in the restaurant here two fitters had the un-nerving experience of seeing the spectre of a man walk across the room and vanish through a partition wall. It was July 23, 1970 and they were so scared that they refused point blank to return.

Little credence would perhaps have been given to this report had it not been for the fact that at the turn of the century a haunted pub stood on the site. The licensees of the inn, The Dutch Hoy, had often seen the ghost entering a bedroom or leaning over a balustrade next to a clothes cupboard. It would vanish immediately any move was made towards it.

But the ghost of the pub was that of a woman, 'dressed in dark clothes'. Unfortunately who she was or who the latest ghostly visitor to the site is, no one knows.

Worlingham

Near Beccles, Suffolk
Open to the public
On A146 (3 miles east of Beccles)
Nearest station—Beccles

Over the last few years several reports have been recorded of a ghostly cyclist having been seen walking beside his machine in the middle of the busy road from Lowestoft.

One of the most convincing statements was by Mr Alan Stevens of Lowestoft in April 1970. He told the local paper *(Lowestoft*

Journal) that he was returning to Lowestoft in the early hours of the morning and was on the Beccles side of Barnby. 'In the middle of the road appeared a man wheeling a bicycle. He was dressed in black knee-length breeches with white stockings.' The machine was fitted with a white mudguard and a red reflector.

The apparitions were about 60ft in front of Mr Stevens who braked hard and nearly hit his head on the windscreen, but 'before I was able to stop and tell the man to move over, he had disappeared'.

When telling friends of the incident he learnt of several others who had experienced a similar incident at the same spot.

Who the rider is no one knows, but from the description of the clothing the ghost could be dated back to the 1920's at least. One suggestion made has been that the ghost is that of a Mr Frederick Davy who owned a jewellers' shop in Howard Street, Yarmouth.

In April 1916 he and his wife had been cycling along the road between Blind Man's Gate and Barnby Church when they were hit by a car. 'He was in the middle of the road, like the apparition, and was wearing the same kind of breeches', said his son, Mr B. Davy, a retired local government officer, 'but he was killed on the opposite side of Barnby from where the ghost was seen. But he could well have travelled some yards before being seen'.

Surrey

The most haunted county in the United Kingdom?

Open to the public during normal hours or by appointment	22
Private houses	9
Clubs, cinemas	1
Historic buildings, museums, ruins	3
Churches, abbeys, rectories	1
Shops, stores	2
Inns, hotels	6
Private houses, offices, factories	11
Open spaces, roads	7
Phenomena	
Smells	1
Noises	15
Moving objects	3
Apparitions	
Females	12
Monks	1
Males	7
Dogs	1
Horses	4
Others	3

Angel Hotel

High Street, Guildford, Surrey
Open to the public during normal hours
On A3
Nearest station—Guildford

During the weekend of January 30 and 31, 1970 a Mr and Mrs G Dell stayed at this historic old hotel and it was in Room 1, a double room, that the ghost of a soldier appeared to them both.

The figure was first seen by Mr Dell in the mirror of a large wardrobe, but it took his wife several seconds to realise the appearance of an apparition. Because it was visible for several minutes, Mr Dell was able to sketch the ghost, which was visible only from the waist upwards, as a middle-aged man with a heavy moustache and a 'compelling expression' wearing an old style military uniform.

The design of the clothing was later confirmed to be that of a 'European army of the late 19th century'.

Although this was the first actual sighting of a spectre in Room 1, a previous guest reported in November 1969 that she had been intensely aware of 'a presence in the room' watching her.

A few reports of an 'unseen something' in the adjoining Room 3 had been made some years ago and during extensive alterations in 1968 a priest's hole was discovered in a room overlooking the High Street. A further intriguing object which added to the mystery was a bullet which was found in one of the old oak beams by Mr Madden of the Surrey Trust.

The building is the oldest inn in Guildford and according to tradition its foundations are of monastic origin and were once linked to the Castle, a few yards away, by an old tunnel.

Antique Shop*

High Street, Bramley, Near Guildford, Surrey
Open to the public during normal hours
On A281
2 miles from Shalford station

In one of the oldest buildings, built in the 18th century, in this small village the ghost of a young lady has often been seen by the proprietress and several customers. She appears standing in an alcove where an old doorway was blocked up many years ago.

Part of the building overhangs one of the many streams that can be found in the area. It flows under the main road and is supposed to be the one in which a young lady in her teens threw herself over a hundred years ago after a broken love affair.

She lived in the cottage which is now one of the most attractive shops in this 16th century village.

Boughton Hall*

Sendmarsh Road, Send, Near Ripley, Surrey
Private property, please respect

The Fletchers have been here in this 300 year old house only about 4 years, but have 'fairly frequently' smelt the strong odour of pipe tobacco in the ground floor rooms.

Some 15 years previously, Mr Fletcher told me, a couple visiting the house had reported seeing the phantom of 'an elderly gentleman walking from one room on the ground floor, up the stairway to the first floor' where he vanished. The current owners have seen nothing but have, as well as experiencing the 'pipe smoke', very occasionally heard 'what sounds like rather slow footsteps' near the stairs.

Brooklands*

Weybridge, Surrey
Open to the public by appointment only
Off B374
Nearest station—Weybridge

One of the best views of this famous, but now derelict, racing track is from a train as it nears the British-Aircraft Corporation's shed sited on part of the circuit. This shed, known as 'the Vatican', is one of the spots haunted by the ghost of Percy Lambert, a renowned and popular racing figure in his time.

During a record attempt in his Talbot a tyre burst throwing him and his machine towards the huge assembly works. Both the sound of his vehicle and the phantom of it, complete with Percy at the wheel, have been experienced fairly frequently on the site and not only by night workers.

One evening a few years ago a mechanic heard the sound of Lambert's car and turned round to see a misty shape of the old vehicle pass the doors of 'the Vatican'. 'There was definitely a figure at the wheel', he told me, 'wearing a skull-tight cap and goggles'. The phantom vanished after travelling about 100ft.

Although not the latest sighting, in May 1963 several workers at

264

Vickers-Armstrong (Aircraft) Ltd, stated that they too had seen the ghost, 'dressed in the helmet and leather coat after the style of a 1920 racing driver'.

Car Park

York Road, Guildford, Surrey
Open to the public during normal hours
On A3
Nearest station—Guildford

Multi-storey car parks are not the usual sites for ghosts yet shortly after completing this new facility in 1969 two workmen reported a few weeks before Christmas that they had seen the ghost of 'The Grey Lady of Guildford' standing on one of the upper levels.

The ghost, seen fairly frequently over recent years, is supposed to be that of Lorna, a 19 year old Quaker girl who died some 200 years ago. She appears as a 'tall grey-eyed girl with light auburn hair tucked under a cap, dressed in long grey robes'.

The cause of her death was due to her father discovering her with a lover of a different faith. So outraged was he that he threatened to throw his daughter out of the house. Lorna, in the heat of the argument, ran away, tripped and fell into a local chalk pit, later dying from her injuries.

Even with this terrible outcome of the affair, her father refused to allow her body to be buried in the family grave.

Guildford is well known for its associations with Quakers. What is believed to be the first property they ever purchased was in Guildford in 1673 and on the south side of North Street, within a few yards of the car park, is 'Quakers Acre' which is a small burial ground where, presumably, Lorna's family rest.

Castle Restaurant*

21 Thames Street, Sunbury-on-Thames, Surrey
Open to the public during normal hours (not Mondays)
Junction of A308/A244
Nearest station—Sunbury

In August 1971 a previous owner of this establishment, which at that time was known as the Castle House Inn, told the *Surrey Comet* that one of the rooms was kept permanently locked 'due to the ghastly feeling'. Mr and Mrs White had both 'on a number of occasions', seen a small white figure pass from their kitchen and living room and had been woken by the sound of footsteps walking up the stairs.

An earlier owner had removed a door which led to the passageway because, despite being locked and barred, every morning it was wide open. Just before the inn was sold an estate agent was examining the property one morning and 'came out of one room obviously scared at the horrible atmosphere', though he had no previous knowledge of the ghost.

The room in question was known as 'the Soldiers Room' for it was established as the sleeping quarters of a troop of Cromwell's forces. The building was constructed in 1640.

Nowadays, however, the room has the title of 'The Ladies', having been conveniently converted by David Newman, the current owner. The chef's wife told me that when it was opened up there were signs of a central fireplace in the room, used presumably by the soldiers some 300 years ago, and the old sloping floor had to be re-laid.

The ghost is that of a young girl murdered by the Roundheads during a drunken brawl and although Mrs Reupke said she had never experienced anything, 'I keep well away from the area'. Several lady customers have been considerably 'inconvenienced' and even upset by the atmosphere and the appearance of a 'pale shadowy figure of a young girl in white'.

The owner, Mr D F Newman, told me that the chef de cuisine, Mr Reupke, was on one occasion in December 1971 waiting for some visitors when he heard sounds of what he thought was his wife approaching the room. He called out but the sounds of the 'rustling of a dress' stopped. The chef turned and felt the strong presence of someone standing behind him and was conscious of a strong breeze yet there is no aperture that would account for this.

The Cedars (Museum)*

Windsor Street, Chertsey, Surrey
Open to the public during normal hours
On A317
Nearest station—Chertsey

This magnificent 18th century house, practically in the centre of the town, is believed to have been at one time an old farm-house which was considerably enlarged and altered in 1780-90. In 1970 the local council bought the property on behalf of a trust formed of local people, altered the building and opened it to the public as a museum.

The previous owner, Mrs Anns, told me that when she lived

there in 1958 the house was semi-detached. Her immediate neighbour was a Dr Hall. She lived with her husband and two children in the house for some 12 years, but it was shortly after moving in that she first heard the sound of 'a child pattering along the corridor to the bathroom'. She naturally investigated, but found no reason for the sound for her two children were fast asleep. Dr Hall, however, had often heard the noise, but was also unable to explain the sound of bare feet on linoleum, especially as the floorboards were carpeted.

In 1970, when the top floor had been converted into a flat, a council inspector visiting the property one evening mentioned the upstairs tenants to Mrs Anns and commented on the sound of children running along the corridor. By that time no youngsters lived there. Friends of Mrs Anns also felt that they were being watched when standing on the first landing.

The curator of the museum, Bob Trett, admits that he has heard nothing, but the building has a very friendly and homely atmosphere.

Chertsey Offset Printers*

Charles Street, Chertsey, Surrey
Open to the public by appointment only
Off A320
Nearest station—Chertsey

Originally a forge, built between 1814 and 1878, the works of this small litho company received considerable national publicity late in 1971 and early 1972 as a result of the unusual incidents experienced by two of the executives and the investigations carried out by the author.

During 1965, shortly after the company moved in, one of the executives, Mr Codman, decided to use a new camera recently purchased to photograph the art work for a sales brochure they were going to print. On processing the negative he was astonished to see the image not of a promotional leaflet but of an old letter heading of the previous occupiers, Hamilton and Birch, a firm of ironmongers. What was more amazing was that no such letter-heading existed in the works and, on checking on the camera, Mr Codman found he had forgotten to remove the lens-hood. What should therefore have been a blank negative showed a letter-heading, all stocks of which had been destroyed months previously.

Continuing to work in the dark-room in the evenings Mr Codman was increasingly disturbed at the impression of someone standing behind him watching intently his activities. So convinced

267

was he that he was being watched on several occasions he turned round to ask the person what they wanted.

He mentioned the incidents to no one until one evening about 6pm whilst working at the sink he was horrified to see a 3 inch magnifying glass rise vertically some 18 inches from the window ledge in front of him and return slowly to its former position. On telling Mr Avery, the works manager, of the incident he was surprised to learn that the other senior executive had also experienced phenomena.

Mr Avery, whilst in the corridor adjoining the dark-room entrance, had seen the door handle to the works move at a time, 6pm, when the works was empty. These incidents have increased in intensity until recently when the door was seen to be opened by an unseen hand on several occasions, usually about the same time.

Several workers in the company have also heard footsteps and noises of someone trying to open the door and, accepting that the place is haunted, have affectionately called the entity responsible 'Henry'.

In the adjoining property—a model kit manufacturers—Mr Vatcher, an executive, has also heard footsteps and the sound of a door opening inside the works when it is empty at night, 'always between 6 and 7pm'.

The author, during a morning in December 1971, interviewed Mr Avery and Mr Codman and was considerably impressed by their sincerity and rational outlook, but noticed in the 'haunted' dark-room a sudden unaccountable drop in the temperature at 11.25am.

It is possible that this haunt is that of a previous employee of the ironmongers as the sales counter of Hamilton and Birch was situated in what is now the dark-room.

What is certain is that the sounds and the opening of the works door continues unabated. The workers, mainly female, have come to accept the incidents and are no longer worried about 'Henry's' activities.

Chinthurst Woods*

Bramley, Near Guildford, Surrey
Open to the public
Off A281
2 miles from Shalford station

On a narrow twisting country road leading through Chinthurst Woods, from Shalford to Bramley, several people have been surprised over the years by seeing the ghost of an old gypsy woman

268

leading a decrepit brown horse down the hill into Wonersh. The couple vanish at the junction of the road by the bridge over Cranleigh Waters.

A recent incident was when in June 1971 a local BEA pilot driving his young daughter home from dancing lessons slowed down as he drew near the couple, which at the time he thought were 'normal'. He turned to the girl and said 'I wonder where they are going'. His daughter looked puzzled and replied 'It's only an old horse Daddy'. It was only then did he realise that something 'was not quite right. My daughter just could not see the gypsy and a few yards nearer home both apparitions suddenly vanished'.

There appears to be no history of any sudden deaths involving gypsies in the locality though that part of the countryside used to be a favourite spot for Romany encampments.

The George*

London Road, Chertsey, Surrey
Open to the public during normal hours
On A320
Nearest station—Chertsey

Situated close to the centre of Chertsey is this 15th century public house owned by Mr and Mrs Hobbs who, although they have not seen the ghost that inhabits the ancient and attractive property, have certainly heard it.

Mrs Hobbs was kind enough to show me round the fascinating house, pointing out where a priest's hole had been covered over, where another existed beside the fireplace and the room from which the ghostly footsteps had originated. I took a photograph inside the priest's hole adjoining the fireplace in the sitting room and was as puzzled as the owner over what appears to be a sealed window half way up the far wall. It is an inside wall, though because of so many alterations during its history it may well have been an outer wall at one time.

The new owners took over in 1968 and were interested to hear the numerous tales of the haunt and to meet the people who had seen the 'lady ghost'.

It was many months however before they began to realise their entity was still in residence, but now only apparently in the junk room.

It's a small room with a sharply angled ceiling and a window overlooking the main road, and, like many haunted rooms, it is much colder than the others in the building.

It was at the beginning of December 1971 that Mrs Hobbs last heard the footsteps crossing the floor. She immediately ran up the stairs only to find the room empty and silent with the door shut.

108 Godstone Road*

Caterham, Surrey
Private property, please respect

This typical Victorian styled house, formerly called 'Scaldshill', the name of the original field, was built in 1859 as part of a row of semi-detached properties in the slowly developing village of Caterham.

For over 50 years a Mrs Betty Sharpes lived there, 'a happy and contented old soul'. She died aged 96 in March 1957 and the property was sold to Mr and Mrs Pratt.

Shortly after moving in, Ed Pratt was surprised to see the figure of an old lady dressed in a shawl and a long dark Victorian frock standing on the upper landing at the top of the stairway. After a few seconds she slowly vanished. He made no mention of the incident to his wife who, a few days later, told him that she too had seen the figure.

Neither were at all frightened, merely assuming that Mrs Sharpes was just curious about them. She has often been seen by the couple, but it was only in 1972 that Mr Pratt's niece surprised them by asking: 'Who is the little old lady on the stairs?' It seems that she too had seen the apparition a couple of times when staying in the house a few months earlier.

One of the first things visitors experience on entering the house is the strong feeling of happiness and warm friendliness, an atmosphere obviously created not just by the current owners but also by Mrs Sharpes.

Golden Grove and St Ann's Hill*

Twynersh, Chertsey, Surrey
Open to the public during normal hours
Off A320
Nearest station—Chertsey

At one side of this attractive public house near St Ann's Hill at Twynersh, in which, I was told, the ghost of a young girl who was murdered used to be seen, lies a large pond with a small island in the middle.

The ghost of a monk has been seen here several times, walking slowly and full of melancholy round the lake. The belief is that he is the murderer of a young nun who was buried alive in the sand pits of St Ann's Hill where once stood a large convent.

A walk through the glorious woods of the public park on this hill is a peaceful and delightful experience. At the junction of two paths one can see the old spring head, partially protected by an arch of old bricks and stones, from which the occupants of the convent used to obtain their water. One of the gardeners told me he was often finding carved stones when digging among the shrubs and assumed they were originally part of the old building which has now completely vanished.

The peace of the area is occasionally disturbed by noises of pitiful moans issuing from the ground near a grass covered bank. It was here that the horrible entombment of the young woman took place some time in the 18th century.

Hayes Lane and Welcomes Road*

Kenley, Surrey
Hayes Lane: open to the public. Welcomes Road: private property, please respect
Off A22
Nearest station—Kenley

During the summer of 1966 members of the Bourne Society carried out an archaeological excavation in an effort to discover the 'lost' village at Watendone. The first mention of this village occurs in the 9th century but it slowly disintegrated under the feet of developers and encroaching weeds.

The chapel of the mediaeval village was burnt down in 1780 though the walls remained until 1808. The present Waddington adjoins what is believed to be the area of the former village and is only a few yards from the famous aerodrome of Kenley.

The 'dig' was mainly successful, revealing ancient foundations and a burial ground thought to be that of the chapel.

It is from this building, now under an estate of fifty new houses, that the ghostly nun, known as the 'Grey Lady of Kenley', is supposed to start her infrequent walks in the area.

She has been seen standing in the back garden of a pair of flint cottages in Hayes Lane, walking down the stairway in a nearby house and in the private drive-way to 'Highleas'.

A little distance away in a house in Welcomes Road, which is claimed to have been built on the old monks walk, the original altar was found and on numerous occasions the smell of candle grease and narcissus experienced in a certain room.

271

The nun is believed to have been the victim of a monk's love for sometimes she carries a bundle which resembles a baby.

She is no 'midnight marauder' for one gentleman saw her on his return from work one evening, and her appearance under a fir tree was during a summer afternoon in 1968.

Heathside Road

Woking, Surrey
Private property, please respect

In a private house in this road lived two sisters named Marshall. The house was built in 1904 and was purchased by the middle-aged couple in which to spend their last years together. Unfortunately, for some unknown reason, the elder woman became insane and was locked up in an upstairs room by her sorrowing and embarrassed sister.

Years went by and finally in 1936 they died, but the ghost of the mad sister continues to pace the floor in towering rage and has been heard as recently as 1963 murmuring and muttering to herself.

So scared were they by the inexplicable noises that at least two 'daily helps' left the household in 1962.

34 High Street*

Old Woking, Surrey
Private property, please respect

This ancient oak-beamed house owned by Munday's, a small firm of builders, has a long history of various hauntings.

Mr and Mrs Alan Munday were reading in bed at 11pm one night in 1960 when their black and white cat which had been peacefully sleeping at the bottom of the bed suddenly and without warning jumped up on all fours, arched its back with fur and tail bristling, and spat and clawed at something the couple were unable to see.

The cat continued to watch the movement of the 'unseen' walk from the door, across the floor to the bedside and apparently disappear through, or at the wall, next to where Mrs Munday was lying petrified with fear. Her husband could feel the hair at the back of his neck tingling at the frightening experience.

Several times doors have opened and closed in the house without logical explanation, and various unusual noises have been heard.

S C Johnson & Son Ltd*

Frimley Green, Near Camberley, Surrey
Private property, please respect

Two years ago one of the temporary factory cleaners employed by this furniture polish manufacturers reported that when cleaning near the mezzanine balcony late at night he saw the figure of a man, dressed in black, standing watching her. 'But the outline was a bit hazy. I said "hello", and the figure just disappeared.'

The lady concerned, Mrs Lily Heppinstall, then found that others had also seen the ghost. Mr Scott of Frimley Green said, 'I thought it was a man until it suddenly disappeared'.

The figure always appeared in the same part of the factory—on the balcony—but seems 'quite harmless. It's just watching'.

Mr Boyd, an official of the company, told me that the building is comparatively new, but it is thought that there were some old farm buildings on the site prior to its construction. It is possible that the ghostly watcher is one of the builders of the premises who is known to have died during its construction.

Lion and Lamb Cafe

West Street, Farnham, Surrey
Open to the public during normal hours
Off A31
Nearest station—Farnham

In about 1500 this attractive little building was the stables of an adjoining inn, but was converted many years ago and is now a popular restaurant.

The unknown ghost appears fairly frequently and as a 'normal customer' though clothed in an old fashioned grey dress. The staff have so mistaken her for a living person that they have offered her the menu or tried to sell her some of the goodies. Only when they look again and find that their potential 'sale' has vanished do they realise that the little old lady has been on the haunt again.

Associated with this phantom are the phenomena in 116b West Street and other flats in other parts of the building. Sounds of someone walking 'heavy footed up and down the passage' were reported in 1963, 1964 and 1965.

In yet another flat footsteps are heard going up a stairway removed over 50 years ago.

In a Queen Anne house in the same street the ghost of a black dog was seen in the 1960's and, in the same building but only on one occasion, the phantom of an old lady who appeared in a bathroom. She was wearing a nightdress—the room was previously a bedroom.

Loseley House*

Near Guildford, Surrey
Open to the public during normal hours
Off A3100
Nearest station—Guildford

One of the few historic houses of Britain that is really lived in and cared for by the owner, Loseley Park has often been used as the site for films and several television commercials. Its real fame, however, has been gained by the fact that Queen Elizabeth slept there (her bed can be seen by visitors). James I and Queen Anne also stayed within its ancient walls and the current resident is a direct descendant of the builder, Sir William More, relative of the the famous Sir Thomas More.

Within the vast rooms one can see some fascinating reminders of its former royal connections. In one corner stands an unusual table brought from Nonsuch Palace set off by panelling from the same home of Henry VIII. Fine furniture and tapestries line the walls and a unique clock, as old as the building, still keeps perfect time from its place on the wall.

One of the many other fascinating items to marvel at is a massive chimney piece carved from one lump of local chalk. It's over seven feet high and is just as wide.

The building, set in a large park, was constructed in 1561-9 partly from stones and other materials from Waverley Abbey, but of the ghost one should speak little. It has been seen several times by the owners and the occasional visitor, but, as Mr More-Molyneux told me, 'it's a family affair which I think should be treated as rather a personal matter'. Just for once, let us respect that and instead admire the home that once heard the footsteps of the Great Queen Bess.

Maldwyns Antiques*

26 High Street, Ewell ,Surrey
Open to the public during normal hours
Just off A24
Nearest station—Ewell

Situated opposite the old village gaol, thankfully preserved like many ancient buildings in Ewell, and on a corner site is Maldwyn's Antique shop. It caters not just for the hunter of objets d'art, but rather surprisingly for the enthusiastic motorist and motor cyclist.

Mr Maldwyn explained the unusual combination by saying 'customers wanting a spare part for their latest speeding acquisition will usually wander around looking at the variety of antiques and furniture I sell. It's the best of both worlds, really'.

The shop itself is crammed from floor to ceiling with thousands of motoring accessories, but the side windows and the 'yard' at the back offers considerable delight for the antique hunter. Copper kettles rub shoulders with Roman tiles, a dressing table is loaded with numerous vases and general clutter. Everywhere it seems there is chaos, but both Mr Sullivan, the manager, and Mr Maldwyn assured me they knew what stock they had.

In living memory the establishment was a corn chandlers and a bakery, but the history of the premises goes back to Henry VIII's time. A tunnel certainly exists from the ancient cellars to the site of Nonsuch Palace, about half a mile away, but the entrance was effectively sealed before 'Maldwyns' moved in twelve years ago.

For a few years up to 1969 a couple of the upstairs rooms were let out and one of the tenants reported to Mr Maldwyn that she was 'pushed aside' while coming down the narrow twisting stairway by 'something she couldn't see'.

No doubt it was a Friday, for here—unlike most theatres—the ghost really does walk between 6 and 7pm at the end of the week—most weeks, anyway. Heavy footsteps are heard upstairs crossing the floor of one front room, through a partition wall and into the back sitting room so regularly that Mr Sullivan now ignores the noises. I was told of one super-sensitive friend (he was the son of a seventh son of a seventh son) who, a few days before I visited the shop, had been so affected by the 'electric atmosphere at the junction of the two stairways he had to be helped down and was shaking with fear for hours afterwards'.

Derek Jones, a friend of mine, told me that he and his wife were also affected by the intense feeling of a presence, 'the hairs on my arms stood out and the nape of my neck must have looked like a brush'.

It is accepted locally that the ghost is of a mistress of Henry VIII for whom the building was constructed, but obviously from the strength and power of the footsteps would it not seem more logical to assume it was the King himself?

Although the owner himself refuses to accept the shop is haunted, he admits that on one occasion he was so convinced someone had entered the shop and gone upstairs he rushed into the room prepared 'to do battle'. When he reached the doorway, the sounds of footsteps stopped.

The shop is practically detached from its neighbour and, although full of ancient oak beams and the original 16th century flooring, there seems to be no logical explanation for the sounds except that offered. It's Henry VIII!

Nonsuch Park

Ewell, Surrey
Open to the public
On A24
¼ mile from Stoneleigh station

Site of Henry VIII's famous and magnificent Nonsuch Palace which was fully excavated in the 1960's is the large park passed by hundreds of London bound motorists every day. The main gateway to the park is situated on a bend on the road where a 'phantom gentleman in a cloak' is frequently seen.

Approximately four reports a year are heard of visitors seeing the lonely figure standing silently and sorrowfully behind the gates looking along the pathway towards the Palace site. One of the latest experiences was of a pair of schoolteachers from the Ewell Castle School, the swimming pool of which is built on part of the dining hall of the Palace.

One lunch time in March 1972 they had decided to take a stroll through the park and saw the figure of a tall thin man: 'He was about 5ft 10in in height', standing on the right hand side of the gate. 'He appeared to be wearing a cloak and when we were about ten feet away he vanished'.

Although no one positively knows his identity, one belief is that he is the forlorn lover of a young girl found murdered in the park in Victorian times.

Old Vicarage

Kingswood, Surrey
Private property, please respect

Early in the 1800's the vicarage of Kingswood was burgled by a pair of young thugs who after gagging the housekeeper, Martha Halliday, with her own stockings tied her up with an unusual type of string. As the vicar had been called away for the night the old sexton had offered to stay in the house with the woman, but she had proudly declined the offer.

The burglars were scared off by the return of a school master to his cottage next door, but they left Martha still gagged and bound to the kitchen chair. On returning in the morning, the vicar was appalled to find her dead—probably from shock or suffocation.

The murderers were traced through the string having been sold only from a particular shop, but they were released on the grounds of their alibi. However, some years later they were arrested in Germany for another murder and before being hanged confessed to the crime in Surrey.

Martha was buried in Kingswood churchyard which adjoined the vicarage grounds.

In 1876 the daughter of the new vicar, whilst listening to a cousin playing the piano, heard the rustle of a silk dress and on looking round across the hallway saw a tall lady in black walking down the stairs.

No one else had seen the figure, but her father admitted that he had heard the rustling several times.

In 1902 the then owners of the vicarage were constantly puzzled by seeing the figure walking about the house. There have been several other reports of a 'woman in black' being seen in the immediate locality more recently.

Old Woking Road

Woking, Surrey
Open to the public
Off A320
Nearest station—Woking

A little over a mile, as the crow flies, from the ruins of the 12th century Augustinian Newark Priory lies old Woking and Hoe Place, ancient home of a former abbot.

In 1965 a lady walking along the Old Woking Road saw a monk suddenly 'come out from the side of a house', stride across the road and 'vanish among the trees of a house opposite'. This is not the first time that the monk of Woking had been seen.

Several times the figure has been mistaken for a live member of a religious order and it is not until he vanishes that the viewers realise that they have seen the local ghost.

Some years ago a Mr Giles fell off his motor bike with fright at seeing the monk and landed up in hospital.

Belief in the locality is that the ghost is that of one of the Augustinian monks from the Priory walking to Hoe Bridge and the abbot's house a few yards further on. Quite often the vague forms of monks have been seen standing on the bridge leaning over watching the stream beneath travelling to join the River Wey.

Parish Church

Farnham, Surrey
Open to the public during normal hours
On A31
Nearest station—Farnham

Not far from the castle, built in the 12th century and owned by the Bishops of Winchester until 1927, is the haunted church of Farnham. The castle is supposed to be the home of the ghost of Bishop Morley, but little evidence for this has been forthcoming.

Witnesses to the apparitions and other peculiar phenomena in the church, however, are fairly numerous; from wartime, when an official heard chanting coming from the empty building, to the more recent experience of a woman who witnessed a High Mass being conducted there. From the description given at the time, it appears that the ceremony belonged to pre-Reformation days.

Some evening visitors, including a former curate, have seen a semi-transparent silk-like screen or veil descend from the roof cutting the altar off from the congregation listening to the sermon.

Puttenden Manor*

Near Lingfield, Surrey
Open to the public during normal hours
Off A22
2 miles from Lingfield station

The owner of this Plantagenet manor, Mr Brian Thompson, who also owns Downe Court in Kent, is a lover of ancient beauty and a devotee of restoration. When he purchased Puttenden in 1966 he aimed at completely renovating the old building and not only opening it to the public, but also living in it providing an opportunity to view practically every aspect of his family life.

He achieved his purpose with such success that the warmth and friendly welcome with which every member of the family greets visitors has become part of the delightful atmosphere of this peaceful and charming establishment.

Most of the time spent on my second visit in 1972 was with Mr Thompson sitting on the front lawn which he had been cutting, chatting about the history of the Manor, the ghosts and his forthcoming book, *A Search for Freedom*.

Puttenden has been featured in numerous television commercials, films and documentaries and must be one of the most photogenic properties that exists in Surrey.

It was built in the reign of Edward IV by Reginald Sondes in 1477 as a 'Hall house'. Eventually the Sondes achieved a title and Sir George became Earl of Feversham in 1676. The younger of his two sons by his first marriage was insanely jealous of his brother and in a fit of rage killed the heir to the title. In remembrance of the lads, the mother planted two weeping ash trees which still beautify the rear approach to the manor. A legend attached to these intertwined trees is that as long as they stand Puttenden will be a happy place.

The murder however caused a change of luck in the family and the male line died out. The 'curse' affected the new owners, the Watsons, in the same way and the splendid titles of Earls of Malton and Marquesses of Rockingham became extinct. In fact every male for 150 years died in tragic circumstances.

In 1901 the Hon Mark Napier purchased Puttenden and started on the huge task of restoration which Brian Thompson has so effectively continued. His feeling for the manor itself seems to have overpowered the evil and the general friendly atmosphere has been restored.

It is in the master bedroom, Mrs Napier's original room, that the apparition of a lady has been seen usually accompanied by a sweet smell of perfume. Mr Thompson has also felt her brush past him when in the study, where the occasional smell of pipe tobacco is also experienced. 'I am quite convinced', the owner said, 'that the old man who used to own Puttenden comes back to sit in his favourite chair and smoke a peaceful pipe'.

Some of the workmen who were employed for the specialist tasks in renovating the house, slept in the master bedroom and complained about having a 'disturbed night'. Footsteps and the sounds of rustling silk kept waking them.

Even though there are at least two ghosts here, the warm homely touch of 'the family' continues as the predominant attraction.

Riddlesdown

Kenley, Surrey
Open to the public
On A22
Nearest station—Kenley

In the late 18th century when the road from Purley into Kenley was slightly to the east of the current main A22 it was used as a route for coaches from London. One of the favourite stops was at the Rose and Crown where the old road joins the new one beside a deserted chalk quarry.

Occasionally reports are received that an old black coach, complete with four horses, has been seen travelling down what is now a pathway and vanishing just before reaching the main traffic line. The locals believe that the haunting is caused by a serious accident shortly before the new road was constructed over a hundred years ago.

Roebuck*

Richmond Hill, Richmond-on-Thames, Surrey
Open to the public during normal hours
On A205
Nearest station—Richmond

'Robbie', licensee of this ever popular pub which is only a few yards from the Star and Garter Homes facing Richmond Park, often accommodates friends in the top attic of the ancient building. 'It's about 400 years old, I believe', he told me in September 1972.

Although he and his wife and 2½ year old son Robert have been living there for some two years, it was only in 1972 that inexplicable phenomena became apparent.

Two of his regular guests, Keith and Ron, are members of the local CID and up to that time had been provided every Monday with accommodation in the small room at the top of the building overlooking the river valley.

However one night both woke at approximately 3.15 in the morning to see 'a pillar of white mist about 5ft 8in high in the middle of the bedroom'. If drifted towards the window overlooking the street and immediately the window burst open and the figure vanished. The sudden drop of temperature in the room could well have been the cold night air sweeping in, but the two policemen were convinced that the room's warmth was reduced before the window opened.

Since then both have refused to sleep in the room and are accommodated elsewhere in the pub.

Shortly before this incident, whilst Robbie was clearing up the bars one night, Ron had asked for the front door keys to 'let the customer out'. Robbie threw the keys over and asked 'What customer?' 'The man who walked through the old bar just now. He went towards the stairway', was the reply.

The barman pointed out no one had passed him working at the front end of the building, though he had seen the figure of a man at the end by the old bar. The place was searched but the unknown customer, with no way out, was never found.

Two other incidents convinced Robbie that the Roebuck has a

ghost, though it 'doesn't bother anyone'. One was in August when he heard heavy footsteps thumping across the bathroom floor. 'Again it was a Monday at about half past three in the morning', and the other was when he was in the bathroom when he heard loud bangs coming from the empty billiard room downstairs.

His wife also heard these sounds but 'prefers not to think too deeply about them'.

Mention of the 'Roe Buck' was made in 1738 when Pope had a garden there with unusual plants and trees amongst which was believed to be 'the oldest weeping willow tree in Europe'. Apparently, when he obtained the cutting he failed to recognise the variety. An even earlier reference to the pub is a painting of it in the local library which is known to have been made in 1710, thus establishing the belief that it is at least of the 17th century period. However, this doesn't help in identifying the current 20th century ghost who was better known some ten years ago. At that time the phantom would move bottles about, the 'clinking' would be heard frequently in the empty bar late at night, and two or three times a glass was found lying on its side in a pool of whisky on the bar counter.

Slines Oak Road

Warlingham, Surrey
Open to the public
On B269 (off A22)
Nearest station—Upper Warlingham

At the 'Y' junction of the B269 with Slines Oak Road, Chelsham and Warlingham, there are two small ponds. From one of these, on the south side, an ancient coach has been seen to 'rise up, all lit up, with passengers screaming at the windows'.

It was some 125 years ago that a report was made of 'a coach with its four passengers plunging into the waters after the horses had been terrified by a highwayman. The coachman and his passengers perished before assistance could be provided'.

Top Rank Bingo Hall*

Bishopsford Road, Rosehill, St Helier, Near Morden, Surrey
Open to the public during normal hours
Off A24
Nearest station—Morden (Underground)

This establishment was originally one of the many hundreds of

Gaumont cinemas opened in 1937 when film-going was gaining in popularity. Complete with Hammond organ it regularly supplied the needs of hundreds of film-fans who would often join in the community singing of the melodies provided by the talented organist.

With the advent of television the attraction of the 'flicks' waned and in an effort to retain some hold on the public by catering for another 'craze' many cinemas were converted, as was this one, to Bingo in 1960.

Prior to this no less than three deaths had been recorded in the building. A night watchman was found dead one morning, a builder was killed during the conversion work and a boiler-man fell down a flight of steps to his death.

Mr Nick Thompson, the manager of the hall, told me in March 1972 that during the previous few months the building had been completely re-wired and during the work one of the electricians working on night shift in one of the upper floors had seen the ghost of a man, 'who had also been witnessed by many others in the same locality'.

Out of the corner of his eye he saw a figure standing silently in the doorway of the room in which he was working and thinking it was his mate made some comment. On receiving no reply he turned to face the apparition which slowly vanished.

This figure of a man in grey has been seen on numerous occasions by members of the cleaning staff between six and seven in the morning. The head cleaner last saw it 'standing in the circle'. 'It always stands a few yards away from the witness, but it never suddenly vanishes, it just withdraws', Mr Thompson said.

He is interested in the history of the old building and established that some 15 years earlier numerous complaints were received from local inhabitants about the organ playing in the early hours of the morning. At that time the instrument had already been removed from the premises.

His own view is that whatever the cause of the haunting, 'it should be left alone, in peace. After all, it is causing no harm'.

Vicarage

Kingswood, Surrey
Private property, please respect

Some 40 odd years ago, just before 6.30 one Sunday evening, two young ladies returning to the new Vicarage built near the church saw the back of a tall figure standing at the gateway of the drive, a long curving path that went round the back of the house.

They thought it was the gardener, although he did not ordinarily use that entrance. When they moved nearer the ghost walked in front of them up the driveway and round the house to a large oak tree.

There is stopped, turned to face them and moved towards the girls 'with a queer loping step'. It was a tall figure in a long black cassock-like garment with a fringe of white at the bottom.

One of the youngsters felt her hair standing on end and wished she 'could poke it to see if it was solid'.

The apparition had a 'huge shock of yellowish hair' but no face. It continued its unusual stride through a little gate at the side of the driveway.

Some years later the new occupiers of the vicarage reported that they too had seen the faceless figure, but had also found the back door of the house open on several occasions, despite having been securely locked and bolted a few minutes earlier.

Unfortunately no explanation for the appearance of this frightening apparition can be offered, though one suggestion has been that it is the ghost of a leper possibly brought in to the household as an act of charity by a former vicar. Another idea is that it is of a gardener who, whilst up in the oak tree pruning some of the upper branches, accidentally fell to the ground badly disfiguring his face as he descended

William the Fourth Inn*

High Street, Ewell, Surrey
Open to the public during normal hours
Just off A24
Nearest station—Ewell

In William IV's reign this fascinating old pub was one of the many coaching inns on the road to London. But the site itself is obviously much older, for current excavations at the back of the car park reveal not only a mediaeval rubbish pit containing bones of horses and pigs but Roman coins and pottery. Unfortunately the building itself is threatened with demolition.

The ghost which is experienced on the road outside the inn is that of the sound of a coach and a team of horses. The creaking of the wheels and clattering of the hooves have been heard several times by local residents who have also reported that they have heard the coach start up and move rapidly off in the direction of London.

There seems to be some indication that it may be connected with the hauntings of Maldwyns Antiques on the other side of the road, for although not heard as frequently the sounds are usually heard on a Friday or Saturday.

Wonersh*

Near Guildford, Surrey
Private property, please respect

This small village with delightful groups of lovely ancient cottages, a 17th century inn (Grantley Arms) and a church which dates from 1050 also has an evil spirit in what was once a studio.

A professor of zoology had in the 1950's purchased the mews flat for his studies, but after only a few months was forced to vacate his home and move to Bramley.

'The feeling was really diabolical', he told me, 'it was getting so bad that I was developing suicidal tendencies. I had to get out'.

Sussex

With one of the most popular coastlines in England

Open to the public during normal hours or by appointment	5
Private houses	3

Historic buildings, museums, ruins	2
Cinemas, clubs	1
Shops, stores	1
Inns, hotels	4
Private houses, offices, factories	4
Open spaces, roads	5
Schools, universities, colleges	1

Phenomena	
Smells	1
Noises	8
Moving objects	1

Apparitions	
Females	5
Monks	1 6
Males	6
Dogs	1 1 1
Horses	1 1
Others	1

Battle Abbey

Battle, Sussex
Open to the public
On A2100
Nearest station—Hastings (5 miles)

Founded by William the Conqueror and housing the site of King Harold's murder by Norman knights, Battle Abbey is one of the most popular historic buildings in the south of England. It was constructed within yards of the site of the famous battle and offers an interesting view of the area from which visitors can visualise the whole picture of the warring troops.

Since 1719 the Abbey has been the home of the Webster family but the largest of the buildings, the Abbot's House, is currently occupied by a girls' school which naturally is not open to the public.

A popular but rather doubtful story that the ghost of Harold, complete with arrowed eye, has been seen near the spot where he was killed, now marked by a large fir tree, continues to be told. But as Harold's death was caused by the swords of knights anxious to retain their own position in William's court, it seems hardly creditable.

More acceptable was the incident which occurred one afternoon in June 1971. In the ruined Great Hall, Howard Shepherdson, a young guide, was conducting a party of visitors round the building and explaining the features to the crowd when a young boy cradled in the arms of his father suddenly enquired 'who is that man over there, Daddy, the one with the long sword?' Only the lad could see the phantom, though one or two others 'felt the presence of something'.

This was not the first occasion that a ghostly knight has been seen in the Great Hall but it has been some years since anyone has stated categorically they they have witnessed it.

Howard was convinced that the youngster could see the apparition, gazing as he had been for some seconds into a blank corner of the huge room. Up to that time the subject of ghosts had not been mentioned, thus dismissing possible sceptical comments of 'imagination'. The description given later by the boy certainly matched that of the phantom believed for some time to haunt the Hall.

One can only hope that this report will prompt others who have been reluctant up to now to divulge their experiences, to report any phenomena they may have seen in this, one of Britain's oldest buildings.

Beggars Bush

Best Beech, Near Wadhurst, Sussex
Open to the public
Off B2100
2 miles from Wadhurst station

Joining the B2100 from Wadhurst to Mark Cross, about 100 yards from the Bestbeech Hill cross-roads, a narrow lane leads back to the secondary road which joins the A266.

Early in the 1960's and occasionally since, the wraith of an old man carrying a heavy sack has been seen in a lane near this private house. He is described as wearing a long brown 'coat' and is obviously labouring pretty heftily under the weight of his load.

He comes from the front garden of the house, walks about 50ft along the road and vanishes on coming to an old gateway.

Seen only during early autumn evenings, he is believed to be the ghost of a local poacher who was shot in the early 19th century by an irate game-keeper, though some state that because the fruit is always ripe when he is witnessed there may well be a simpler explanation. An old tramp was found in the garden of the house many years ago suffering from a bad fall after 'scrumping' a few pounds of apples. He died before reaching the hospital.

Blackboys Inn*

Blackboys, Sussex
Open to the public during normal hours.
On A265
4 miles from Uckfield station

Built as a farmhouse in 1389 this large inn must be one of the most popular in the area judging by the number of cars seen outside and the number of customers who pack the bars inside.

I asked the journalist owner, Mr A Johnstone Smith, whether he had witnessed the ghost that reputedly haunts the pub. 'I'm afraid not', he admitted. 'Perhaps I'm too sceptical, but there is most certainly a "feeling" of someone around sometimes. My wife has experienced this unseen presence and a Mrs Cooke of Uckfield felt something a couple of years ago.'

The belief is that the silent phantom is of Anne, a woman who became pregnant by a cousin and died in childbirth in 1804.

Busheygate*

Battle Road, Robertsbridge, Sussex
Open by appointment only
On A21
Nearest station—Robertsbridge

Home of the author Built about 1725 as a pair of tied farm cottages on the Egerton estate, this rather attractive cottage was practically rebuilt in 1971 when the conversion was made into a single building. A rear wall built with stones from the mediaeval villa known as Glottenham Castle, the site of which is about two miles away, had to be removed and reconstructed with modern brick. The stones, however, have been retained in the garden.

Within three feet of the pair of privies in the back garden a copper powder flask was found which suggests that at some time flintlocks were used to defend the privacy of the occupier, though part of a Roman glass bottle was also found in the area.

Whilst working in the garden early in 1972 the present owner felt that he was being watched by a pair of 'old characters' standing on what had been, up to 1934, a public footpath leading across the fields to Brown's Farm. On another occasion a 'vague shape like a white dress hurriedly "flitted" past a hall window.

Three local residents have stated that the property was haunted by a 'woman in white'. Experienced by visitors, however, is the occasional smell of strong pipe tobacco which wafts around the dining room, close to the inglenook fireplace.

The building had been derelict from 1968 to 1970 and neither the owner nor any of the visitors since it has been re-occupied smoke a pipe, but the phenomenon suggests that someone there did once.

Classic Cinema*

King Street, East Grinstead, Sussex
Open to the public during normal hours
On B2110/A22
Nearest station—East Grinstead

One of the many cinemas built in the heyday of film going was the Classic sited practically in the centre of this busy Sussex town. Following the tradition of the theatre, owners and managers continue to wear immaculate formal suits complete with sparkling white shirts and bow ties. Although after the war the habit began to die out, many old style conventionalists continue to appear in 'evening dress'. One of these traditional owner managers was Mr Christopher of the Classic who died in the 1950's.

Twenty years later in February 1970 Mrs Chamberlain, an usherette in the Classic, was in the balcony one evening and during an interval felt someone pass her.

She turned to look into the body of the cinema and saw the figure of a man leaning forward over the balustrade looking down into the stalls. On walking down the stairs towards him to ask him to sit down, she noticed he was wearing a 'very dark suit with a white shirt and bow tie', but just as the usherette reached him the apparition 'vanished into thin air'.

The full description she gave later exactly fitted that of Mr Christopher whom she had never seen or heard of. Other members of the staff have also occasionally reported similar incidents of the tall man in the balcony, and sometimes in the coffee lounge looking down the centre circular stairway.

Being a conscientious executive the owner would often 'help out', even to filling the boiler with fuel at night to ensure the temperature was maintained for the following day's performance.

In January 1970 a hinge pin from the door of the huge boiler was found to have been removed and it took 'five men several hours to replace the door'. The sounds of someone filling the boiler at midnight have also been heard by cleaners and night staff, despite the fact that this job is now done in the morning.

Eridge Green*

Sussex
Open to the public
On A26
Nearest station—Eridge

Over a hundred years ago in this small hamlet a 16 year old servant girl from one of the large manors, probably in Eridge Park, used to meet her boyfriend in a barn next to the village hall.

Unfortunately the love affair ended in disaster with the young lad deserting his lover on finding her pregnant and the girl hanging herself from the beams in the loft.

Often in the ensuing years ghostly screams and despondent moans have been heard issuing from the empty building as unpleasant reminders of the incident.

Mrs Turner, now of Heathfield, was one of the villagers to have heard the cries as recently as 1969 and told me it was really most distressing. The sounds are heard just before ten in the evening.

Farm Cottages*

Salehurst, Sussex
Private property, please respect

Built on a shelf of land beside a minor country road between Bodiam and Staplecross is a terrace of three cottages, the centre one of which is haunted.

Originally built in the late 17th or early 18th century they have been considerably altered on numerous occasions. The gabling and extended front wall of the middle cottage was added in 1936 to act as a buttress against a slip towards the road, and the internal construction re-arranged before the three were re-sold early in 1972.

Above the centre gable end is a stone plaque with the letters 'ESC' embossed on its face. These are the initials of a former owner of the property and is not indicative of a local council.

The haunt here is of an old man seen standing at the entrance of a bedroom usually about 10.30 in the evening.

No horrific crimes are the cause of his appearance for the apparition is of a local farming land-owner whose land was 'stolen' by the builder of the cottages who 'chopped off' a piece of his land to construct his home some 200 years ago.

It used to be legal in the olden days to 'acquire' property by building a cottage on the verge of roads. Provided that it had been constructed in one night and four walls were up and smoke issuing from the chimney it was considered habitable and owned by the builder. Many squatters' cottages built under these old laws can still be found, for with a team of friends working hard during a long winter evening it was comparitively easy to comply with the conditions. One in the west annoyed the lord of the manor who owned the ground, but he accepted the situation and charged 2/6d (12½p) a year 'ground rent', but this was soon forgotten.

The reason for this old Sussex character continuing to inhabit the building is one merely of pure rage at losing some of his ground. He has been seen only a few times, but as recently as February 1972.

George Inn*

Battle Road, Robertsbridge, Sussex
Open to the public during normal hours
On A21
Nearest station—Robertsbridge

It is perhaps coincidence that another haunted pub in Robertsbridge, the Seven Stars, was originally known as the George and is situated practically opposite this magnificent inn. Shirley and Gordon Mannering have held the licence here for some 8 years and having 'thoroughly cleaned' up the place' and improved the lighting and heating, have turned the pub into one of the most popular eating places in the area. Their appetising cold buffet is renowned for its variety, and the sincere friendliness of the Mannerings and their staff make a visit here a welcome occasion.

One of the puzzles for Shirley, however, has been the inexplicable bumps heard in the large room over the bars. 'It sounds like someone with his legs tied together moving around the empty room', she told me in March 1973.

But many people have heard the noises which occur 'nearly always at lunch time'. The last occasion was in November 1972. The room is used for weddings and other similar functions and the belief is that the unseen entity does not agree with marriage.

The building was constructed in the 17th century and was originally an old coaching inn. Who the 'blooming bumper' is, however, no one knows.

Fletcher's House★

Lion Street, Rye, Sussex
Open to the public during normal hours
Junction of A268/A259
Nearest station—Rye

John Fletcher, dramatist and contemporary of William Shakespeare, was here in 1579. His father, the Rev Richard Fletcher, who had resided here some years was aggrieved at not being appointed vicar of Rye because of the refusal of the Rev Richard Connope to resign, despite the latter's continued absence, and left the town when John was only two years old. Richard eventually became Bishop of London.

The house had been a private house for many hundreds of years, but in 1932 it became a restaurant. Like the majority of buildings in this attractive, popular centre few alterations were made and even the original front door of the vicarage with York and Tudor Roses carved on its lintel has been retained.

At 4 o'clock one afternoon in 1951 Mrs Betty Howard, one of the current owners of the restaurant, was walking up stairs and on hearing a noise turned round and saw on the landing a few feet below a youngish man in a dark lounge suit.

Thinking it was a customer, she went to speak to him but he just disappeared. He was about 6ft tall and appeared to be in his early thirties. The figure was never seen again, but the manageress told me that 'what sounds like footsteps going up the stairs' are heard sometimes in the evenings.

Lion Hotel★

Nye Timber Lane, Nyetimber, Near Bognor, Sussex
Open to the public during normal hours
2 miles from Bognor Regis station

It is not known exactly when this old building was constructed, but it was repaired in 1407 and is believed to be on a site mentioned in the Domesday Book. It has many romantic associations, if one considers smuggling as 'romance', for it is claimed a three-quarter mile long tunnel incorporated into the foundations leads to the site of a former church and Barton Manor on the coast. This manor was often used by the 'free traders' as a headquarters and temporary cache before using the tunnel to bring in the contraband.

The pub, complete with a 'spy window' on the top floor as a safeguard against unexpected calls by the customs men, also has a rambling staircase and crazy floors, only one of which seems to be level.

Dudley Newman, the proprietor here in the 1960's, reported that the well-established ghost is more heard than seen. The sounds of rustling heavy robes and silk are far more often experienced than the witnessing of the phantom owner, a tall lady in dark robes who frequents the ground floor rooms.

One explanation offered as to her identity is that she was the mistress of one of the smugglers and was murdered as a result of 'knowing too much'. Or maybe she is still looking for the 50 kegs of brandy that are supposed to be hidden in the tunnel.

Reg Allatt, the current proprietor, in describing the layout of the building, told me that 'behind the bed in Room 5 there is a door which has been filled in and there is no information about the room behind it, whilst in Room 7 there is an entrance to another at the top of the house which has remained sealed for 40 years.'

The ghost walks through Room 5 and into Room 6, usually at approximately three or four in the morning. Reg points out that all machinery is turned off by time clocks and therefore could not account for the noises of footsteps.

He has often heard the inexplicable sounds, 'but', he admitted, 'I'm afraid I bury my head beneath the bedclothes so I don't know if there is anything to be seen'.

Michelham Priory*

Upper Dicker, Near Hailsham, Sussex
Open to the public during normal hours
On B2108, just off A22
3 miles from Hailsham station

Surrounded by a moat encompassing some six acres of land, the 13th century priory of Austin Canons currently offers visitors a unique opportunity of seeing a fascinating example of Tudor adaptation. Adjoining the parlour and buttery below the prior's room and incorporated into the Dining Hall a Tudor wing and kitchen can now be seen.

Because of the Sussex Archaeological Trust's interest in the property numerous excavations have been made, and some are still being carried out to identify the remains of a huge building in the grounds on the edge of the moat. There are many problems connected with this sort of work, however, for the water level has risen and every hole deeper than 18in immediately fills with water.

The priory itself now stands on what must be an underground lake.

There are four ghosts here that have been witnessed in recent years.

After the dissolution in 1536, Michelham and its lands passed through numerous hands until Herbert Pelham obtained it in 1587. He was responsible for restoring some of the original buildings and also added the Tudor wing; but in doing so was compelled to sell the property to Thomas Sackville, Earl of Dorset in 1601.

For some 300 years the Sackvilles let out the priory to tenant farmers and in 1897 J E A Gwynne of Folkington purchased the estate. It was this that created one of the ghosts for the 'selling over the head' of one of the tenants created such absolute rage with the farmer he threatened to kill the new owner. Nothing happened apparently, but a phantom white horse has been seen and heard riding through the arches of the gatehouse. Rupert Gwynne used this mode of transport when visiting the occupier.

During the war the army used the priory for 'D Day' conferences and an interesting reminder of those days is the pencil drawing of the English Channel to be seen in the first floor of the gatehouse.

Another ghost is that of one of the Sackville family. The curator, Mr Harrison, told me that a lady in a grey gown leading a small brown terrier approached the ticket office sited in the gatehouse and on being told by a member of the staff that dogs were not allowed, turned back along the driveway and vanished. That was about three years ago, since when she has been seen several times, always during the opening hours of 11am to 5.30pm.

The other ghosts were seen in the main ground floor Tudor room. In 1969 a couple of visitors reading an explanatory notice on one of the walls turned to relate the information with the objects and saw a man in a black cloak slowly descend from the ceiling diagonally to the floor in front of the ingle-nook fireplace and glide through the end doorway. Stunned by the sight of the apparition, they stood there for some seconds when another phantom, a lady in a Tudor gown, ran silently past them apparently in pursuit of the cloaked figure.

The woman has been seen several times since and the explanation of the 'descending man' may well be, according to Mr Harrison, that before the Tudor alterations were made a staircase existed on the site leading from the mediaeval kitchen, but the connection with the lady is unknown. The room concerned unfortunately suffered severe damage from a fire some years ago and was completely rebuilt. There was no trace of a staircase, but future excavations may confirm the theory.

Nan Tucks Lane*

Buxted, Sussex
Open to the public
Off B2102
Nearest station—Buxted

This narrow twisting lane which leads from Buxted to Blackboys is the site of a pitiful suicide and a genuine haunting, though this is so infrequently seen that the casual tourist is unlikely to witness anything, but there is always a chance.

I was travelling this curving hedge-lined route one evening in September 1971 and thinking of nothing in particular when I noticed a black shadow running along the ditch a few feet in front of my car. I slowed and the figure, indistinguishable other than being human-shaped, speeded on.

Reaching a corner, the apparition, if that is what it was, just melted into the hedgerow. There was no chance to stop or turn round for the lane is far too narrow.

The story concerning Nan is that, like many simple young girls on their own in the country in the 17th century, she was terribly shy and perhaps a little frightened of people. Because of her lack of conformity and wan looks she gained the reputation of being a witch.

Some slight incident turned the local villagers completely against her and, enraged with her actions, they pursued her through the village to the church.

Here poor little Nan, hoping for sanctuary, was mystified when the vicar, perhaps seeing the screaming mob and not wishing to risk their fury, turned her away. The crowd grabbed her and carried out the usual trial by water, ducking her shivering young body into a local pond to see if she would float.

The girl survived and in terror ran into a nearby wood like some half-crazed animal.

In the morning her cold body was found swinging gently from the bough of an oak tree. But, like some unremitting conscience, she continues to rush down the lane named after her—the site of her last journey.

There have been reports that the poor demented phantom has also been witnessed on the Hadlow Down Road.

St Michaels School*

Moat Road, East Grinstead, Sussex
Open to the public by appointment only
On A22
Nearest station—East Grinstead

In the spring of 1965 several young pupils at this Anglo-Catholic school for girls, once connected with a nearby convent, were frightened by seeing the ghost of a former occupant.

She appeared at 10.30 in the evening in a suddenly created 'aura of an evil atmosphere' on the ground floor looking silently up the stairs. According to one of the girls, she was about 5ft 4in tall with long white hair and with an 'incredibly evil face'.

The atmosphere remained for some minutes, long enough for the figure to be seen by three girls walking through the hallway, one of whom stated that she felt it brush past her.

A few days later several other girls and a member of the staff reported that they had heard footsteps pacing up and down a passage leading to the hall.

Seven Stars Inn*

Battle Road, Robertsbridge, Sussex
Open to the public during normal hours
On A21
Nearest station—Robertsbridge

This ancient building was constructed in 1380, only 30 years after the earliest music manuscript of the associated Robertsbridge Abbey was written, and about 170 years after the founding of the Abbey.

The associations of the public house with the ruins of a religious sect are varied. An entrance to one of the tunnels from the Abbey site can be found in the cellars (another arched entrance, now bricked up, is on the side of the main road about 500 yards south) and a ghost has recently been heard walking through the upstairs rooms.

One of the rooms of the pub is said to be where Charles II was kept prisoner and an unusual 70ft deep shaft from the loft to the cellars adds an intriguing mystery to this hotel.

When the Cistercian Abbey of St Mary's was moved to its present site, about ½ mile to the east, a chapel was left on the original spot which was later to be used as the foundation of the George Hotel. The local archaeological society state in their journal that it was 'built as a high class building which is extremely pleasing and obviously expensive'.

In 1567 it was the only house to be held on the demesne of the Manor and is the largest and most elaborate of the existing mediaeval buildings in the attractive village.

Over recent years the story of a haunting by 'The red Monk' has been developed, but no substantiating facts have been traced. However, during November evenings the sounds of footsteps have been clearly and definitely heard on several occasions walking through empty upstairs rooms.

So definite were they in 1969 that David Barden and another local resident went to investigate, but found no cause for the sounds.

Ruth Parkes, wife of the licensee, told me that her two large labradors had watched something unseen to her walk through her sitting room from the narrow corridor leading to the minute room where Charles II was supposed to have been kept. Adjoining this room is a small flight of vertical stairs at the top of which, in the loft, is the entrance to the mysterious shaft.

Another local resident was disturbed when trying to open the door leading to the corridor she felt that 'someone was pushing against it'. Other visitors have noticed a 'cold corner' in the bedroom and a young Canadian girl staying at the inn during 1972 mentioned seeing a figure in the corridor and 'thought it was that of a monk.'

Turkey Cock Lane*

Rye, Sussex
Open to the public
On A268
Nearest station—Rye

A tragic romance is believed to be the cause of the main ghost here. In 1379 an Augustinian Friary was built to replace an original house of 1263 which was washed away by the sea. After only a few years one of the brothers, known as 'Cantator' because of his 'divine-like singing', fell in love with Amanda, a young and beautiful girl who lived at the Dormy House. This building can still be seen behind what remains of the Friary, facing out to the desolate Romney Marsh.

However, so strong was their love for each other that the couple decided to elope, possibly across the channel, but their illicit scheme was crushed when the plan was discovered and the monk condemned to death. It seems a favourite punishment of those days was to be bricked up alive and this method was used to dispose of Brother Cantator. Before death finally quietened him, madness took control and he was heard 'gobbling like a turkey'. The incident was perpetuated in the name of the street.

His death did not end his being seen for quite recently a cowled monk was observed in the chapel garden, and some years ago reports were received of seven phantom figures gliding across the grass towards the encircling brick wall. It is thought that they were the men responsible for the cruel punishment.

Part of the gardens were converted to shelters during the war and in the course of the work several skeletons were found on part of the old foundation floor of the monastery. They were all found to be in a kneeling position.

All that remains above ground is what is known as the Monastery Hall which is used for social gatherings.

The sounds of the turkey noises have not been heard for many years, but one of the witnesses, Miss Marjorie Pillers, told me that at Easter 1952, when in a guest house adjoining Dormy House, she saw the figure of a 'monk in a brown habit' standing by the party wall of the next-door property. She was not scared, just intrigued, for it was many years later that she learnt of the history of the locality.

Winchelsea*

Sussex
Open to the public
On A259
Nearest station—Winchelsea

In September 1970 I had spent a week's holiday touring the south coast and, returning home by way of Sussex, had decided to spend a couple of nights in Rye giving me an opportunity to enjoy the old world charm of the area.

On the afternoon of the 23rd I visited the nearby town of Winchelsea, admired the ancient ruins of the Franciscan monastery and the interesting museum and was about to drive back to my hotel when I heard what sounded like a large number of horses galloping up the hill from Rye.

Because I was just on the verge of turning right into the main street, I reversed back into the road beside the ruins. The horses

297

hooves came nearer and I expected to see them come into view at any moment.

Suddenly the sound stopped and all was quiet. I moved forward slowly but there was nothing—no horses, no cows—just the peaceful road.

On my return to the hotel I mentioned the incident to the proprietress and was surprised to learn that I was merely one of many motorists who had experienced similar phenomena.

Apparently there is some connection with the sound of the unseen horses and the Weston brothers who, as gentlemen and men of honour, lived for many years in Winchelsea under assumed names.

At night they became highwaymen terrorising the area for miles around but they were eventually caught and executed in 1782.

The headless ghost of George Weston continues to be seen under a tree near the ancient ruins waiting, it seems, for the opportunity of holding up another coach.

Wyke Gardens*

Worthing, Sussex
Private property, please respect

In August 1951 whilst on business in Worthing I decided to see whether some wartime friends, the Richardsons, still ran a guest house here. Unfortunately they had left many years before, but as it was late in the evening I took advantage of the 'bed and breakfast' facilities and arranged to stay the night.

At 8am the following morning I was woken by a young lad bringing in a cup of tea. I thanked him, but finding the liquid cold and horribly sweet looked up at him to make some comment to find that he had gone.

He had appeared to be very ill with a small thin grey haggard little face and huge brown eyes like saucers accentuated by dark circles. What heightened his general appearance of misery and neglect was the bedraggled older style brown suit that hung rag-like from his shoulders.

Over the breakfast table I questioned the owners as to the identity and health of the boy. They assured me that they never provided morning tea and had no children in the house. An elderly resident guest confirmed this and told me later that he and a couple of other 'boarders' had experienced the same incident when sleeping in the front bedroom.

The proprietress of the guest house explained the half empty cup of liquid syrup by saying that it would have been my 'evening refreshment' supplied the previous day.

Unfortunately I had no time to pursue enquiries, but recalled that the Richardsons, who ran the small guest house when I first visited it during the war, told me that their 11 year old son had been killed in a car crash some five years previously.

I cannot believe, however, that the youngster I saw could have been their son. They were a friendly generous couple who would never have neglected a child to the extent that this boy had been.

It's still a mystery to me.

Wales

A land of ancient beauty riddled with mediaeval folk-lore

Open to the public during normal hours or by appointment	8
Private houses	2
Clubs, cinemas	1
Shops, stores	1
Inns, hotels	2
Private houses, offices, factories	2
Open spaces, roads	4
Phenomena	
Smells	1
Noises	5
Moving objects	2
Apparitions	
Females	1
Males	4
Horses	1
Others	2

Beach House Club*

Mumbles, Swansea, Glamorgan, Wales
Open to the public by appointment only
On A4067
6 miles from Swansea station

Late in 1967 whilst on a business trip to South Wales, I was taken by a colleague to this rather exclusive and ultra-modern clubhouse overlooking Swansea Bay. Although the main purpose was to discuss in pleasant surroundings the latest industrial developments at Port Talbot, the conversation eventually got around to the topic of psychic phenomena.

It was whilst we were chatting that the owner, Mr J Gaunt, told me that the club was genuinely haunted. Footsteps of an unseen person were often heard walking through a corridor and doors would mysteriously open and close.

Mr Gaunt assured me that the incidents had been occurring for some years and were corroborated by the previous owners.

Although no one actually knows the reason for the sounds or the doors opening, the owner had been told that a young man who stayed at the club 'some years ago' had 'either drowned himself or was drowned accidentally' near the famous Mumbles Lighthouse. Most of the locals associate the phenomena with this death.

It interested me to see that in Obtober 1967 the *Herald of Wales* reported the incidents which apparently had increased in number.

Blue Lion Inn

Cwm, Near Rhyl, Flintshire, Wales
Open to the public during normal hours
Off B5429
6 miles from Rhyl station

There are several villages in Wales with the name of Cwm, but only one I believe with a haunted pub called the Blue Lion. Like many old buildings that have witnessed a murder it has a long history of phenomena.

Locals believe, and one has no cause to doubt them, that the ghost is of a farm labourer, John Henry, who was murdered here after a fight in 1646.

Stan Hughes, the landlord in 1969, has a keen interest in small mammals and has created his own private zoo. On no less than five occasions during that year he found the cage doors open and the animals missing. No common thief could be the culprit for a layer of sand covers the floor of the menagerie and no signs of footprints or disturbance of its surface were found.

As well as several customers here, the landlord himself has seen the apparition of 'young John' in the bar on more than one occasion.

Cegin-y-Mynach

Rhrs Fynach, Rhos-on-Sea, Denbighshire, Wales
Open to the public during normal hours
Off A546
3 miles from Colwyn Bay station

Three miles from the popular sands of Colwyn Bay lies an ancient 16th century house at one time associated with a monastery. Adjoining the building is what was known up to July 1971 as the Blue Dolphin suite, a very pleasant restaurant.

The suite is still there, but it has now been re-named and opened up as a tea-room for the hundreds of tourists and trippers attracted by the nearby country and the seaside.

Miss Shaw, in charge, first realized the building was haunted when she saw the figure of 'a short man in a black suit' vanish 'into thin air. I was convinced at first that it was a customer, but when I spoke to him he just disappeared'.

Girls working in the sparkling new tea-shop have often heard the sound of footsteps walking along the passage outside the ladies' toilet which, at one time, was part of the original old building and may well have been a portion of the monastery—not as a ladies' lavatory, I hasten to add.

Clwch Dernog

Llanddensant, Carmarthenshire, Wales
Private property, please respect

Practically in the heart of the Black Mountains lies a small Welsh village called Llanddensant six miles south of Llandovery. One of the ancient houses on the outskirts has a long tradition of haunting and poltergeist activity by an unknown and unidentifiable entity.

Sometimes let out for holiday periods, it has an 'aura of mystery' and an increasing variety of phenomena.

In 1969 an occupant at the time returning from a visit to friends in the locality heard the creaking of a gate as she approached the building. There are no such luxuries in the area.

A previous temporary resident recalls that he awoke one night to see 'a pair of close-set eyes at the window' which were lit by a soft glow illuminating the face of an elderly man.

During 1972 I heard of a family of four who had stayed in the house for only two days, though they had planned to spend three weeks there. The reason for their speedy departure was due to the 'fearful atmosphere' experienced. The two children had also been

302

scared by 'the figure of an old man with piercing eyes' who had approached them in the garden but had vanished as soon as the front door had been opened by one of the parents.

There are some rumours in the village that the house was owned by 'an old warlock' in the 18th century, but no evidence of this has been forthcoming.

Farm

Abergavenny Road, Monmouthshire, Wales
Private property, please respect

Stephen Clarke, an archaeologist and writer for the *Monmouthshire Beacon*, in a series of articles reprinted in a collection under the title of *Ghosts and Legends of Monmouth and District*, tells of a phantom cow 'which haunts the fields on a farm just off the old Abergavenny road'.

He met one of the numerous witnesses of the ghost who described to him her own experience on carrying out the normal early morning duties of bringing in the herd for milking. Because the animals are often asleep they have to be woken by a slap on the rump, but several times the milkmaid has found that her hand has 'passed right through it and the cow vanished'. Several workers have experienced the same incident.

The farmhouse itself is also haunted in a number of ways. Unexplained noises have been heard in the building and lights go on and off mysteriously.

It would perhaps be interesting to find out whether the previous owner had a pet cow.

Glynne Arms

Hawarden, Flintshire, Wales
Open to the public during normal hours
Junction of A55/A550
6 miles from Chester station

Early in 1971 Mr Jakeman, the landlord here, reported that this 17th century pub is well and truly haunted. Not only has he experienced the phenomena but several customers have also heard and smelt the ghostly manifestations.

The most frequent occurrence is that of a 'peculiar smell rather like some form of perfume' that becomes noticeable in a particular area. This is probably connected with the sounds of 'light footsteps' heard walking along a landing that stop at a bedroom door which is then 'tapped' by an unseen hand.

Penalt

Monmouthshire, Wales
Open to the public
Off A466
15 miles from Chepstow station

About five miles south of the county town of Monmouth lies the tiny hamlet of Penalt and it is here, near the area known as 'The Argoed' that an apparition of a 'lady in white' is occassionally seen.

The 'semi-transparent wraith' has been witnessed at dusk gliding towards the original site of an old mill pond adjoining The Generals. Stopping for an instant, she falls forward and vanishes.

The identity of the woman is not known nor the date of her obvious suicide.

Rockfield

Abergavenny Road, Monmouth, Monmouthshire, Wales
Open to the public
On B4233
15 miles from Chepstow station

Some five miles north west of Monmouth lies the small village of Rockfield where some 125 years ago a major crash killed three people. During one pitch dark storm ridden night, with rain lashing down as if to wash the road away, a coach party was returning to Monmouth, but urging the driver to take care.

Horses though are often scared of lightning and on an unsure surface of a near flooded road must have been practically uncontrollable.

Several witnesses have stated that under similar conditions whilst travelling the same road on stormy nights, they have seen the vague shadowy form of a 'coach and four' silently swaying and careering down the road like some 'weird creature'. Reaching a sharp bend however the horses being unable to stop, shatter themselves against a wall near Ancre Hill and the disintegrating coach and screaming passengers fly over the wall to land in a field on the other side. Once the wreckage of the wooden vehicle reaches the ground, the complete apparition vanishes without trace.

Watery Lane

Monmouth, Monmouthshire, Wales
Open to the public
Junction of A40/A466
15 miles from Chepstow station

An unusual building for this part of the country is the Nelson
museum devoted to purely naval matters, yet some 15 miles from
the nearest port of Chepstow. One of the unusual sights though is
an old coach seen occasionally at dusk moving rapidly along
Watery Lane, through Bailey Pit Farm to Wonastow Court, about
three miles south-west of the main town.

Although seen more frequently years ago, no one has carried out
much investigation into the apparition perhaps because part of
the old roadway itself has become covered with grass and practically hidden from the general public.

Writing in *The Monmouthshire Beacon* Stephen Clarke also
reports on another incident in Watery Lane which, initially reported in 1948 by a young man after walking home late one night,
has been seen by a couple of other residents in the locality.

The man had just passed an old well on the roadside when he saw
the figure of a man 'seemingly leap out of the air at him'. As he
raised his hands to protect himself the figure vanished.

Despite the unnerving experience the youngster investigated
and found that before the road was constructed several pools
existed well below the current level though with high banks either
side. In one of these pools the body of a local man was found. But
whether he had accidentally fallen in and drowned or had committed suicide by jumping from the bank has never been established. From the reports, the latter sounds more feasible.

White Hill

Near Monmouth (2 miles), Monmouthshire, Wales
Open to the public
Off B4293
10 miles from Chepstow station

The wind-raked shrubland of this lonely hill mounted by an old
tower has a ghost never seen, never felt but, without question,
heard.

The sounds are those of a young baby coming from a thorn bush.
Diligent searchers, hearing the pitiful cries of a child, have often

spent much time hunting for the source but without success. Locals, however, waste no time for they know the story which is associated with the heart-rending sobs.

Although possibly inaccurate, the belief is that a gypsy stole a young child from a local farm many years ago, perhaps with the intention of claiming a ransom, but for some reason killed it and hid the body in the bush.

Warwickshire

Known as Shakespeare's county

Open to the public during normal hours or by appointment	4
Private houses	–
Inns, hotels	2
Open spaces, roads	2
Phenomena	
Noises	1
Apparitions	
Females	2
Males	1 1
Horses	1

Ettington Park Hotel

Stratford-upon-Avon, Warwickshire
Open to the public during normal hours
On A34
Nearest station—Stratford-upon-Avon

In 1963 one of the best films ever made on the subject of haunted houses was made by 20th Century Fox in this ancient building, formerly known as Ettington Court. The film entitled 'The Haunting' was based on a novel by Shirley Jackson and was re-shown on television early in 1972.

The tale was of a party of psychic researchers carrying out an invesigation into the poltergeist activity and the associated haunting by an unseen suicide. One of the highlights of the story was when a woman member of the team, who had become affected by the atmosphere and the frightening incidents, ran up an old iron spiral staircase to the room where the suicide occurred.

All ended happily however, but what was not realised when the film was being made was that the house itself has a long history of hauntings.

Ettington, mentioned in the Domesday Book as Eatendone, is the original ancestral home of the Shirley family, claimed to be England's oldest family. The present building with 40 bedrooms stands in 40 acres of magnificent country, and has its own private chapel and old coach house which, up to recent times, housed the family coach. The chapel is accessible only through a concealed door of the dining room and there is another 'secret door' leading from the library to the ballroom. It is the third manor house to occupy the site: the original was Saxon, the second Tudor which was practically rebuilt in the 18th and 19th centuries.

Philip, the youngest member, is 34th in male descent from Sewallis, a Saxon who held the manor of Ettington at the time of the Norman conquest. He and his parents now live in Kildare, having rented the property as a hotel.

The site of the haunt is the cloister-like terrace beside the main arched entrance.

Several times a figure of a lady in a long white dress has been seen through the decorative wrought iron panels gliding along the corridor over the tiled floor, in which is inscribed the family motto 'Loyal je suis'. Her appearance is always at dusk.

Although her identity is unknown, she is believed to be associated with a family crime committed over 200 years ago which caused the illustration of a 'bloody hand' to be incorporated into one of the heraldic crests of the Shirleys.

Other incidents reported have been locked doors of servants bedrooms in the turret rooms being opened and closed by unseen hands.

Harrow Hill

Longcompton, Warwickshire
Open to the public
Off A34
5 miles from Moreton-in-the-Marsh station

Situated practically in the centre of an area once strongly associated with witchcraft (Whichford and Great Rollright are only a couple of miles away) is the village of Longcompton.

This spot is one where an occasional report is made of a phantom coach and horses. The driver and the six steeds, all headless, are seen at dusk travelling at an uncontrollable speed down the hill. The incident no doubt recalls a fatal accident in the 17th or 18th century when perhaps the horses bolted or the brakes of the vehicle failed, probably in foul weather.

The apparition is only seen in the winter months during or just after a heavy rainstorm.

Jack and Jill Inn

Newland Road, Lillington, Warwickshire
Open to the public during normal hours
On B4453
2 miles from Leamington Spa station

Mr Graham Boulton some years ago was the licensee here and often used to sit on the 'roof garden' over the patio accompanied by his dog during warm summer evenings. Eventually he died and, although not forgotten, memory of him faded until 1971 when the current landlord, a Mr Watson, was gazing out of his bedroom window one 'still and humid June evening' and suddenly saw a figure of a man standing on the patio roof.

'It looked just like the reflection of a television picture on glass', he said, 'but the window was open at the time'. The description of the apparition certainly seemed to fit that of the former licensee. Among the duties of publicans is to examine the cellars and pumping gear from the barrels, and it is not unreasonable therefore to assume that a phantom of Mr Boulton might sometimes be seen there. It was only a few weeks after the first appearance that a barmaid, checking on the bottles in the cellar, was frightened at seeing what sounds like Graham's ghost moving silently around the barrels.

What scared the young lady even more was that the shape of the containers could be seen through the apparition. She left shortly afterwards.

Mr Watson, a 'student of psychic research', believes that one cause for the haunting could be that his predecessor was inadvertently buried under a wrong name.

Warley Abbey Grounds

Warley Park, Abbey Road, Smethwick, Near Birmingham,
Warwickshire
Open to the public during normal hours
On A457
Nearest station—Smethwick West

Demolished in 1968 Warley Abbey itself had rather a vague history though the popular belief is that it dated back to 1308 when it was known as Wernlegh or Wernleigh. It was held on a 'kitchen tenure' payment to the King's kitchen by supplying pheasants and wooden platters.

It was certainly linked with the history of Hales Owen. One idea is that it was built in the 18th century by Sir Hubert Gatton, a prominent Catholic who used materials of the original manor house together with stones from a nearly ruined farm worked by Hales Owen Abbey.

In 1905 the area was purchased for use as a public park and the building itself served as a restaurant, offices, and later a golf clubhouse. The responsibility for the existing grounds is that of the Warley County Borough who have laid it out as a public open space with grass and flower beds.

Evidence of a subterranean passage was found some years ago, but no indications of the identity of the ghost that haunts the grounds at twilight.

She is known as 'The Grey lady of Warley' and is thought to be the phantom of a murdered heiress of the castle. Occasionally visitors walking through the grounds in the evening have reported seeing her glide over where the old Abbey once stood and vanish half way along a path.

Westmorland

For magnificent lakes and mountain scenery

Open to the public during normal hours and by appointment	1
Private houses	1
Apparitions	
Females	2
Dogs	1

Levens Hall*

Near Kendal, Westmorland
Open to the public during normal hours
On A6
5 miles from Kendal station

Probably the most complete example of a Tudor house in the north-west of England, Levens Hall is virtually a treasure house. Every room is panelled with decorative ceilings and some of the musical instruments displayed are unique. For example, Mr Robin Bagot, the present owner, often plays a harpsichord which he made himself. So perfect is it that both the BBC and ITV have borrowed it for some of their television programmes.

One of the main attractions of Levens Hall, however, is the fabulous gardens that were originally laid out between 1689 and 1705 and were designed by Monsieur Guillaume Beaumont who was renowned for this type of work. Unfortunately all his garden designs, including that for James II at Bagshot have disappeared except for traces at Forde Abbey in Dorset.

The current owners revere the memory not only of the originator of the gardens but also that of succeeding gardeners and list all of them in their attractive and colourful guide written by Annette Bagot, FSA. They are also justifiably proud of their home which, in earlier days, was called Lewens or Leavens.

Founder of the family which occupied the Hall for some 400 years until the purchase by Allan Bellingham in 1562 was Norman de Hieland, who later became known as 'de Redman'. The mediaeval portion of the present building is believed to be the remains of an earlier Hall and Pele Tower, though William de Lancaster was the first to mention Levens in about 1170.

The building and the owners and occupiers have a fascinating history in themselves, but unfortunately only a little is known about the three ghosts that are seen fairly frequently on the premises.

Pure superstition is the story that when an albino fawn is born in the herd of black fallow deer, which roam freely in the park, some change will take place though the tale is connected with the appearance of 'The Grey Lady'.

This apparition is believed to be that of a gypsy who was turned away when begging for food from the owners in the early days. Before dying of starvation she cursed the family who lived at Levens at the time, saying that 'no son should inherit the house until the River Kent ceased to flow and a white fawn was born'.

The birth of Alan Desmond Bagot heralded the new era, for the river froze solid and a white deer was found in the herd the year he was born.

The gypsy however, if that be the 'Grey Lady', continues to be witnessed. She was seen by Lisa Bagot, the owner's second daughter, when a child of seven, but the most recent occasion was in 1971 when the figure was seen standing on a narrow bridge and 'nearly caused a motor accident'.

Another phantom of a woman in a pink dress and mob-cap has been seen in the Hall several times, but like so many ghosts her identity is unknown. Annette Bagot told me in August 1972 that a party of Womens' Institute members visiting Levens Hall saw the Pink Lady on the stairs and a man belonging to another party complained of the family's black dog pushing past down the stairs and being a danger to the public. 'None of the rest of his party saw the dog and it was, we suppose, our ghost as we have no black dog ourselves'.

Annette continued by saying that she did not know whose black dog it was and could not tell me anything more about him, but he is 'our much most frequent visitor'. Among human visitors to the hall who have witnessed the 'black woolly animal' are Mr Raymond Leppard, Miss Rujickora, Harry Killard and Mrs Bagot.

The dog is practically a booby trap for he suddenly appears in front of peoples legs and, in dodging him, many have lost their balance. He also 'trots up the stairs in front of unwary guests and disappears into their bedroom, leaving them to hunt unavailingly for him'.

Wiltshire

Dominated by Stonehenge and Salisbury

Open to the public during normal hours or by appointment	5
Churches, abbeys, rectories	1
Shops, stores	1
Inns, hotels	1
Open spaces, roads	2
Apparitions	
Females	3
Monks	2
Males	1

King and Queen Inn

High Street, Highworth, Wiltshire
Open to the public during normal hours
Junction of A361/B4019
6 miles from Swindon station

A few yards from this old coaching inn (it's believed to be over 500 years old) is the site of an ancient monastery and some say that tunnels exist from the nearby church to it. Is it from one of these that the apparition seen by so many originates?

The ghost has been seen by the landlord's Alsatians which were obviously 'scared stiff, literally', by one or two customers, but more especially by the licensee, Mr Richard Nelms himself. 'It was that of a monk', he says, 'and moved rapidly across the courtyard towards the site of the old stables'.

This incident occurred in 1969 when Mr Nelms was clearing up one night, but Mr Ivor Hawkins, verger at the church, witnessed the phantom in the daylight some 35 years ago.

The description of the ghost is given as 'about four feet tall', for 'it is crouched, like a hunchback'.

In Pentlands Lane, not far from the King & Queen, groups of teenagers have been scared by a 'bent white figure drifting above a field'. One van driver described his experience when he went to investigate. This thing seemed to by laying on top of a tractor by the hedge in the field. 'It was shining white and seemed to follow us when we moved.'

Another couple who have seen what may be another form of the hunchback monk in the locality saw 'a grey shape about two or three feet from the ground on the verge beside the road. It was all hunched up'.

During this period some two dozen people witnessed 'the thing' in the field and surrounding hedgerows.

The licensee of the pub has been so concerned at these sightings that he has taken out an insurance policy against shock caused to his customers. But that doesn't cover the residents using Pentlands Lane.

It is possible that the same phantom is that seen at St Michaels Church in the High Street. (See separate entry).

Maddington

Shrewton, Wiltshire
Open to the public
Junction of A360/A344
10 miles from Salisbury station

Hardly a village, more of a hamlet, is the description that can be given to Maddington. Other than a farm, a church, a vicarage and a manor there are a few buildings that can be classed as being within its confines. Yet a couple of ghosts have been well recorded here.

Late in 1970 Mr Alexander of Shrewton with his daughter saw the spectre of a young woman wearing a long white costume standing only a few feet away from the barn in which they were working. Seconds later they heard footsteps and the swishing sound of feminine clothing. This was not the first and only occasion that the young lady had been seen for the Rev Barnard, a former vicar, had also experienced her visits to his church, usually 'late in the evenings'.

Two ladies of the manor house have also seen the young woman glide past their kitchen.

There is evidence that Maddington Manor was used at one time in its ancient history as a 'training school' or novice house for the nearby Amesbury nunnery and there is strong belief that the lady in white is one of the novices who was unable to 'make the grade'.

The other ghost claimed to have been seen in the manor is that of a crusader from Shrewton who passes through the building on his way to the churchyard. But there are only a few people who have seen this character for his appearances are limited to 1.30 in the morning.

St Michael's Church*

High Street, Highworth, Swindon, Wiltshire
Open to the public during normal hours
On A361
Nearest station—Swindon

In 1910 the Master of Balliol College wrote to the Society for Psychical Research enclosing an account of an apparition seen in the parish church of this charming old Wiltshire town. One of the interesting objects within the building is a monument to Lieutenant Warneford VC who destroyed the first German Zeppelin in the first world war.

The church is recorded in the Domesday Book and served as a garrison for Royalists in the Civil War. There is a record of the clergy and patrons from 1290 onwards, and visitors can see some fine Anglo-Saxon and Elizabethan work within its precincts and possibly a ghost, for the apparition reported over sixty years ago has been seen in the 1970's.

The first sighting was reported by Graham Arkell who, with his brother now Sir Noel Arkell, his sister and a friend saw by the south door the figure of a man leaning forward towards them. Instead of an ordinary face there was a 'featureless grey blank' and where the eyes should have been were 'sunken dark shadows'. Within seconds the spectre disappeared behind a pillar with 'a jerky movement of its arms'. This incident occurred at 11.30 in the morning with the sun shining on to the open doors.

What was unusual at the time was that a lady arranging flowers at the font saw nothing, though standing only a few yards from the ghost.

On pursuing the matter Mr Hawkins, the verger who died in 1970, also admitted to seeing the figure in November 1936 at 7.45 in the evening. In his statement he tells of the apparition 'coming up the centre aisle' and going through some curtains near the west end door. 'It did not appear to part them, but went straight through them.'

The ghost, dressed in a long white robe, was of medium height.

Mr John Read, the organist and choirmaster, also saw the spectre about the same time. Nothing more was heard or seen of the spectral visitor until 1970 when a woman saw the apparition move across in front of the alter during Evensong and a Mr Phineas Archer saw it outside the church.

On one warm evening in the summer he was sitting on his front door-step in Sheep Street when he saw what he thought was a monk glide from the direction of the old monastery at the east end of the High Street into the church.

More recently a Mr Vardy saw the same figure when walking home one night.

Sir Noel Arkell confirmed the first sighting and told me 'the event is still quite clear in my memory and mind'.

Savernake Forest

Wiltshire
Open to the public
On A436/A4/A338
3 miles from Hungerford station

Parts of this ancient mediaeval forest, once a favourite hunting ground for royalty, appear to have lain untouched since its formation. The lichen-covered twisted curves of the old beech trees and the wrinkled, gnarled branches of the oaks must on moonlit nights present a weird, ghostly atmosphere for any visitor. Imagination could really run riot in the creepy cluster of clawing arms, albeit wooden ones.

The 2,000 acre forest, now leased to the Forestry Commission, contains many long avenues of trees one of which, the Grand Avenue is some 4 miles long and is divided on the south by the river Kennet.

Over the years reports have been made of ghosts having been seen roaming the woods, both at night and during the day. Many of these can surely be dismissed as live 'gentlemen of the road' looking for a quiet spot for a nap, but consistently one hears of a headless woman rider dashing through the trees on her white horse. The latest occasion was in 1969 when a couple of afternoon picnickers, who had wandered into the forest from the south, saw the apparition careering through the ancient oaks.

She is believed to be the ghost of a member of one of the Royal hunting parties who was killed when her horse bolted through the low hanging branches of the forest.

Pestle & Mortar

Mere, Wiltshire
Open to the public during normal hours
On A303
4 miles from Gillingham station

The village of Mere with its two coaching inns and a marvellous view of three counties from Castle Hill is where Charles II hid while fleeing after the Battle of Worcester in 1651.

It is not known whether this restaurant is of the same period, but in 1965 Mrs Campbell was surprised to see the figure of a lady in a long white gown' glide through one of the rooms one evening shortly after closing. A waitress, Rosemary Haslutt, saw the figure the following day.

The residents also found that a large table, stored in a locked room, was turned over and pictures have been moved by unseen hands.

Worcestershire

A county of much beauty

Open to the public during normal hours or by appointment	3
Private houses	1
Historic buildings, museums, ruins	2
Inns, hotels	1
Private houses, offices, factories	1
Phenomena	
Noises	1
Apparitions	
Females	3
Males	1
Horses	1
Others	1

Dudley Castle

Dudley, Worcestershire
Open to the public during normal hours
On A457
1¼ miles from Dudley Port station

To say that this massive ruin has had a long and chequered history rather understates the facts, but one thing is clear, it has seen a few battles and numerous deaths. Dudley itself was named after Dudda, though no one knows who he was.

The castle, one of the very few included in the Domesday Book, was first created by William Fitzansulph, one of William's followers. The earthworks of this, although since built on, remain complete and nearly as perfect as when they were thrown up nearly 1,000 years ago. Of the usual Norman motte (mount) and bailey type, the castle is currently linked with a thriving zoo run by the Dudley Zoological Society.

In 1175, because of Prince Henry's rebellion against his father, the castle was dismantled and by 1321 John Sutton had gained ownership and occupied it for over 30 years. He was probably responsible for much of the restoration and the chapel and hall.

Some time in 1533 the castle was seized by John Dudley, Duke of Northumberland, who remodelled the whole of the dwelling area under Sir William Sharington. Sir William wrote to Sir John Thynne in 1553 concerning the building of that other famous establishment at Longleat.

Following the execution of the Duke, the Crown held the castle until 1554 when Queen Mary granted it to Edward Dudley, a relative of the Suttons.

In 1575 Queen Elizabeth visited the castle and the preparation for her stay necessitated the building of a withdrawing room, a warder's tower and an angle tower. Although ten years later there was much talk of placing the Scottish Queen Mary at Dudley, nothing came of it and in 1643 ownership passed to the Ward family.

Thomes Leveson holding the castle for the King at the time of the Civil Wars rather than cause more bloodshed, for there had already been two fierce battles, offered to surrender to Sir William Brereton and in 1647 the building was made 'untenable'.

At the end of the 17th century more building took place, but in 1750 came the disastrous fire which created the ruin. For four days flames swept through it and the molten lead from the roof made it look as though the whole hill was burning.

For a complete and fascinating history of the castle I would recommend readers to the official guide published by Herald Press and obtainable from the current trustees for it is unfortunately impossible from the wealth of information that it contains to identify the ghosts seen here since 1934.

The phantoms have been described as 'two elderly people dressed in 17th century clothes' who appear to walk arm in arm up to the 12th century gatehouse and vanish. Numerous odd sounds of voices and the clash of steel have also been heard, and occasionally a peculiar sudden gust of wind experienced.

Mount Pleasant Hotel*

Worcester Road, Great Malvern, Worcestershire
Open to the public during normal hours
On A449
Nearest station—Malvern

There cannot be many hotels with an orangery listed as an ancient monument. The Mount Pleasant, however, sited near the Festival Theatre, not only has a famous orangery but also magnificent terraced lawns.

It is a Georgian house, notable for its 'charming atmosphere'.

In January 1964 a Mrs Gillis, whilst on a business trip, stayed the night here and was woken at 'about 2.30 in the morning'. On looking round the room to see what had caused her to wake she was astounded to see the figure of an old woman in a long black dress standing by the window.

'As I looked at her', she told me, 'she turned to face me and in doing so grew fainter and finally faded away. I wasn't frightened, only a little puzzled'.

Over the breakfast table Mrs Gillis discussed the matter with another overnight guest and learnt that another unusual incident had occurred in the next room at the same time.

Mrs Gillis said that her table companion told her of waking at what she thought was about 2.15 and feeling 'absolutely paralysed, not with fear, but physically. I told her that she had probably been lying awkwardly, but she assured me that it wasn't that'. Suddenly after about 15 minutes the phase passed and the guest was able to move. 'She had been pinned down for all that time trying to call out for help. Even if it was just coincidence, it was a peculiar one'.

I agree, especially as there is a belief that at one time the two rooms were one and that an old woman smothered her daughter there many years ago.

Old Court House

Shelsley Walsh, Worcestershire
Open to the public by appointment only
Off B4204
10 miles from Worcester station

In 1965 two late arrivals at a Christmas Eve party were astonished to see a large vague shape silently rushing across the lawn and apparently plunging into the moat surrounding the house. Before joining their friends, they walked to where the object had disappeared, but found nothing.

On enquiring as to the reason for the phantom they learnt that they were two of the lucky few who have seen the phantom carriage and four sent by relatives of Lady Lightfoot in an attempt to rescue her in the 16th century.

The local tradition is that her Ladyship was imprisoned here for her outspoken criticisms of Henry VIII's policy. She proved too much of an embarrassment and was finally murdered, unbeknown to her friends and relatives. One Christmas Eve an attempt was planned to take advantage of the festive period and with a sudden bold move to gain entry into the courthouse and release the Lady. Unfortunately, either the horses bolted or the driver had already partaken of too much Christmas spirit and the four horses, the coachman and the rescue party all plunged to their death in the murky waters.

3 Walcott Lane

Drakes Broughton, Worcestershire
Private property, please respect

Disposing of the belief that 'modern houses don't have ghosts' is the case of an apparition of 'a little old lady' frequently seen entering through the back door of this pre-war home, gliding across the kitchen floor and who on passing the living room turns and vanishes.

The tenants of the council owned property, the Moores, have seen the ghost 'practically every month' for the 20 years they have occupied the house. Both their son and daughter have also witnessed the haunting as have several visitors.

Unfortunately there is no logical explanation for the site used to be an orchard. Mrs Moor told the *Worcester Evening News* in August 1970 that there is usually a 'look of sheer terror on the face of the old lady'.

One clue could be that a coffin maker used to carry on his business at the end of the lane some many years ago, which might suggest the burial of a live body.

Mrs Moore stated emphatically that the ghost didn't frighten her and would make no attempt to get rid of it.

Yorkshire

Once part of Northumbria, a huge Saxon kingdom

Open to the public during normal hours or by appointment	12
Private houses	1
Clubs, cinemas	2
Historic buildings, museums, ruins	3
Churches, abbeys, rectories	1
Shops, stores	1
Inns, hotels	1
Private houses, offices, factories	3
Open spaces, roads	2
Phenomena	
Noises	5
Moving objects	1
Apparitions	
Female	4
Males	5
Others	1

Air Heating Ltd*

1 Gill Lane, Yeadon, Near Leeds, Yorkshire
Open to the public by appointment only
On A658
1¼ miles from Guiseley station

Early in 1970 the regional manager of this company, a subsidiary of Leith Cardle & Co, reported what were obviously typical poltergeist phenomena which had been occurring over an eight month period in the offices.

The executive concerned, Mr J V Caulkett, told me two years later that the incidents reached such a climax during the hours from 11am to 4pm that 'we were unable to continue work in one particular office due to the furniture moving about, such as heavy filing cabinets falling over and a very heavy desk moving right across the office'. A tin of paint, which had been left, was thrown across the office, bouncing off a wall and making a dent in a flush door and bursting open on the carpet. Telephones were continually having to be repaired due to being thrown on the floor. Coins were thrown around and a stationary cupboard crashed to the floor.

Although the local vicar carried out an excorcism and the Rev Bacon repeated the service, 'unexplainable occurrences' have continued, though considerably abated.

Mr Caulkett feels that the phenomena were linked to a particular female member of the staff, for when she left the majority of the experiences ceased.

The building was constructed about 1834 and was used initially as a church and then as a church school. During the last war it became a small industrial factory and now houses this heating organisation.

Locals told Mr Caulkett that the owner of the building, when it was a sheet metal workshop some years ago, often held seances there. Another incident that may be connected with the haunting was an accident in 1905. A brewers' dray rushed down the street out of control and the driver, when the vehicle collided with one of the buildings, was flung through a window of the offices and died on the floor. The relevant aperture was blocked with 'very thick stone slabs' for some reason—perhaps, with a peculiar quirk of logic, to prevent another similar incident—but these were removed when Air Heating moved in.

Mr Caulkett said that, although very sceptical, he was now fully convinced that a poltergeist was active in the building and supplied a photograph taken when papers were flying about the room. He points out that this is not definite proof, but 'we can assure you that when this was taken, there was no air movement whatsoever'.

Bailey Club

Monk Bretton, Barnsley, Yorkshire
Open to the public by appointment only
On A62
Nearest station—Barnsley

Named after the nearby priory, the small village of Monk Bretton has become a favourite spot for Barnsley businessmen who are attracted to this entertainment venue offering varied facilities for their enjoyment. Adjoining the property and possibly continuing below its foundations is an old Quaker burial ground, and it is this that has caused the regular haunting of the establishment.

Manager of the popular club, Brendan Mulligan, working in his office late one night looked up to see a vague outline of a man in what looked like an 'old Quaker style hat', but as he watched it the figure 'swayed to the middle of the room and disappeared'.

Other members of the staff who have witnessed the apparition over a period of several months include Mrs Sally West who 'went icy cold' at seeing the figure, and Arthur Whitehead, a maintenance mechanic. He was walking through the premises late one night in 1970 when he 'heard the concert room door open and shivered as a dark misty figure glided past'.

Another incident was when he heard the club's organ being played by unseen hands producing, not the normal 'pop' tunes so much in demand by the club members but, 'religious music'.

Bramham

West Riding, Yorkshire
Open to the public
Off A1
12 miles from Leeds station

In 1408 Henry IV defeated the Percy family and their allies in a rebellious attempt to overthrow the monarchy. Numerous battles were fought out all over the north, the west and the midlands, though the battle of Shrewsbury was one of the most prominent.

There was, however, another blood-letting episode near Bramham Park where several hundred met their deaths.

For several years now, near the village cricket pitch, the sound of horses had been heard usually at dusk though no such animals have been seen in the locality, except for the odd farm horse, for a long time. One local resident described the sounds as 'about half a dozen horses galloping at full speed across the meadow in the direction of Boston Spa', heading north away from the battle site.

One can only assume that the terror and ferocity of the fighting there over 400 years ago has left its eternal mark on the surrounding atmosphere.

Brompton Road

Attercliffe, Sheffield, Yorkshire
Private property, please respect

Only a few yards from the river Don on the east side of Sheffield, a 'house of fear' has been causing the occupants considerable worry.

Books and ornaments have been hurled around the rooms, pets refuse to enter certain parts and a puddle of water has been found in the shape of a horse shoe on the floor.

The incidents could be classed as typical poltergeist phenomena were it not for the fact that an apparition of a 'small old lady about 80, wrinkled and walking with a stoop' has frequently been seen in the house by the residents, friends and relatives.

Mr Jackson, the occupier, told the *Sheffield Star* in November 1970, 'the trouble seems to run in cycles, starting at the end of the year'.

Fountains Abbey

Near Studley Park, Yorkshire
Open to the public during normal hours
Off A61
12 miles from Harrogate station

The ruins of what was once the wealthiest Cistercian house in the country are still among the most magnificent to be seen. The Abbey was founded in 1132, but after personal enemies of the abbot had destroyed most of the structure it was reconstructed between 1148 and 1179. Its prosperity has been associated with the involvement in the wool trade, but it was one of the first abbeys to be sold by Henry VIII in 1540.

There were only two major additions—the north tower and the Chapel of the Nine Altars. This chapel at the east end was built between 1204 and 1250 and, thanks to the upkeep by the Department of the Environment, the whole of the ground plan of it has survived. Also the site of the refectory and lay brothers' quarters can be clearly seen.

Although no apparitions have been reported here, the sounds of a male choir have occasionally been heard by evening visitors.

Glebe Cottage

Guiseley, Near Leeds, Yorkshire
Open to the public by appointment only
Off A61
12 miles from Harrogate station

Another example of rather an uneventful haunting, though what must have been rather disturbing when first experienced nearly 20 years ago.

In June 1967 the occupier, the Rev Victor Dawes, and his wife reported to the *Yorkshire Evening Post* that they had both heard 'inexplicable thumps and bumps whenever the lights are switched off at night', and several times in the early hours they have felt a weight on the side of the bed 'as if someone was sitting on it'.

This was no news to a tenant of the cottage of some years ago, Mrs Edith Busfield, for both she and 'numerous visitors often heard footsteps going up the stairs at night' though no one was to be seen.

Golden Lion

North Street, Leeds, Yorkshire
Open to the public during normal hours
On A61
¼ mile from Leeds station

For several years reports have been made that this pub is haunted by 'a gentleman in a Victorian suit' who frequents the cellars. Not only did Thomas Scott, the landlord, see the ghost but his two daughters have described how, for several nights during August 1968, they saw 'an old lady with her hair done in ringlets' bending over their bed.

Previous landlords have experienced similar phenomena and have linked the two figures together, believing that they are a husband and wife who used to live on the premises in the early 1800's.

Shortly before going to press it was learned that this pub will probably soon be demolished under a redevelopment scheme But because ghosts never move—only fade away—it will be interesting to see what transpires in any new building that may be constructed on the site Or will it become a roadway ? Motorists had better watch out!

Haworth Parsonage

Haworth, Yorkshire
Open to the public during normal hours
On A6033
12 miles from Bradford station

The rough path from Haworth Parsonage to Far Withins must have been walked hundreds of times by Emily Jane Bronte whilst compiling her books during the 1830's.

In the bleak Georgian house where they lived and worked for some twenty years, visitors can see some of the personal effects and a few of the manuscripts written by the three sisters. The house has been perfectly preserved and appears precisely as it was when it was the home of the author of the famous *Wuthering Heights*.

Far Withins, the original building used as the pattern for the Heathcliffe residence, is also still in existence and is owned by the Keighley Corporation.

Emily, the quietest of the three girls and probably the most intense in character, has been seen on occasions wandering 'with her head bowed deep in thought' along the narrow path leading from her old home.

There seems to be no regular time for the phantom's appearance as she has been witnessed in the evenings and early afternoons, but mostly during the latter half of the year.

Howley Hall Golf Club

Near Batley, West Riding, Yorkshire
Open to the public by appointment only
Off A650
Nearest station—Batley

This popular golf course, on the slope of a hill between Batley and Morley, is 'like a tree set in a desert of concrete' for practically surrounding the haven are the hard outlines of mill chimneys, factories work-shops and the general impedimenta of industry.

The headquarters of the golf club is a peaceful place and was once the farmhouse belonging to the ruined 16th century Hall.

The hall itself was built by Sir John Savile, the first mayor of Leeds, and when his son, Viscount Savile, joined the King during the Civil War, he left the estate in the hands of a near relative, Sir John Savile of Lupset.

In June 1643 the Duke of Newcastle demanded that the house

be handed over to the King, but Sir John refused. A siege ensued, but finally the Hall was blasted into ruins and several of the defenders killed.

What was left was let out to various families, one of them being the famous Villiers. It is believed that Lady Anne Villiers left the Hall one Palm Sunday to bathe in a nearby spring, but accidentally fell and was drowned. The spring is still known as 'Lady Anne's Well' and the water from it is supposed to cure rheumatism.

Whether this lady is the ghost seen recently by a Mr and Mrs Bunney of Leeds cannot be established. One afternoon in 1972 the couple were walking near the ruins of the Old Hall when Mrs Bunney commented on the unusual appearance of a woman walking towards them. 'She had a long dress with a dark top and a curious red mantilla veil over her face and shoulders'. Mr Bunney had just agreed there was something strange about the woman when the figure faded and vanished.

Other ghosts have been seen practically on the same spot. Mr Gomershall, a mill worker, saw two men and a woman one evening. 'I thought they were golfers', he said, 'but when my dog barked and growled at them they just vanished'. The apparitions wore dark loose clothing 'of an early period'.

The director of a Dewsbury mill had experienced a 'most peculiar feeling of being watched by a crowd of invisible people' at one spot on the course a few days earlier.

The area certainly reeks of violence for a few hundred yards from the golf course the winding Scotchman Lane takes its name from the murder of a Scottish innkeeper. The publican, a Mr Fletcher, was killed by a highwayman, William Nevison, who stabbed him with a cobblers' knife in the 1670's. Nevison was later caught and hanged in York Castle.

Long Marston

Marston Moor, Yorkshire
Open to the public
Unclassified road between A59 and B1224
7 miles from York station

In 1644 the Battle of Marston Moor was one of the many incidents that had long reaching effects on the Civil War.

One can imagine the horrific scene of battle and the aftermath resulting in pitiful groups of weary men wandering aimlessly around the area. Lost, beaten, often wounded, they would probably resemble the modern day soldier suffering from shell-shock.

It was in 1968 that a locally accepted incident was finally recorded, that of seeing ghostly human relics of this battle trudging the roadside.

Some motoring tourists, lost in their search for the road to Wetherby, had found themselves on this small country road. They noticed what they first thought were a small group of 'half-a-dozen tramps' stumbling silently along the ditch. Realising that there was something unusual about their clothing, they slowed down to look more closely. One suggestion made at the time was that they were drunken actors dressed in 17th century costume, but their appearance was really one of 'exhausted campaigners'.

On checking their experience later, the tourists realised that they had been travelling the road that ran through the site of the ancient battle and that the 'silent crowd' were the oft-seen ghosts of the area.

It is possible they were apparitions of local men conscripted into service for the occasion and, having suffered the fate of so many, were returning to the peace of their own homesteads.

Spofforth Castle

Near Harrogate, Yorkshire
Open to the public during normal hours
On A59
4 miles from Harrogate station

Although at first glance the ruins of this fortified manor, now in the care of the Department of the Environment, appear to be uninteresting, there are various intriguing aspects to be examined by the archaeologist, the historian or, more to the point, the ghost hunter.

William de Percy, a leading Norman Knight and prominent supporter of The Conqueror arrived in this country only a year after the initial landing of the invaders in 1066. Because of his character and bold attitude he was highly esteemed by the King who showed his gratitude by giving him 86 Lordships in Yorkshire including Bottom Percy, Wetherby and Spofforth.

The latter consisted of a huge area and it was here that the Percys established their headquarters. Within a short period the desolation was turned into a fertile and productive manor and the family remained in the house, built primarily as a home rather than for defence, for some 300 years.

It is believed that Richard de Percy, one of the leading signatories of Magna Carta, held a meeting of the barons here where the details were drawn up in 1215.

The direct line of the Percys died out at the beginning of the

14th century, but the name was retained as a result of a condition on the marriage of the last Percy, Lady Agnes, to the Duke of Brabant. It was their son, Henry, who obtained a licence in 1308 to fortify his house and it was the resulting work that is still visible, though renovation was made in 1559.

It was shortly after this, when the Percys had become prominent in Northumberland, that Spofforth gradually declined and was reduced to ruins during the Civil War.

Over the last few years several visitors have witnessed an unidentifiable phantom which appears at the top of the early 13th century tower, the stairs of which are blocked.

Only guesses can be made as to the identity or sex of the spectre, for it is seen only as a vague half-human shape; 'half-human' literally, because it is cut off at waist level.

Bluish-white in colour, it is seen standing on the narrow parapet, only inches wide, and after a few seconds falls rapidly down the stonework on to the grass path surrounding the ruin.

Efforts to establish whether there has been a suicide at the castle have proved fruitless.

One of the last occasions when the apparition was seen was in October 1969 when a group of children, accompanied by a teacher, were more than a little horrified to watch the apparent death of a ghost.

Synagogue

Donisthorpe Hall Woods, Moortown Estate, Leeds 17, Yorkshire
Open to the public by appointment only
Off A6120
Nearest station—Leeds

What was probably a 'once only visit' by a ghost was experienced by a team of Gas Board workmen in August 1970 when laying a new main to the synagogue now on the site of the Donisthorpe Hall.

Three of the four men saw the figure, which they thought to be of a Quaker, watching them dig the trench carrying the main pipes. During the laying process human and animal bones were discovered in the grounds.

The foreman of the team, a Mr Edgar Lupton, was the first to see the apparition. 'It was just the top half of one of those old Quakers, dressed in a charcoal-grey cloak and wearing a wide brimmed hat with a flat top.' As he watched it, 'it seemed to melt away'. The next day another member of the team saw the figure in a different place and drew the outline on a stone. The description matched that seen a few hours earlier.

At the side of the old hall was a mausoleum in which was a large slab of marble which was used as a laying-out table, and some of the work force believed that in moving it they had disturbed a ghost of one of the former occupants of the building.

But the old hall was in fact a home for aged Jews, not Quakers, for many years. The rabbis used to wear tall flat-topped hats very similar in design to the drawing and the description given by Mr Lupton. 'The charcoal grey colour would also be consistent with this', said a Leeds Councillor, Mr Harold Levey.

White Rose Salon

Whitefriargate, Hull, Yorkshire
Open to the public during normal hours
Junction of A63/A1079
Nearest station—Hull (Paragon)

Not far from Paragon Station in the city centre is this smart hair-dressing salon owned by Mr and Mrs Hardy who were so disturbed in 1971 by mysterious noises from an upstairs room that they called in the local police.

The sounds heard both by the staff and numerous customers are that of someone slowly pacing the floor of the empty room then 'dragging something towards the door, followed by more sinister shufflings'. The constabulory locked the door of the room, fitted trip wires but were mystified when the sounds continued unabated.

On opening up, the room was found to be undisturbed but the light had been switched on.

The noises are not now so loud and continue to puzzle the owners, but only a few of the customers: one cannot hear much under a hairdryer.

SOME MORE BOOKS ABOUT GHOSTS

A Case-book of Ghosts	Elliott O'Donnell ..	Foulsham
Apparitions and Ghosts	Andrew Mackenzie .	Barker
Apparitions		Faber &
and Haunted Houses	Sir Ernest Bennett	Faber
Elliott O'Donnell's Ghost Hunters		Foulsham
Four Modern Ghosts	E J Dingwall &	
	T H Hall	Duckworth
Gallery of Ghosts	A MacKenzie......	Barker
Gallery of Ghosts	James Reynolds	Creative Age
Gazetteer of British Ghosts ..	Peter Underwood ..	Souvenir
		Press
Ghost Hunter's Game Book ..	J Wentworth Day ..	Muller
Ghost Hunter's Road Book...	John Harries	Muller
Ghost Tour	Jack Hallam	Wolfe
Ghosts and Apparitions	W H Salter	Bell
Ghosts and Hauntings	Denis Bardens	Zeus Press
Ghosts and Witches	J Wentworth Day ..	Muller
Ghosts, Ghouls and Gallows ..	G F Marson	Rider
Ghosts I've Met	Hans Holzer	Jenkins
Haunted Britain	Elliott O'Donnell ..	Rider
Haunted England	Christine Hole	Batsford
Haunted Houses	Joseph Braddock ...	Batsford
Haunted Houses	G C Harper	Chapman &
		Hall

Haunted Inns of England	Jack Hallam	Wolfe
In Search of Ghosts	J Wentworth Day ..	Muller
Lively Ghosts of Ireland	Hans Holzer.......	Wolfe
Lord Halifax's Ghost Book		Fontana
Mysteries of London.	Andrew Green.....	Napier
Mysteries of Surrey	Andrew Green.....	Napier
Mysteries of Sussex	Andrew Green.....	Napier
New Lights on Old Ghosts...	Trevor H Hall	Duckworth
Phantom Footsteps..........	A Alpin MacGregor	Robert Hale
Phantoms of the Sea.........	Raymond Lamont Brown	Stephens
Real Ghosts, Restless Spirits & Haunted Minds.......	Brad Steiger.......	Tandem
Realm of Ghosts	Eric Maple........	Pan
Screaming Skulls & Other Ghosts	Elliott O'Donnell ..	Four Square
Stately Ghosts of England ...	Diana Norman.....	Muller
Strange Stories of the Chase..	Countess of Faversham	Garnstone Press
Unbidden Guests............	William Oliver Stevens...........	Allen & Unwin
World's Strangest Ghosts	R Thurston Hopkins	World's Work

ACKNOWLEDGEMENTS

To all those kind people who have helped me compile this collection through writing detailed experiences, lending me their personal notes, supplying valuable material, carrying out searches or spending time discussing phenomena, may I offer my sincere thanks.

In particular I would like to acknowledge the great assistance provided by the following: Colonel Campbell Adamson of Brechin, Mrs Vera Akers of Willesborough, Alan Ambrose of Pluckley, Sir Noël Arkell, Annette Bagot of Levens Hall, Gordon Baker of the Environmental Consortium, Her Grace The Duchess of Bedford, Una Broadbent of Coulsdon, John Bristow Bull of London, E W Butler of Belfast, William Cade of Castledermot, Stephen Clarke of Monmouth, Robin Cooke MP, of Athelhampton, Sir John Craster of Craster, M J Digby of Chiswick, the Rev J A Woodhead-Keith-Dixon of Lorton Hall, Keith Dobney of Hitchin, Ray Eaton of Essex, E J Evill of Buckingham, Christina Foyle of Maldon, N K Gale of Castletown, Donald Good of Lincolnshire Newspapers, Jack Hallam of Reigate, Lauretta & John Harrison of Torquay, Margaret Hawarth of Goosnargh, Paula Hemmings of Douglas, Mrs Betty Howard of Rye, Wyn Hughes of the *Luton Evening Post*, Gemma Hunter of Richmond, R Forbes Hutchinson of Edinburgh, Derek Jones of Ashtead, Captain Kennett of the USAAF, P W Lawson of Speke Hall, M Lloyd of Missenden, Captain Alex McAdam of Glasgow, J McLellan of Blackburn, Dermott McManus of Harrogate, Lieut. Colonel George Malcolm of Poltalloch, Mr Maldwyn of Ewell, Mrs D Margary of Lympne Castle, John Medina of Walton-on-Thames, Sir David Ogilvy, Bt of Pencaitland, S D Pomeroy of Ford Motor Company, Mrs Campbell-Preston of Taynuilt, P H Reid of Mobil Oil Company, Raymond Richards of Macclesfield, Sheila St Clair of Lisburn, Maurice Simpson of Stonehaven, T Stewart of Mobil Oil Company, Adrienne Tiidus, Brian D Thompson of Puttenden, P J Weston of Ballygally, D B Wills of Littlecote House, Josephine Manning Wilson and Joan Wright of Rhynie.

I am indebted to Messrs Frederick Muller for letting me quote from *A Ghost Hunter's Game Book* by James Wentworth Day and

The Stately Ghosts of England by Diana Norman and to Oriel Press for allowing me to extract material from *North Country Squire* by Sir John Craster. May I also thank Miss Driver of the *Journal of Paraphysics*, Paraphysical Laboratory, Downton, Wiltshire for permission to reproduce much of Suzanne Padfield's report on Shepton Mallet and of course to Miss Padfield herself for her permission to publish her experience there and for details of the Butleigh, Somerset case.

I am also extremely grateful to Mr W H Downes of the Clacton Ghost and Occult Research Society for his detailed reports on several Essex cases, to Michael Neale for so kindly handling my photographic requests, to John Palmer of Richmond for lending me much valuable material and especially to Mr William Perrott, Member of the Society for Psychical Research for providing me with his personal files, and to Mr Eddie Pratt of Caterham for his help with many London cases.

My deepest and heartfelt thanks go to my niece, Deirdre Borner of Whyteleafe who so patiently accepted the complete disruption of her home, provided so much vital assistance and typed practically the whole book.

PLATES

Mobil's Refinery, Coryton, Essex. *Mobil Photo Library*
The Brocket Arms, Ayot St Lawrence, Herts. *Keith Dobney*
Boys Hall, Willesborough, Kent. *Andrew Green*
Elvey Farm, Pluckley, Kent. *Andrew Green*
Hall'i'th'wood, Bolton, Lancs. *The Bolton Corporation*
16 Montpelier Road, Ealing. *Andrew Green*
Castle Restaurant, Sunbury-on-Thames, Surrey. *D. F. Newman MHCI*
Chertsey Offset Printers, Chertsey, Surrey. *Andrew Green*
Busheygate, Robertsbridge, Sussex. *Andrew Green*
The Seven Stars, Robertsbridge, Sussex. *Andrew Green*
Air Heating Ltd, near Leeds, Yorkshire. *J. Norman Preston*

Fontana Books

All Fontana books are available at your bookshop or newsagent; or can be ordered direct. Just fill in the form below and list the titles you want.

....

FONTANA BOOKS, Cash Sales Department, P.O. Box 4, Godalming, Surrey, GU7 1JY. Please send purchase price plus 7p postage per book by cheque, postal or money order. No currency.

NAME (Block Letters)
_____

ADDRESS
_____

_____

_____